Dear Mike,

   Thank you indeed for honor of presenting at ICMI 16. I am certain I will remember this for the rest of my life. An extraordinary and very gratifying experience.

♡ Janet

FEMINISN'T
A Compendium of Blog Posts by
Janet Bloomfield

Dedicated to my crazy bitches:

*Jessica Valenti
Amanda Marcotte
Lindy West
Zerlina Maxwell
Clementine Ford
&
Anita Sarkeesian*

You make mocking feminism so easy!

Men 8

    What would happen if no men showed up for work today? 9

    Men talk about their feelings all the time. They just don't use words. 13

    Man-shaming. It should be a word. 14

    Yippee-ki-yay, motherfucker. John McClane and the redemption of masculinity. 17

    Attention middle class men: please stop inventing and producing all the useful shit we need and just die already. 21

    Oh look. It's Janice fucking Turner again. Men = Malign? 24

    First I feared him, then I loathed him, then I forgave him and now I take care of him: the story of my Father and me. 30

    60% of married men carry the primary financial burden for their families. 35

    Asperger's Syndrome: is it just another way of pathologizing creativity? And genius? Especially MALE creativity and genius? Let's get on our tinfoil hats. 38

    Hanna Rosin says we are witnessing the end of men! Oh yeah? How about we look at the facts? 45

    How do civilizations commit suicide? By elevating women at the expense of men. It doesn't have to be this way. 51

    #GamerGate is fundamentally a fight for men, for masculinity and for male spaces. 57

    When the world goes to hell, it's men who die to save others. Remembering the first responders of 9/11 61

    Attention men struggling with mental illness: man up you whiny suckholes! 62

    You don't need to care about men to care about men's rights. You just need to be fucking human! 65

    Of course you can blame the victim. Who else are you going to blame? 67

Feminism 71

    The moment I knew feminism was a crock of shit. 72

    Jessica Valenti admits she is obsessed with what men think of her. 75

    Jessica Valenti coughs up a ball of full retard 76

    It makes me laugh when feminists love Jane Austen because I'm pretty sure she would spit on them. Politely, of course. 80

    Babies? We don't need no stinking babies! The genius of Amanda Marcotte. Again. 83

    Feminism is a voice that speaks for all women. As long as you're white. And rich. And you work outside the home. The rest of you bitches can step off. 88

    Jezebel solves the problem of women's inequality! It's about bloody time. 90

    Attention feminists: please stop being so sexy and start being more shrieky and angry! 93

    How to spend a ton of money being a "woman" and still be a shrill bitch at the same time. 96

There are more male nurses than ever. Highly specialized, technically qualified male nurses, who get paid more than female nurses because SEXISM! 99

Men: stand up for yourselves and we WILL hate you. The new feminist war cry! 100

Bitter old feminist is bitter and old. 113

There never was a patriarchy, and there isn't one now 120

The real face of domestic terrorism? Radical white feminists. It's not about equality and they're not afraid to say it. 127

Gang of female rapists abuse male prisoners and they are not even being charged! Oh, okay. That seems fair..134

Feminists agree, at least in theory, that women MUST face the consequences of deciding to have sex. 139

Married to a feminist? Congratulations. By the way, your baby is really sad and your wife will never be happy. 145

Legal Parental Surrender is NOT morally equivalent to an abortion and no amount of bitchy sarcasm will make it so, Amanda Marcotte...149

Men's desires, women's desires. Sometimes they aren't all that nice. But only men's desires are wrong. How to be a joyless feminist. 155

Wanna be a Male Feminist? Okay, here's what you have to do..160

DO NOT give feminists cookies. Feminists hate cookies. NO COOKIES!...........................168

Richard Dawkins hands feminists a fabulous argument and not one of them touches it. I wonder why not?...173

Dating, Sex and Relationships 178

Dating single mothers? Just say NO! A note for all the single dudes...............................178

Sluts lower the value of all women. Here's how to compete with them. 181

Slutty feminist WOMEN with fucked up personal lives are heroes. Slutty feminist MEN with fucked up personal lives are mentally ill traitors. 183

Hook-up Culture is a thing white kids do? Why are more than 70% of black children born out of wedlock then?..188

Attention high school girls: please don't fall in love with a boy because that is an excellent way to get abused. Just give blowjobs instead. 196

I went to college and there aren't enough men! Wah! I stayed home and there are too many men! Wah! Jesus, bitches, could you pick one? 202

Katie Roiphe thinks online relationships are more real than real ones, explaining once again, why she is single..204

Sluts tend to be fat and ugly, so stick to the pretty girls, lads. Unless you want to get laid, that is. 206

Valentine's Day is bullshit. Except for chocolates. I'll take those....................................208

Zerlina Maxwell says we need to teach men not to be sexually aggressive. All the other women say "fuck that". 211

Sex contracts? Sounds like so much fun. How do you enforce defaults? 214

Hey, Ivy League ladies: if you want to marry up, you need to marry young, so get out there and nail down a freshman! 217

Yoo hoo! Hey all you career ladies with no time for a husband! And all you single mamas! And all you older ladies hitting the wall! I have the solution to all your man-hunting woes! 221

Ladies, stop being so mean to sluts. Sluts make excellent friends! Said no woman ever, including other sluts. 225

All teenage girls need advanced training to understand they are NOT sexually entitled to their male classmates. 228

Is there no subject feminist writers can't turn into a bitchfest? Now there are gender rules for where you have to sit on a date. 230

How to be attractive to other people? Be really self-absorbed and don't make any efforts to please anyone else. 235

Ladies, are you short a little cash? Here's a quick and easy way to beef up your bank account and it's filled with LOL, too. Fun for everyone! 242

Marriage 246

How to pick a wife. Advice for single men. 246

How to Pick a Wife – 2.0 249

Katniss Everdeen is an awesome role model for girls because her life is all about children and family. And she will kill you if you try to fuck with her. 252

A decade of dishes will turn a girl into a woman, and a sensible one, at that. 253

No, my husband doesn't do any housework. Why the fuck should he? 255

It takes a village to raise a child? No, it takes a family, but that doesn't make the village unimportant. 257

The best gift for a stay at home wife and mother? Being at home, of course. But these things are nice, too. 259

How many men want a marriage proposal from a woman? None! 263

Want to protect yourself from domestic abuse? Be a stay at home wife and mother. 264

My husband pays all the bills, so I OWE him blowjobs, right? 266

Shit, I'm doing this housewife thing wrong! 269

Hey married dudes! Want to have more sex? With your wife, I mean. STOP DOING HOUSEWORK! 271

It's been fifty years since Betty Friedan tore apart her home. Thanks for nothing, you whiny bitch. 274

Women change their names when they get married precisely because identities DO matter. And for most women, husband > daddy. 278

Yes, I take my husband for granted. What do you want anyways? A standing ovation every day? 281

Work for THE Man = Freedom. Work for YOUR Man = Slavery 286

Feminist Housewife? I don't think so. 291

"Lean In", says Sheryl Sandberg. That way you won't miss when you chuck your husband and kids under the bus. 294

Husband ≠ Friend 298

Rocket scientist figures out that a woman's life isn't rocket science. 301

Should greedy wives walk away with all the spoils? 305

Sulky little bitch can't manage her money, threatens her husband with divorce if he doesn't give her more. Sulky bitch is clearly also a stupid bitch. 309

What do women want from marriage? Oh, everything. Is that so much to ask? 313

Being a mother isn't a job? Bullshit. Is it the toughest job? Hahahahahahah! Nope. But it's definitely a job. 318

Appease the shrieking feminists and they will STILL piss and moan. Jane Austen is the WRONG sort of woman to grace a bank note. She liked men. And she understood economics. Obviously, Jane sucks. 322

Advice for Women Who Don't Want to get Divorced 327

Food = Love..336

Introduction

In October of 2010, my very best friend called me weeping, from outside an operating theatre in the UK. She had just been asked to write her four year old son's obituary, by a well-meaning social worker, who thought it might help her come to terms with the fact he was unlikely to survive his most recent round of surgery to correct a life-threatening condition he was born with.

It was an utterly devastating moment in her life.

Pixie and I met in college, and have been best friends for almost 20 years. When her son was born, she became a stay at home mother, like me, albeit for very different reasons. Pixie had a wonderful job that she absolutely loved, and that would have integrated with motherhood very nicely, but when her son was born critically ill, she found herself a necessary caregiver with a child who had needs so intense, they permitted no work of any kind, other than the desperate struggle to keep him alive. She spent most of his first year in intensive care units, and the sensitivity of the various machines keeping the babies alive meant she could not use electronic devices.

So we wrote letters to one another.

Old fashioned, pen and ink letters. Just nattering about the various aspects of our lives, and commenting on popular culture and Jennifer Aniston's endlessly complicated relationship with her hair and her love-life. Many of these letters addressed feminism, and the scorn we both felt from other women about our choices to be stay-at-home mothers. Pixie's choice was not a choice at all, which leant the criticism she faced a whole lot more sting. On that ill-fated day in October, to take her mind off what was happening in the operating room, I suggested we create a blog, and our letters to one another would become blog posts that we would invite the whole world to read.

We had no expectation, honestly, that anyone other than ourselves would read the blog, but we seemed almost instantly to attract readers hungry to hear what we had to say. In 2010, openly critiquing feminism was a radical act, and there were not many commentators in the media willing to do so. Inevitably, we also attracted haters, and my inbox began to fill with violent threats and suggestions that I should be killed, raped, shot, stabbed ... all manner of unpleasant things. These threats did not frighten me.

They pissed me off.

They made me more determined to speak, and posting to the blog became a daily ritual. I discovered that I had a lot of the same ideas as men's rights activists and soon began writing for the most prominent men's rights website in the world: A Voice for Men. Over the course of three years, my readership has grown steadily and the blog is closing in fast on 5 million views. With over 700 posts, most in the range of 1500 – 2000 words, there is a whole lot of writing on www.judgybitch.com.

This book is a collection of blog posts, arranged into sections. All of these posts are available online, for free, but keeping the blog tidy, organized and easy to search was never a huge priority, so many of these posts can be difficult to find. This book organizes some of my favorites, and there are many more posts on the blog for readers to explore, if interested. In some places, I have reduced the length of titles, but a Google search of any title will bring you to the post, where you can investigate all the references and articles to which I refer. I have included important sources as footnotes, but for a full list, readers will have to visit the blog.

The book begins by discussing men, because our cultural attitudes towards men have been utterly disgusting for a good many years, largely the result of relentless efforts by feminist media to paint men as monstrous, bad, ugly and toxic. I then go on to discuss dating, sex, relationships, feminism and marriage. A lot of readers will find my perspective refreshing. Plenty will find it infuriating. Both are perfectly fine with me. At the end of the day, I don't care if you are offended. Your feelings are not my problem.

If you purchased this book because you are interested in learning about men's rights, you will find much here to explore. Many people wonder why men's rights activists are so opposed to feminism, and as you travel these pages, that opposition should become quite clear: feminism is the most powerful cultural force that opposes rights for men. Many years ago, that was not the case, and feminism actually supported equal rights for men and women both. Not anymore. Feminism fights tooth and nail to deny equal rights to men, and I fight back, insisting that men and women are equally deserving of care, compassion, understanding and basic human rights.

Why?

Because men are human beings.

What other reason do you need?

I hope you enjoy the book.

Love, Janet

Men

Let's start at the very beginning
A very good place to start
When you read you begin with A, B, C,
When you sing you begin with Do, Re, Mi ....

And when you begin exploring why femin**isn't**, you begin with men. There's a very good reason for that. In order to truly appreciate what modern feminism has become, you're going to need to unpack a lot of ideas about men, and replace them with better ideas. These better ideas can be summed up with two general maxims:

Men and women are different
Men are good

If close your eyes, and breathe deeply, and let your mind relax into a comfortable state, you already know these things are true. You're just afraid to say them. Feminist culture desperately wants you to believe two totally contradictory things at once: that men and women really aren't different, and that men are bad. But if men and women are the same and men are bad, doesn't that mean that women are bad, too? How can women be good, and men bad, and yet be the same? Feminist logic makes no sense, because feminism isn't about logic, it's an ideology that wants to declare women superior. And in some ways, we *are* superior. In other ways, not so much. And that's okay.

Many of my personal favorite posts iterate the goodness of men, not because I think men are *always* good, but because we hardly ever see the goodness of average, every day men acknowledged. If a man does something bad, his actions will be plastered across the media, and all men will be condemned for the actions of some. When the only thing we see in the media are representations of men as violent, callous, monstrous, evil – it becomes that much easier to believe all men really are monsters.

They're not.

The overwhelming majority of men are good, kind, loving, decent human beings, just as the majority of women are. Human beings are social creatures who need and love each other, and the narrative feminists promote actively and deliberately sabotages the natural love and affection men and women have for one another. This is a tragedy for all of us. So let's begin by reminding ourselves of the goodness of men. Let's begin by recognizing that our whole world depends on the work ordinary, average, regular men do, day in and day out. Men create civilization, in a way that women simply don't. Don't be afraid. It's okay to acknowledge it.

Come with me, and we'll go explore.

What would happen if no men showed up for work today?

Commenters have often mentioned that if men didn't show up for work one day, the entire world would screech to a halt. Using data from the US Department of Labor, I want to take a look at just how true that is. Hearing about "male privilege" is so common in the media, but perhaps the reason men have historically had the privileges they do is because they EARN THEM BY MAKING OUR LIFE POSSIBLE?

Just a thought.

And in the same breath, women have historically had the privileges they have because they GIVE BIRTH TO LIFE. Modern, feminist inspired liberal democracy has destroyed women's role, by and large, with plunging birth rates across the developed world, but they CANNOT destroy men's traditional work, or we all perish. What they want is for men to do the work silently. With no acknowledgement. For no reward.

There's a word for that: *slavery.*

Let's see what happens when the slaves revolt, shall we?

All information taken from Bureau of Labor Statistics[1], United States Department of Labor, 2013, except where noted.

First up, the entire power grid is down. 100% of power plant operators, distributors, and dispatchers are men. Now, it's possible that there are a few women working in these occupations, but however many there are, they do not make up even 0.6% of the total workforce, so statistically, 100% of the workforce is male.

91% of the nation's electrical engineers are men, and if they don't show up for work, there is no one to monitor and manage the nation's electrical supplies. Assuming some automation (designed by men, naturally) kicks in for the day, we had all better pray there are no problems. 97.6% of electrical power line installers and maintenance workers are men.

Lights out, ladies and gentlemen.

Don't bother turning on your taps, either. Or flushing your toilets. 95.5% of water and liquid waste treatment plant and system operators are men.

Think you might be able to get out of town for the one day the men don't show up?

Think again.

Planes are out.

95.9% of aircraft pilots and flight engineers are men. If you happen to find a plane with a female pilot, don't get too excited. 98.4% of aircraft mechanics and service technicians are men. You can, however, be assured of your comfort as you sit on a pilotless aircraft that has no mechanic for pre-flight clearance, because 77.6% of flight attendants are female.

Should you be lucky enough to find a female pilot and a female technician to clear you for take-off, you still have some praying to do. Statistically, 0% of airtraffic controllers and airfield operations specialists are women[2]. Of course, that doesn't mean there are ZERO ladies working in air traffic control. There just aren't enough to constitute even 0.6% of the workforce.

Trains, of course, are also out.

---

[1] http://www.bls.gov/cps/cpsaat11.htm

[2] http://www.bls.gov/cps/cpsaat11.htm

100% of locomotive engineers and operators are men, as are 100% of the workers who operate railroad brake, signals and switches. 94.4% of railway yardmasters are men, but if you chance upon a female yardmaster, it won't help you much. She can't operate the trains.

You might have better luck with bus drivers, almost half of whom are women. But the streets are likely to be chaos. And there won't be anyone on hand to help you navigate that.

87.4% of police and sheriff's patrol officers are men. 96.6% of firefighters are men. 68.8% of Emergency Medical Technicians and Paramedics are men, so if it all goes tits up and you get hurt, there's a small chance you might make it to a hospital.

I hope you don't get too badly hurt, though. 65.7% of all surgeons are men.

Maybe you should just work from home? In the dark, mind you. With no running water.

Uh-oh. Looks like that might be a problem, too.

For all computer and mathematical occupations combined, 74.4% of the workforce is male. Computer network architects, who design and implement all our computer based communications systems are 91.9% men. And 94.2% of radio and telecommunications equipment installers and repair technicians are men.

Looks like that plan is fucked.

Hope it doesn't get too hot, or too cold the day men don't show up for work. Even if you had power, which you don't, you would be hard-pressed to get anyone in to take a look at your wonky air-conditioner or furnace.

98.4% of heating, air-conditioning and refrigeration mechanics and installers are men.

Oh well. Guess you'll have to mosey on down to the local café, which has no power either, but what's logic and consequence anyways? Be careful when you step over all that accumulating garbage! Remember that most EMTs are men, and they've taken the day off. Don't want to get hurt now.

Most garbage collectors are men, too. 93.4%, to be exact.

You'll need to stop at the bank first, for a little cash injection.

Oops. Don't bother.

The machine hasn't been filled with money today. 81.5% of security guards and gaming surveillance officers are men. It's unlikely the banks would be functioning anyways, with no men at work. 72.1% of all securities, commodities and financial services sales agents are men. 72.6% of the nation's CEOs would be taking the day off, along with 70.9% of all the general and operations managers.

Don't count on getting a weather report today. Statistically, 0% of the nation's atmospheric and space scientists are women.

Actually, don't plan on acquiring pretty much anything today. The workers in the entire production, transportation and material moving occupations are 78.2% men. Not only will no goods be moving on the day men go on strike, they won't be made, period. 82.4% of all the industrial production managers are men.

Nothing will be built or extracted from the earth in terms of raw materials. 97.5% of that workforce is male.

Nothing will be installed, maintained or repaired. 96.8% of that workforce is male.

If men took a collective day off, we would instantly be without power, without the means to communicate, without protection, without water, without trucks bringing us the food and products we take for granted, because men are the ones who provide all those things.

Where in our culture do we EVER see that acknowledged? If women took the day off, with the sole exception of NURSES, nothing would happen. No one would die. The world would continue to function. The hair salons and primary schools and retail clothing stores would close, and the male management structure would have to find some way to answer their own phones for a day, but essentially, nothing would happen.

You will often hear feminists barking on about male privilege, usually in a well-lit room, comfortably warm, with her iPhone close at hand, buzzing with updates from her latest #mensuck Twitter feed, with zero awareness that every single one of those luxuries is provided by men.

Male privilege is the idea that men have unearned social, economic, and political advantages or rights that are granted to them solely on the basis of their sex, and which are usually denied to women.

Unearned.

UNEARNED?!?

The Department of Labor says otherwise, bitch. It is women who have failed to earn their privileges. We live in a world powered and created and maintained by men, and yet feminists have created a whole philosophy and ideology that insists women and men are equal.

We are not equal. We do not need to be equal. We can't be equal. What we can be is grateful.

And we can pray men never, ever take a day off.

Lots of love,

JB

Men talk about their feelings all the time. They just don't use words.

A common cultural trope is that men don't like to express their feelings, and women's magazines and websites devote enormous amounts of space teaching women how to correct this "flaw" in men.

This irritates me for two reasons:

First, it is based on the assumption that the way women communicate is automatically best and everyone else (read: men) should be forced into accepting and imitating that excellence. If women like words and tears and dramatic gestures and consider all of those things perfectly acceptable forms of communication, well then, dammit, men should, too. If women like to use their words to show how they feel, then everyone else should use their words, too.

This falls in line with the general effort to define men as not just DIFFERENT, but WRONG and quite possibly BAD. Acceptable men are the ones that act like women, accept women's moral superiority and strive to imitate women in their thoughts and actions and beliefs. Some men are like that naturally and good for them. But most men are beaten into submission by the ubiquitous cultural message that they are flawed and must be fixed. I hate my son growing up in a world that tells him his natural instincts and proclivities are bad and that the only solution is to leash himself to a woman who will civilize him. Correct him. Improve him. I hope LittleDude grows up to see how much bullshit that is.

Which leads to my second point: men talk about their feelings ALL THE DAMN TIME, they just don't use words. Men show you how they feel by WHAT THEY DO. Sometimes, very rarely, Mr. JB is a dick and when he is, we don't have a long conversation about it. He brings me flowers, and he hates buying flowers! Those flowers say everything though. They say, "Honey, I'm sorry. I know I upset you and I feel terrible about that and I'm sorry and I know you will forgive me because you love me and I want you to know how much I love you, too". No words exchanged, but so much said.

When he sends you a picture he snapped with his phone of a beautiful sky or a crazy traffic jam or the sauce he spilled on his tie, he is telling you how he feels. "Look at this sky! It's gorgeous and it makes me think of you. I want to share this with you." Or "Christ, look at this traffic. Man this pisses me off. I feel frustrated and angry and I need to think about you so I can calm the fuck down and not kill everybody."

When he scootches over on the couch so you can have the warm spot, he is telling you "I love you and I think about your comfort and I want to make sure you feel warm and cozy". When he unloads the dishwasher, he is telling you "you look tired and you have had a long day and I want to pitch in and help you out because I care about you". When he walks past you and stops to give you a peck on the cheek, he is telling you "I can't imagine my life without you."

Men don't typically use words to describe how they feel. They use actions. A man's love is in what he DOES, so before you take a breath to start bitching about how he never talks to you, stop for a second to consider what he does for you, and listen. Listen to the silence. All his feelings are in it. Acknowledge it. Say "thank you". And remember that for most men, the inverse is true, too. He watches what you DO for him to see if you love him. Your actions speak volumes.

So be nice. Do nice things. Don't talk. Do. Talk a walk on his side of the communication divide and you might just realize that he never shuts up about how he feels. Even if he never says a word.

Lots of love,

JB

Man-shaming. It should be a word.

Call out someone for being an overweight slovenly pig, and you're fat-shaming. Call out someone for dressing like a whore and wandering completely shit-faced drunk down a dark alley where – surprise! she gets raped! – and you're slut-shaming. Call out someone for expressing contempt and straight up hatred for men and masculinity, and you're …. well, now. We don't have a word for that, do we?

Let's make one: *man-shaming*.

Man-shaming is not the same as emasculating. Emasculation means to literally remove a man's genitals (castration is to remove the testicles), and in a more colloquial sense, it means to humiliate a man by denying him the qualities that define masculinity – strength, vigor, confidence, courage, boldness and virility. Not a definitive list, obviously.

Man-shaming is something different: it's an effort to cause men to feel shame for their very natural feelings. To make them feel as if being a man, or being masculine is somehow wrong and disgraceful. And it starts very early, in our culture. Our current school system is rigged to benefit girls at the expense of boys, and students are graded and evaluated "objectively" on how well ALL students can imitate a typical girl's behaviour. At six years of age, students are expected to sit quietly, follow instructions and read and write and cut and paste and color and cover everything in glitter and always remember to use your words! They are NOT expected, or in some cases even ALLOWED, to track the trajectory of objects in motion, disassemble and reassemble physical structures, learn rules and fairness and victory and defeat, interact with the world and other people physically, display confidence or boldness or courage, and if they do, they will be diagnosed with some sort of bullshit "condition" and drugged into submission with a glue stick in one hand and a ribbon just for showing up in the other. I use the word "they" because girls who quite naturally display characteristically male traits will be forced into submission as well, but the fact is that most Ritalin prescriptions are filled for BOYS.

Assuming a boy survives the near continuous man-shaming of schooling, he goes out into a wider culture that paints men and masculinity in an equally harsh and derisive light. He confronts himself as violent, stupid, arrogant, ruthless and cruel. The alternative is apathetic, aimless, unmotivated, uncivilized and still really, really stupid. He sees men discarded like used Kleenex by the women around him and may even have grown up without a man in his own life. He meets head-on, the message that he is superfluous, easily sacrificed, unnecessary and possibly even dangerous.

And yet, men still account for almost all of the engineers, scientists, mathematicians and computer programmers in the world. Men are the engine that drive our modern, high technology society further ahead at speeds that astonish and delight. As Camille Paglia once said, without men, we'd all be living in grass huts.

Mike Buchanan calls for a renewed interest from the MRM in activism: stop debating and start taking on specific issues, one at a time. He wants to see naming, shaming and ridicule heaped on feminists, and this is where women like myself can help. Building awareness starts by pointing out, in very specific ways, when the people around you are engaging in man-shaming.

Here's an example:

Mr. JB has three close friends, all male and all single. JudgyAsshole, an accountant, CleverBoy, an engineer and PrinceCharming, a senior manager in the healthcare field and an adjunct professor at the local university. They are all accomplished, intelligent and worthy men. A fourth man, PansyAss, had joined the guys one day and the conversation turned to women and the men's physical preferences for how women should look. PansyAss was adamant that a woman's worth was only properly taken by evaluating her MIND and nothing else mattered. He argued that focusing on a woman's looks was superficial and objectifying and dehumanizing and all the usual feminist blah blah blah. PansyAss was raised, of course, by a strong single mother who had him in daycare from day one and who proudly raised her son to be a feminist and a friend to women everywhere.

Here's the thing: teaching women that it does not matter how they look, and teaching men to feel ashamed of caring how women look is doing no one any favors. Biology always wins. Men have a very strong preference for women who look lush and fertile and strong and fit, and the waist to hip ratio on a woman communicates all those things. Ladies who bury their waists under 60 extra pounds of lard are deeply unappealing to most men, and when men are made to feel that it is some flaw in their fundamental character that revolts at the idea of stroking those fat rolls, that is man-shaming. Stand a slender woman with breasts and hips and a small waist next to an overweight woman solid from neck to cankles, and most men will prefer the slender woman. The entire Fat Acceptance Movement is an attempt to shame men for a very natural preference for slim women, because the alternative would be to lose some goddamn weight, and that puts the onus and responsibility on women, and we all know how much women like being held responsible for anything at all. Yeah, not a whole lot.

I entered the conversation with the guys and pointed out that their desire for a healthy, fit, strong body (in addition to all the other qualities a sane man wants in a woman) was not some personality flaw and that PansyAss was attempting to shame them for being normal, healthy men. Asshole, Charming and Clever can't wake up one morning and just magically find fat chicks appealing, and trying to make them feel bad for that is man-shaming.

Don't feel bad, guys. The shame belongs to the women stuffing cupcakes down their gullets and ordering bigger stretchy pants on the internet because regular stores don't carry their size. PansyAss and his ilk can have those women. Have fun!

I find that men are so much more open to seeing when they are being subjected to man-shaming and much more willing to change than women are. Even when shaming techniques are pointed out to women, most women have an attitude of "So what? Who gives a shit?". It's not that women can't see that they are deliberately and openly mocking or discrediting or ignoring men and masculinity – they can. They just don't care. Masculinity has become a set of qualities that feminism is determined to stamp out, which is obviously completely absurd given that our entire society and economy functions as a result of a group of hypermasculine men who are on the cutting edges of science and mathematics and engineering and programming. Those men create the world we live in, and they do it by being bold, fearless, confident and taking risks that would make the rest of us blanche. Of course, there are a FEW women who participate, but they are outliers. The majority of women don't produce anything particularly useful, except other human beings of course, and that is just as it should be.

Popular media, swallowing feminist dogma hook line and sinker, likes to try and make stay at home wives and mothers feel shame, too. We aren't contributing anything, apparently. Just making a productive man even more productive, raising happy children, creating safe communities and making life worth living, but NOTHING ELSE. Well, fuck that nonsense!

I won't accept any shaming of my life. Being a wife and mother is the highest manifestation of a psychology and set of needs and desires that has evolved over millennia to ensure the survival of humanity. And no man should ever accept that his psychology and set of needs and desires, similarly evolved, is shameworthy. There is honor in the feminine and in the masculine. It's time to call out everyone, men and women alike, who refuse to acknowledge the value of both.

> *Honor and shame from no condition rise;*
> *Act well your part, there all the honor lies.*

ALEXANDER POPE,
An Essay on Man

Lots of love,

JB

Yippee-ki-yay, motherfucker. John McClane and the redemption of masculinity.

Back when I was a lowly undergrad student in film theory, I irritated the shit out of my classmates and professors alike by insisting that *Die Hard* was the best movie ever made. There is an unspoken assumption in film theory that Hollywood cinema is plebeian – something for the unwashed masses to enjoy in all their mind-numbing cluelessness. Film theory majors are deeper than this, people! We enjoy the moving complexity and artistry of the black and white post-World War II Albanian avant-garde. The French New Wave! The cinema of the Weimar Republic!

Die Hard? **DIE HARD?!?!?!?!**

Are you fucking kidding me?

No way, motherfucker. Not kidding you at all. *Die Hard* is the best movie ever made. Sit back, relax and I will tell you why.

There are only seven stories in the world: the entire world of literature and film can be boiled down to these seven basic plots.

Overcoming the Monster
The hero must destroy the monster and restore balance to the world
Rags to Riches
The hero is an everyman whose natural talents finally triumph
The Quest
The hero must overcome terrific odds to capture a prize
Voyage and Return
The hero is thrust into a strange and alien world and must find his way back to reality
Comedy
In this sense, comedy doesn't mean "haha funny", but rather that the hero must overcome obstacles to getting the girl
Tragedy
The hero doesn't get the girl
:(
Rebirth
The hero is transformed in some profound way and becomes a better person

Die Hard is the greatest film ever made because it combines all SEVEN plots into one heroic story of redemption and triumph.

Let's start with a little context. *Die Hard* premiered on July 15th, 1988 into a culture undergoing some dramatic transformations. Globalization was beginning to look pretty threatening to the manufacturing based US economy, women were entering the workforce *en masse* and the divorce cult was just taking hold. Americans in particular felt the ground quivering under their feet, for good reason.

Jobs were evaporating, families were disintegrating and men were getting sidelined by perky chicks in shoulder pads and high heels, who seemed to have the upper hand in the new world order where strength and stamina and sheer brute force was no longer required.

Enter John McClane.

He's a cop, on his way to LA to spend Christmas with his wife and kids. McClane's wife Holly has gone back to using her father's name (which she pretends is really her "own" name) in her professional life. She works in the vaguely threatening Nakatomi Plaza and the film starts with her office Christmas party.

And quickly goes straight to glorious hell.

Let's look at the seven stories again:

In *Die Hard*, the monster takes the form of German terrorists hell bent on avenging some compatriots being held hostage by the state. The terrorists want them released! Except not really. They're actually just plain old thieves, but their foreignness is both unsettling and doubly threatening.

The terrorists are sophisticated and well-armed and have exotic accents and names, and John is just a cop from the rough street of NYC. He's every man. Just a guy trying to get along as best he can.

The odds are stacked dramatically against John. The corporate crowd is laughably useless. They sit around wondering when they're going to be allowed to pee, while John takes on the whole group of bad guys by himself. One coked up guy in a suit decides he might be able to outwit the terrorists and ends up with a bullet in his head for his effort.

Nope. It's just John. And one by one, he takes the bad guys down. In his bare feet.

Nakatomi Plaza, like the global economy, is a work in progress. John's world spans lush lobbies and oak-panelled boardrooms, glassed in computer workstations and concrete rooftops littered with chains and pulleys and strange boxes and metal containers. He moves through elevator shafts and bathrooms, under conference tables and across marble foyers, each floor representing a different stage of development, for both the story and the culture. John needs to adapt instantly to every circumstance, and he does.

John still loves Holly, despite her misgivings about him. When he is at his most vulnerable, digging chunks of glass out of his feet, his thoughts are with her. He wants her to know that he loves her. The obstacles to love are not just dangerous criminals with loaded guns and no qualms about using them, but a wider culture that whispers to Holly: *He isn't good enough. He's just a cop. You deserve more. You need more.*

Then again, there's nothing like being dragged by the hair to make a girl appreciate her well-muscled husband with a gun in his hand and a fierce instinct to protect, backed up with courage and the willingness to risk everything.

Funny that, eh?

Watching the movie, we can see how honest John's heart is, how much he really does love Holly and how confused he is by her seemingly greater attachment to her professional life, and at the end, she falls into his arms, grateful and welcomed, but we all know in our hearts that she is responding to the circumstances.

Is anyone the slightest bit shocked when the sequel comes along and Holly and John are divorced? Nope. The writing is on the wall in the first film. John gets the girl, but only because she happens to need him at that very moment. The minute life returns to the normalcy of laundry and breakfast dishes and late night meetings, we know that Holly will discard John. He doesn't fit in her world anymore.

John's profound sadness comes from his realization of that fact, but he can't stop himself: he has to try. He has to save her, come what may.

This is the foundation for John's transformation. He realizes that the world, his world, is out of control. His life is careening down a path he doesn't want to be on but is powerless to stop. All he can do is react. He cannot change the circumstances he has found himself in, but he can react to them, and he sure as hell can fuck up what other people are doing.

Hans: Do you really think you have a chance against us, Mr. Cowboy?
John: Yippee-ki-yay, motherfucker.

Does he have a chance? Does any man have a chance against a force that is both overwhelming and diabolical?

It comes down to a simple question: can evil be defeated?

> "The only thing necessary for the triumph of evil is for good men to do nothing."
>
> — Edmund Burke

John McClane is an ordinary man in extraordinary circumstances, and he travels every hero's path on his way to redemption. He takes every masculine virtue and amplifies it: courage, intelligence, a willingness to take great risks, an instinct to protect, physical power, perseverance, defiance and a tolerance for pain, and he sets those against the feminized men and women who live in glass towers and pursue money and material gains over all others.

And he kicks their asses.

John doesn't just exist, he exists as a man. He insists on the value of masculinity and demonstrates his power in defiance of every force against him, right to the bitter end. Even after he has defeated the terrorists and rescued the hostages, the authority of the state in the form of the FBI still excoriates and criticizes him. He is mocked and scorned and the gratitude he ought to have earned is nowhere to be seen.

He finds his solace in the arms of his wife, but that solace is tinged with betrayal. She will not stay. Her gratitude is fleeting. She will discard him when he is no longer useful.

Ultimately, *Die Hard* is a tragedy. John cannot win. His redemption is overshadowed by rejection. The world does not want him, no matter how clearly he demonstrates his value.

Men have a number of choices when they confront a culture that refuses to acknowledge them: give up, give in, drop out altogether or stand up and refuse to be cowed. Do you really think you stand a chance against a tide of opposition and a chorus of disapproval?

Yippe-ki-yay, motherfucker.

Live free or die hard.

Lots of love,

JB

Attention middle class men: please stop inventing and producing all the useful shit we need and just die already.

Sensational headline much? I thought I would do Janice one better and make her point even more clearly. According to Janice, middle class men are "useless" because they don't read Martha Stewart and STILL get all pissy about screechy harridans living in the house with them[3].

Come on now, lads. What is your problem?

---

[3] http://www.thetimes.co.uk/tto/opinion/columnists/janiceturner/article3675766.ece

Turner's article is all the usual tired clichés about men and housewives and why women are awesome and men suck, but I found this statement particularly delightful:

"...it seems easier to train a bonobo monkey to play Chopin than a human male to pick up his own pants."

Oh my. Lucky Mr. Turner, eh? You know Janice, this is actually a really easy problem to solve. Your husband leaves his pants on the floor? Leave them there. It's his house, he lives there, too, he clearly doesn't give a shit, so why should you?

Why indeed!

Janice seems to be operating under a few assumptions that lay bare how she feels about her husband, her marriage and men in general, and sadly, I think she is indicative of an entire generation of women who really do think men are "useless".

Her first assumption is that the home belongs to her and she has the absolute authority and right to dictate how it looks and how it runs. It's interesting, isn't it, that on the one hand Janice rails against the idea that women could ever have found leading a pampered, sheltered life in a cozy cocoon of domesticity that a man paid for fulfilling, and then on the other hand, she still demands the right to command that space with unconditional decree.

Pants on the floor? VERBOTEN! Pick them up, useless man, and put them where I tell you to!

It's beyond me why Janice's husband doesn't tell her to fuck off.

Her second assumption is that whenever a man protests the requirement to meet his Princess's household standards, he must be in the wrong. Janice has lots of love for the Scandinavian model, which forces men to take a portion of leave after a baby is born or lose it altogether. The personal preferences of the family in question play no part in the dictates of the government. What does the baby want? Goodness! Who would ever consider that? What does the mother want? Who gives a shit? Back to work, bitch. What does daddy want? Oh please. Who cares?

Here's an ugly little reality that women like Janice refuse to even contemplate: most of the "work" that women do is complete and utter bullshit. What's the number one job category for women? Same as it was in the 1950's: **Secretary**. So basically, women have mastered the alphabet, and know how to use a telephone, a calendar and a keyboard. Wow! So much accomplishment!

Across all the Western, feminized world, productivity rates have soared, but wages have stagnated. Part of that is thanks to a movement within capitalism to return most of the proceeds of capital to shareholders and not workers, but an even bigger part has to do with women flocking *en masse* into the labor market and destroying the family wage. You see, there are way more jobs now than ever before, but there isn't way more money. Instead of one man doing something relatively useful and productive and earning a wage he could use to support a family, there are now endless towers of cubicles filled with women filing shit alphabetically and updating their Facebook status and taking a wage for doing so. Wages that would otherwise have gone to their husbands. And therefore to themselves.

It cannot possibly come as a surprise to anyone with a heartbeat and a single brain cell that our world runs on the power of science, technology, engineering and mathematics. Every single useful thing we have or hope for comes from the STEM fields, which have always been and continue to be completely dominated by men. Need a marketing strategy for scented candles? Hire a woman. Need the human genome sequenced? Oh, oops. You'll need men for that.

Oh, of course, there are a few women in the STEM fields. Our society has almost always made room for female genius to rise. There just aren't many of them to be had. #sorryfeminists. The Nobel Prize was established in 1901, and since its inception women have flooded into colleges and universities and we've had every opportunity to shine. 553 Nobel prizes have been awarded to 835 individuals, and that includes the wishy-washy Peace and Literature prizes[4]. And how many have been won by women? 44 prizes awarded. 50% of the population has secured just over 5% of Nobel Prizes. When you get rid of the peace and literature prizes, the number falls even lower. 16 prizes. Not quite 2%.

Way to go, ladies! Whatever will the world do without your genius?

So we've wrecked the family wage, destroyed the labor market, created a generation of fat, depressed, unhappy, stressed out children and for what? So women can utterly fail to compete with men in any meaningful way and then declare men "useless"? Women are not men. We do not have the same talents or interests or desires or motivations and the past 70 years has shown, if anything, that we are nowhere near to catching up with men, although the culture has done an amazing job of convincing both men and women that it's the end of men and the rise of women!

Yeah, right. My iPhone, dishwasher, antibiotics, vacuum cleaner, computer, car with auto-starter and every other useful thing I own begs to differ. The end of men? We better hope not. And this is not to say women aren't capable of genius. We are, in our own ways that complement and do not compete with men. We'll chat about that tomorrow. For now, let's be grateful all the men have gone off to work today. Women haven't shown themselves to be capable of doing what men do.

Why, some might even call them useless!

Lots of love,

JB

Oh look. It's Janice fucking Turner again. Men = Malign?

You remember Janice, right? She of the "why are middle class men so useless" tirade? *(see above)* Well, she's back at it, this time claiming that men are a malign influence we need to stamp out pronto[5].

As always, Janice *in italics*.

"While he was on remand for the murder of Tia Sharp, Stuart Hazell wrote a letter to his father: "You know I'm not a bad person," he said. "It's the Hazell curse." Not his fault: the internet searches for "violent forced rape" and "little girls with glasses". Attacking a child who trusted him, penetrating her with a sex aid, strangling, then posing and photographing her 12-year-old corpse: not his fault at all."

Wow! There's a leap of logic. Saying you are not a bad person is not the same as saying you are innocent. Hazell is simply identifying a pattern of behavior within his particular family as a contributing factor to his horrific crime, and most evidence bears that assertion out: adults who commit shocking crimes against children were almost always abused themselves as children, and very often by women[6].

[4] http://www.nobelprize.org/nobel_prizes/lists/all/index.html

[5] http://www.thetimes.co.uk/tto/opinion/columnists/janiceturner/article3768313.ece

[6] http://bjp.rcpsych.org/content/179/6/482.full

"Forces beyond his control made him commit this horrible crime. Hazell claims that he was abused as a child and thus powerless against an almost occultish desire to visit his own suffering on the next generation. He was a mere puppet of his innate drives and sexual impulses, a victim of destiny."

He wasn't a victim of destiny, he was a victim of childhood abuse that left him so profoundly damaged, he became a perpetrator of the very crimes that blighted his own childhood. Again, that's not terribly unusual. It might surprise you to know that a significant percentage of men who were abused as children were abused by women, and that abuse by a female relative correlates very highly to becoming a perpetrator. There is an alarmingly high rate of sexual abuse by females in the backgrounds of rapists, sex offenders and sexually aggressive men – 59% (Petrovich and Templer, 1984), 66% (Groth, 1979) and 80% (Briere and Smiljanich, 1993)[7].

"A curse is a magnificent excuse. It not only obviates all blame but dismisses the need for any further analysis. And it struck me that in this bizarre and grisly year, in which stories of sexual violence — from Jimmy Savile and Stuart Hall to Rochdale and Oxford — have saturated the news, that our examination of such events has been just as worthless and hollow."

Well, your examination certainly constitutes worthless and hollow. Why is it that you seem to have noticed all the nasty, evil men, but you make no mention of the nasty evil women who were up to murder and mayhem during the same period?

Fiona Andersen killed her three small children, and is hailed as a "beautiful girl". Sheri Torkington killed a woman she didn't even know after a screaming argument with her boyfriend. Michelle Mills stabbed her boyfriend to death in a brutal attack that was so frenzied she broke the blade right off. She then sat and watched him die for 20 minutes. Melanie Smith set fire to a house and killed five members of a young family because she wrongly believed the mother was having an affair with her partner.

"The endless assaults, rapes and dressing-room gropings exposed by Operation Yewtree were put down to 1970s sexual mores and celebrity indulgence. The "grooming" cases in which vulnerable girls were trafficked at rape parties were blamed on our dismal care system and the imported culture of Pakistani Muslims. The most arcane acts, committed by Hazell or Ariel Castro, the Ohio basement kidnapper, were filed with the likes of Fred West or Ted Bundy under "evil"."

I like how you left Rosemary West out of your analysis, there, Janice. I guess she was just an innocent dupe under the spell of darling Fred? Under a curse of some sort?

"Meanwhile, wherever I go, whichever women I speak to — my hairdresser, my old ma, friends at my exercise class, a gazillion strangers on Twitter — all are asking the same uneasy question: what is it with men? I can foresee the outraged, defensive online comments gathering now under this piece: "man-hating feminist", "how dare you blame the whole male gender". But seriously, guys, have you never stopped to wonder hard why members of your gender do so many vile things to members of ours?"

Why, yes, Janice, I'll bet they have. Have you ever stopped to wonder why so many members of your gender do equally vile things to their husbands and boyfriends and especially to children? I always wonder how it is possible to be evil and such a fucking coward at the same time. How hard is it to strangle a baby? Why not pick a more equally matched opponent? What is it with women that they go after the smallest, most vulnerable of victims?

---

[7] http://www.canadiancrc.com/PDFs/The_Invisible_Boy_Report.pdf (p.28)

"Because, let me tell you, womankind is a permanent state of Maoist self-criticism. If, say, some new study suggests that kids in nurseries are the tiniest bit disadvantaged compared with those cared for by mummies at home, we must pull on our hair shirts, wring our hands at our whole sex's selfish ambition. Daily we are berated for female shortcomings: we drink too much, break up the nuclear family with our pesky financial autonomy, are too promiscuous, cause our own cancers with frivolous lifestyle choices. And that's on top of our workaday self-flagellation: we're too fat, too old, are wearing unfashionable pointy shoes during a round-shoed summer . . ."

Selfish
Neglectful
Drunk
Slutty
Broken families
Frivolous
Fat
Old
Concerned about shoes

Yeah, that about sums it up, Janice.

Perhaps the reason women spend so much time thinking about these things is because it takes a lot of energy to defend such shallowness and superficiality.

People hardly ever feel guilty about doing the RIGHT thing, now do they? And based on your photo, Janice, you are definitely too fat.

"So it seems only fair that, just this once, men do a little uncomfortable soul-searching. Apply your larger, more rational male brains to a very big conundrum: why do men commit almost all of society's crime? It is a question so seldom considered that when the sociologists Cynthia Cockburn and Ann Oakley tried to analyse it, they found the Ministry of Justice does not even routinely break down offences by gender."

Men don't commit all of society's crimes. They get charged and prosecuted for all of society's crimes. Women have long received preferential treatment from the justice system, and continue to do so, masking the true extent of women's criminal proclivities. Domestic violence, for example, tends to be mutual, but men are far more likely to be charged and convicted of an offence both genders take part in equally.

Men who kill infants will not be seeing the light of day for a long, long time. Women who kill infants get a pat on the head, the address of a therapist and a prescription for Prozac. Indeed, there is a call for even MORE leniency for mothers who murder their infants[8]. According to one report[9]:

> Fathers were more likely than mothers to have killed their infants using violence which wounded. Nonetheless sentences were unrelated to the brutality of the offence: mothers who had killed with wounding violence received less severe penalties than fathers who had killed in a non-wounding way.

---

[8] http://www.independent.co.uk/news/uk/crime/scrap-outdated-infanticide-law-say-judges-495016.html

[9] http://www.ncbi.nlm.nih.gov/pubmed/8264367

"With persistent digging they found that in the year to June 2012, 85 per cent of all indictable crimes in England and Wales were committed by men. Moreover, the more serious the offence the more male offenders: 88 per cent of crimes against the person, 98 per cent of sexual offences and 90 per cent of murders were by men. And although theft is seen as the domain of female shoplifters, women were responsible for only 21 per cent. Taking into account that 19 out of 20 prisoners (each costing around £40,000 a year) are male, Cockburn and Oakley calculated that if men committed the same amount of crime as women, we'd save £30 billion a year."

You mean of course if men were CONVICTED of the same amount of crime as women and sentenced to the same amount of time. Even when women are convicted, they get less time in jail. Why, Vicky Pryce announced the day she was released from jail that she would be writing a book discussing the economics of jailing people women, and who wants to bet she thinks it's a bad, bad thing?

"That's a fat chunk of the deficit paid off right there. You mean we're clawing back a pittance from disabled folk with spare bedrooms when dealing with the root cause of male violence could save the defence budget? So why is this is not a key government strategy, except that men's brutality is seen as a given – an unavoidable downside of superior physical strength and sexual urgency, a by-product of that dark Y chromosome and the sloshing rocket fuel that is testosterone."

Indeed, why is not a priority? Let's get to the root cause of male violence, shall we? How about we start by looking at these men's earliest years. The first few years of life have a dramatic impact on how people come to perceive and react to the world around them. Uh-oh. Can we see the problem here? Who cares for small children during their earliest years? Who is primarily responsible for shaping their minds and experiences? Who governs whether their lives are filled with love and affection and stability, or abuse and neglect and violence? Oh, that would be women.

Hello, Mummy!

Let's take all these violent, terrible men and NOT blame their hormones, but look at their earliest experiences. Where are their mothers? Oh, right. Janice already answered that. They're off at the pub getting sloshed and worrying about their footwear.

"But is it really a given? As I'm sure male Times readers are bursting to tell me, not all men are rapists or wife-beaters. Then why not focus on what turns innocent boys into dangerous men? This week Diane Abbott, the Shadow Public Health Minister, made a much-heralded speech about the crisis of masculinity. She described modern man as lost in a post-industrial landscape, functionless, suicidal, porn-addicted, racked with performance anxiety in a "Viagra and Jack Daniels" culture, having "moob reductions" while unable to articulate his feelings."

Nice! What a sweet characterization of men. Well, I suppose if Janice is going to portray modern women as fat, drunk sluts more concerned about fashion than their own children, it's only fair that she portray men as fat, drunk, emotionally crippled porn-addicts who can't get it up.

Gosh her love of humanity just shines like a beacon in the night, doesn't it? But she still hits it. What turns innocent boys into dangerous men? What is it, Janice? Or more accurately, WHO is it?

"It was a somewhat broad brush picture. Blue-collar manual jobs were lost decades ago and today's young men who greet each other with "bro" hugs are certainly less restricted by masculine norms than boys at my school who believed it was effeminate to study English A level. But putting the spotlight on masculinity felt timely in 2013, the year of the sex crime."

Let's just go back for a minute and consider:

> There is an alarmingly high rate of sexual abuse by females in the backgrounds of rapists, sex offenders and sexually aggressive men – 59% (Petrovich and Templer, 1984), 66% (Groth, 1979) and 80% (Briere and Smiljanich, 1993).

Oh, dear. Looks like our fat, drunk slutty mothers have been up to a little bit of alarming behavior when the lights are off and no one is looking.

"At the heart of her speech was a welcome affirmation of fatherhood, hitherto absent from Labour thinking for fear of sounding judgmental about what constitutes a family, and all the more powerful from Ms Abbott, a single mother. "We need to say loudly and clearly, that there is a powerful role for fathers," she said. "Loving fathers are a benefit to children, loving families are a benefit to men."

How rich, coming from a single mother. Yes, indeed. Loving families are a benefit to our entire society. Why then do we have so many social programs to benefit single mothers, who, by definition, have made sure their children have no fathers in any meaningful sense? Why does the UK offer tax incentives to mothers who farm their children out to day orphanages and punish women who care for their own children?

"Maybe what is required is a Ministry for Men to focus on building healthier, happier men and in doing so guarding against the tragic consequences of malign male libido. (It would be self-funded by the resultant fall in crime.) A minister to oversee the provision of mentors for fatherless boys, to ensure those who witness domestic violence do not abuse themselves, to promote sex education based upon consent and respect. A male leader saying categorically that men are masters of their own lives, not slaves to their sexual appetites or victims of a curse."

You've got that ass-backwards, bitch. There is nothing malign about the male libido. What is malign is the abuse boys are subjected to, often by women, that results in the kind of anti-social behaviors you rail against. Monsters are not born, honey. They are made.

Made by whom?

That's the real question. Maybe we need a Minister for Women to teach women not to sexually abuse boys, to teach them not to have children if they don't intend to care for them, to teach them how to behave like mothers and wives and sisters and daughters and friends. Stop thinking about your fucking shoes and start thinking about someone other than yourself.

No one is saying that sex offenders should get a pass for how they have decided to act as an adult. The word adult is synonymous with autonomy and responsibility. Being the victim of an abusive, loveless childhood peppered with sexual assault is not an EXCUSE for how adults behave. It is an EXPLANATION. In order to understand why innocent boys become dangerous men, we are going to need to bring women into the conversation. How have these boys been mothered? Where are their fathers? What, exactly, have their experiences been?

That means we need to listen. Listen to what damaged men have to say. Discover how and by whom they were damaged. It's easy to just blame men for being men. It's the testosterone. Nasty stuff, that is. It's also a complete cop-out.

No baby is born determined to grow-up to be a child rapist. Those that do deserve our condemnation, absolutely, but that does not automatically exclude compassion. No, Hazell should never see the light of day again. Perhaps his mother shouldn't either. He wasn't born that way. He was made. The hand that rocks the cradle is the hand that rules the world. And the hand that decides to beat the ever-loving shit out of that baby is the hand that slays the world.

That hand often belongs to a woman.

If we really want to know what is up with men, we'll need to start by asking *what the fuck is up with women*?

Lots of love,

JB

First I feared him, then I loathed him, then I forgave him and now I take care of him: the story of my Father and me.

My father was born in 1938 during WWII in a small town outside a large city in Germany. He was the only son in a family of ten children. He was six years old when the war ended in 1944, and his earliest memories are of houses burning, being painfully hungry and soldiers marching.

Dad and his sisters suffered through extreme food deprivation, as did countless others. Indeed, he experienced such severe malnutrition that his growth was permanently stunted and he reached an adult height of only 5'4, despite the fact that his father and grandfather and uncles were all well over 6'. He has huge hands and incredible upper body strength, a testament to the physical man he might have been.

He witnessed horrors we can barely comprehend, including the deaths of four of his sisters. They did not just die, they died in front of him. Dad is not forthcoming with war stories, and I have never heard the exact circumstances under which he lost his sisters. It is simply too painful, all these years later, to recount. One story he will tell is watching a Russian tank burn, and seeing desperate soldiers escape through the hatch, only to be beaten to death at the roadside by old women with shovels and hammers.

Those experiences made him a profoundly religious man, and sadly, his views of pain and suffering were always ones of comparison. Dad was offered a place at the gymnasium in Stuggart (a university preparatory), but his father, a former SS officer, forbade it. He would learn a useful skill, and he was sent to agricultural college. His father didn't see the Green Revolution coming, and by the time Dad graduated, industrial farming was well under way.

Dad married in Germany, and had two sons. Like many others, he turned his face towards the New World, seeking opportunity and greener pastures. When his children were ten and eight, he set forth for North America, leaving his sons and his wife in the care of his mother and sisters, promising to return for them when he had secured a job and a home for them.

He never went back. He abandoned them.

He met my mother when she was just nineteen years old and he was considerably older. He never told her about his family back in Germany, and they married and had four children by the time my mother was 25 years old. My three brothers, and me.

And they were fucking horrible parents. There is no nice way to spin it. They embraced a religion that encouraged extreme violence against children. Their philosophy was that a child's will must be completely broken so that the child will then accept the will of God. My mother was ecstatically violent, and my father less so, but they were both culpable. Their particular brand of religious violence continues in America to this day.

To compound our suffering, my parents also believed that any demonstration of physical affection would "spoil" a child, and I have not one single memory of my mother or father kissing or hugging us, or showing any sign whatsoever that they loved us.

When my father came towards me, as a child, all I felt was ... fear. I wondered what pain was in store. And no matter what it was, I knew it would pale in comparison to the pain he had suffered. I was supposed to feel grateful for that.

I didn't.

We lived on a farm, growing our own food, making our own bread, with chickens and cows and bees (for honey) and pigs and endless fields of potatoes. Whatever money my parents managed to earn, they turned over to the crazy church. It was an interesting childhood, to say the least.

And then....my mother discovered feminism. She exchanged one violent, irrational, dehumanizing ideology for another, and she soon decided that she needed a man like a fish needed a bicycle. After countless physically violent arguments with my father, including one episode where she hit him in the head with a cast iron frying pan and left him for dead on the front porch, he turned his back and walked away from us, just like his first family.

One day we woke up and he was gone. My mother was quick to inform us that he simply walked away, and left us to starve in the streets, and that she alone would be the sole reason we survived and prospered. She never missed an opportunity to curse him. She told us about his first family, and how she did not need to divorce him, because they were never married in the first place. She hated him and hated all men and our daily lives were filled with her anger and vitriol and violence. She never gave a moment's thought to what her hatred of men and our father was doing to her sons. She gave us daily rations of rage and blame and every bad thing that happened was always his fault.

Being a child, I believed it. So did my brothers.

And we loathed him for it. How could he leave us with such an evil woman? My mother once held a knife to my throat and made me beg for my life. When I was eleven. And I remember going to bed, thinking not how much I hated her, but how much I hated HIM for leaving us to her devices.

Needless to say, coming in to my own as a person was a difficult and very fraught process. When I finally made it to university, I had literally no idea what a loving, affectionate, decent relationship looked like. I was lucky enough to meet Pixie almost immediately, and although her material circumstances were much more comfortable than mine, she too had experienced a horrifically traumatic and abusive childhood. I will leave it to Pixie to reveal any details. Suffice say, at our posh university, we were definitely outsiders.

Interestingly enough, I was never attracted to men who behaved badly. I never sought to enmesh myself in relationships that replicated the worst of my father. Quite the opposite. I didn't seek out pain in an effort to work through what I had suffered. I had a lovely boyfriend who was all kindness and sympathy. He was the gentlest man I have ever known. And I cannot adequately articulate how his gentleness and caring healed me.

He proposed marriage, but ultimately, he was far too compliant and mild, and I was disconcerted by his willingness to acquiesce to what I wanted, even though I never wanted anything bad. I could trust him to treat me with the utmost kindness and care, but I could not lean on him. That was impossible. I declined his proposal and moved on.

I eventually landed at graduate school, in an MBA program, where I met my husband. From the time my father left and all throughout my twenties, I never saw him. I knew he was working overseas and only landed stateside a couple of times a year, but I never sought him out and he never looked for me. I married and went overseas myself, and after a year in Australia and another year in China came back to North America with a young daughter and my son only months away from being born.

And then I received a phone call. It was my father, calling to tell me that my mother's mother had passed away, and that I should let her know. So much of the pain had seeped away that I felt confident confronting my father, and I asked him why he had done it.

Why did you just turn your back and walk away?

And then the truth came to light. He hadn't walked away. He certainly had not left us to starve. My mother had filed for an annulment and requested a restraining order, which she was granted. When I finally saw my father again, he had two boxes with him. One was filled with income tax returns showing that he had never missed a child support payment, and court orders preventing him from seeing us based on his violence towards my mother, along with supervised visitations that were all scheduled for when he was overseas, working to meet his child support payments.

The other box contained cards and letters. Birthday cards and so many letters. All returned. By my mother. He never stopped sending them, hoping one of us would one day get the key and fetch the mail, but my mother was always adamant that the mail was her business. It was one of those community mailboxes, where you had to go and fetch your mail, and since I never got any mail, it never occurred to me that there was anything untoward about my mother's insistence that only she would have access to it.

As an adult, it makes so much sense. How did we continue to live in our house? How was my mother able to afford food and clothing and YMCA memberships for four children without my father's support? Of course she had his support. But she hid it from us, and poisoned our minds against our father. It's called parental alienation, and she is not the first, nor the last woman to destroy her children in this way.

It's a special kind of evil.

It has been many years since I have had any contact with my mother. She hated Mr. JB with a passion, and saw that she could not control him. She forbid me to marry him. I told her to go fuck herself. With the birth of my own children, I have truly come to grasp the depths of her depravity. It is unthinkable for me to hurt my children. I would die before I ever whipped them unconscious with a wet leather belt. I would kill anyone who tried to do such a thing.

It was not just my mother who was violent during my childhood, though, and a huge part of the reason I have a relationship with my father is owing to the heart-felt, tear-soaked apology he offered me. My father does not cry. It was an intensely emotional experience, to listen to him express his regrets for what he had done.

"If I could do my life again, I would have showered you with love, and never lifted a hand against you".

He gave no excuses, no justifications, no defenses. My father looked at me and apologized for being wrong. So very wrong.

And I forgave him. I cannot turn back the hands of time and restore his children to him, but I have three beautiful children of my own, and he is a wonderful grandfather to them. He gives them all the love and attention he denied his own children. And I understand profoundly how important that is. In being the mother to my children that I wished I had, I have erased so much of the damage she inflicted. In being a loving, perfect grandfather, my father is able to forgive himself for being a terrible father.

The most amazing relationship has blossomed between my Dad and my husband, too. Mr. JB is the son my Dad wishes he had. They go fishing and do home improvement projects together and sit in the sun and have cold beer and talk about football. My Dad holds forth on his crackpot conspiracy theories and my husband laughs at him and tells Dad he's nuts and they laugh and watch the kids race up and down the street.

Today is Father's Day. Millions of fathers will wake up to pancakes and glitter covered construction paper cards and new socks and ties. Millions more will wake up to a quiet house, their children only ghosts that haunt the corners of the room. This post is for those fathers. I am a living testament to the fact that children grow up, and they look back and see truth that they could not see when they were only children. Estrangement from your children is the most unbearable pain, and to see your children twisted against you is pure agony.

But there is hope. Children are not children forever. The brutal reality is that the women who injure their children in this way will never face any punishment from the law. Their own children may not be so forgiving.

My mother stole my father from me and blighted my childhood in so many ways. My revenge has been to refuse to allow her to influence my life, to refuse to carry out a cycle of abuse and to be a good mother to my own children. My revenge has been to marry a good man, and be a good wife. My revenge has been to find my father, forgive him, and be a good daughter. I cannot give him back the days past, but I can give him this day, and all the days to come.

Never lose hope. The future could be so different.

Happy Father's Day.

Lots of love,

JB

60% of married men carry the primary financial burden for their families.

This story is everywhere today, and I'm finding the various spins on it so fascinating. First of all, I have yet to see any major media outlet put men at the center of the narrative: I can't find any stories that talk about the 60% of MEN who are supporting their families. All the focus is on the 40% of WOMEN who are now out earning their husbands.

Feminist websites are all rah rah rah – ladies be kicking ass so hard!

Instructively, Jezebel (linking in from a fellow Gawker site) follows their sneering piece with a gif showing a scantily clad woman punching a man in office setting, with the headline "Woman Shows How To Kick Ass At Work". One can imagine the outcry if it were a man doing the same thing to a woman.

Double XX at Slate has two stories, both trying so hard to spin the 40% as some kind of feminist triumph. Hanna Roisin confesses that the numbers are a teeny bit misleading, since economic factors (such as the wide scale decimation of male dominated manufacturing jobs) are one of the principle reasons men are unable to make a living wage anymore.

Women didn't magically acquire more skills, or learn to use them in more productive ways. Men lost their jobs. That's not exactly a triumph. Winning a race because your main competitor broke his leg at the starting line is not winning. It's taking first by default. A victory dance might be premature.

Amanda Marcotte has nothing to contribute to the conversation, really, other than to mock another news site for their reactions. She pays at least passing lip service to the idea that stripping men of economic power leaves FAMILIES worse off, but can't quite bring herself to suggest that, oh, men just might be good for something after all.

"It's true that these new breadwinner stats are not all good news, but the real problem is that men earning less means less money overall for the average American home. What's really hurting Americans isn't female equality, but growing income inequality between the rich and everyone else. Pitting men against women is simply a distraction from the real economic issues facing us all."

Amanda doesn't really want to address the whole income inequality issue in any depth because the first fact that will leap out is that single mothers make up 25% of the so-called "breadwinners", and single mothers tend to be dirt poor. Single motherhood remains a terrible choice for women and children, and for the fathers who are shut out of the picture from the get-go.

Income inequality highlights that little niggling fantasy of the "patriarchy", too. When the top income earners, both men and women, are taking ever larger slices of the economic pie, it looks a lot like aristocracy and not patriarchy.

What nobody really wants to discuss is the actual Pew Study itself[10], but I think we should take a look because there's some pretty interesting stuff lurking there.

Let's leave aside the number of women who are currently working outside the home and look at how people FEEL about that situation. How many people think the ideal family is a male breadwinner with a full time mother at home?

51% think having a mom at home makes children better off.

74% think having moms work has made it harder for families to do a good job raising children. 50% think having moms work has made it harder for marriages to thrive.

And pretty much no one thinks being a single mother is a good idea.

People over 30 seem capable of understanding that having women work outside the home is bad for children and bad for marriage, but they don't seem to grasp a very simple economic fact: women flooding the labor market has been a key reason men's wages have evaporated. The number of "jobs" may have increased over the past few decades (mostly housewife or paper filing jobs), but the amount of money available to pay for those workers has not. Instead of having one very productive (usually male) worker earn a family living, we now have two workers fighting over the same wages.

---

[10] http://www.pewsocialtrends.org/2013/05/29/breadwinner-moms/2/#chapter-2-public-views-on-changing-gender-roles

People under the age of 30 seem to get that: having two people work doesn't make it easier to live a comfortable life. It makes it harder. More people scrabbling for the same resources will obviously make workplace competition cutthroat, and no is better off in the long run.

What we are seeing is a Tragedy of the Commons playing out. We have a finite (more or less) set of resources in the form of jobs and money. We need those jobs and money to support families and children. Rather than maximize our potential as a family unit, we have set up a situation in which any given individual has to fumble after limited resources the best way they can, leaving everyone worse off.

The supply of money is not limitless. It really comes down to that. We can work together as families to maximize how much money we get in two ways: both adults compete and both take home less of a finite resource, or the two adults specialize. One takes care of the money and one takes care of the home and children.

Specialization wins every time. And it looks like lots of people know that instinctively, but the train is picking up speed on the way to Disasterville and no one seems to understand where the brakes are located.

It's under the desks where all the women are sitting.

When the US government wanted to encourage home ownership, it made the cost of interest on mortgage payments a tax deduction. Lots of reasons that was a good idea, and lots of reasons it was a terrible idea.

But the economic adage "if you want less of something, tax it; if you want more, subsidize it" holds true. Putting the brakes on the train could be as simple as offering generous tax deductions to men supporting families at home. Basic personal amounts, amounts for dependants, income splitting – there are lots of ways to reduce men's tax burdens for the years they are winning the bread their family eats.

And that's the sticking point for feminist culture in particular. Depending on men. It's a strategy that has worked for thousands of years, and based on my iPhone, 3G wireless network, dishwasher, flush toilet, push-up bra and every other luxury I have access to, it looks like men are pretty damn dependable.

But that isn't a story that gets told very often, anymore. Once upon a time, there were men who were loving fathers and husbands, who spent their lives toiling to bring home the bread.

Once upon a time? 60% of men still do exactly that. My guess is 100% of men would gladly be the family breadwinners, provided there was both opportunity, and rewards in doing so. In a culture that can't bear to demonstrate even the tiniest slice of gratitude or acknowledgement towards the majority of men who continue to support and provide for their families, why on earth should they continue to be beasts of burden? Why march out daily to compete for resources against the very person with whom you are going to share those resources?

It makes no sense.

40% of women are the family breadwinners. Peachy, ladies. Let's all fight over crusts.

And in the end, we'll all starve.

Lots of love,

JB

Asperger's Syndrome: Is it just another way of pathologizing creativity? And genius? Especially MALE creativity and genius? Let's get on our tinfoil hats.

For a long time, CleverGuy has been encouraging me to read Temple Grandin, assuring me that I would really like her writing. I know who Temple Grandin IS, but I never felt terribly compelled to read her books. She designs cattle management and slaughter facilities, and she is a very high-functioning, yet profoundly autistic genius.

Well, I ordered her book *Thinking In Pictures*, and finally got around to reading it this weekend. The book is fascinating, and her descriptions of her childhood and how she functions and thinks as an adult are truly remarkable. And also eerily familiar.

I suspect that is just what CleverGuy anticipated I would feel. As you recall, CleverGuy is a software programmer who decided to up his skills by taking a degree in electrical engineering, and for his final project, he built a 3D printer from scratch. CleverGuy has lots of experience working with (overwhelmingly men) who have been diagnosed as having Asperger's Syndrome, or who otherwise fall somewhere on the autism spectrum. In fact, I suspect CleverGuy himself might be somewhere on the spectrum, and hence is able to recognize the traits in others.

True story: last summer, me and CleverGuy had a conversation that went on for days in which we tried to determine whether either of us had any flaws in our personality. No, really. We did. Any potential candidate for "flawdom" was recognized as one that we share, and therefore could not possibly be a flaw.

Irrational optimism? Check

Self-aggrandizing logic? Check

Complete lack of regard for social niceties? Check

Total indifference to rank or social status? Check

Cringe inducing conversational style? Check

Preference for truth and bluntness over diplomacy and deceptions? Check

Difficulty getting along with peers because we find them all so fucking stupid? Check

Obsessive interest in fictional worlds and characters? Check

Ability to not take criticisms personally and focus on the veracity of insults? Check

Basically, we are totally unbearable socially unless we go into Bald-faced Painful Lying mode, pretending to find other people interesting and their conversation something less than retarded, which neither of us particularly like to do.

So I read Temple, and decided to take a few on-line "Do you have Asperger's" tests. Here is one from Wired[11].

When I filled out the questionnaire, I did not answer in terms of how I am NOW. At some point during my early twenties, I realized that I was not like other people in that I was far more socially awkward and offensive. I assumed that was the result of growing up, isolated, with violent assholes for parents,

[11] http://www.wired.com/wired/archive/9.12/aqtest.html

disregarding the fact that my brothers had all grown up in the same family, and had none of the problems I did with getting along with my peers.

Almost always, I was able to find another nerdy, "different" girl with whom I bonded, and we created our own little social world in which our bizarre and obsessive interests, while not necessarily shared, seemed perfectly normal. The summer I spent with Christina collecting, cataloguing and naming frogs was particularly memorable. Many long arguments over whether we had re-captured Mabel or Eloise ensued.

Fun times.

Compared to my friend, everyone else seemed stupid and mean.

But eventually, I matured enough to realize the problem wasn't with other people. It was with me. I could see that I lacked certain understandings of how relationships worked, and I set out to learn how normal people interacted. It was a Social Studies Project, and I used different resources to learn what was considered proper, acceptable behavior.

I studied etiquette manuals. I skipped all the shit about forks (who gives a crap?) and went right to how to respond when someone says their grandmother got hit by a bus. Hint: don't laugh. And I read psychology books. Lots and lots of psychology books. I found Abnormal Psychology the most helpful. Like a laundry list of what NOT to do. And I watched films and read fiction books, dissecting exactly how people responded to certain situations. I examined the musculature of facial expressions, not so I could read them in others (which I can do, to a limited extent), but rather so that I could reproduce them.

It's actually a very interesting subject. Try this: pull the inside of your eyebrows up, like a baby who is about to cry. Turn the corners of your mouth just slightly down. You should feel a lump, a tightness forming in your throat, and feelings of sadness may suddenly come to you, because you have tricked your brain into thinking you are sad.

Neat, huh?

Am I sounding psycho? I hope not. It's not that I don't have feelings, I was just really inept at conveying them and even though I could READ those expressions, more or less accurately in others, I had no idea how to respond.

So I learned.

Like Data, learning to be human.

I honestly thought everyone had to learn those things, and I was just a bit late to the game.

So, no surprise, I tested a teensy bit high on the "Do You Have Asperger's" quiz. But I answered the quiz as if I were responding BEFORE I had studied appropriate responses to emotional situations. If I answer as who I am now, given that I have studied and learned how to respond, I'm perfectly normal. None of the questions ask if I have to make a special effort to "find social situations easy".

In fact, I do find almost any social situation easy now. Because I have a set of instructions and responses I can access to tell me how to behave. And I'm constantly improving on them. I think a lot of people still find me abrasive and impolite and far too blunt, but that's because I generally don't give a fuck what they think. When I'm entertaining my husband's colleagues, I can put on the Perfect Hostess Apron just fine.

It's an effort, but one that I'm generally capable of.

And "thinking in pictures". Isn't everyone capable of doing this, to a certain degree? Temple is unique in that she can ONLY think in pictures, but surely most people can visualize their thoughts with little effort? My default is to think in pictures, but I have excellent memory recall of written words. I can remember and find links for posts with little effort. If I've read something in the last two to three years, I can find what I'm looking for almost down to the page number. But it takes a conscious effort.

Sometimes I MUST think in written words, and when I fail to do that, it's a disaster.

True story: like every other 15 year old in my highschool, I wrote my Beginning Driver's Exam and got a Learner's Permit. I read the Rules of the Road book to the point I had it memorized, and I used that book to help me to drive.

I passed my exam on the first try, and then proceeded to be one of the worst fucking drivers you have ever been on the road with. Our garage door was covered in dents because I could never figure out the boundaries of the car. Many poles in parking lots had chunks out of them thanks to my superior parking skills. I parallel parked exactly ONCE, and that was to pass my test. Nearly had a heart attack doing so. The three times I attempted a left turn, I crashed into oncoming traffic. I only ever made right hand turns after I smashed up the surgeon's Jaguar in a busy intersection.

When I drive, I have to constantly recite the road rules. I cannot accurately judge the speed of objects in motion, so I can only use rules that don't require that (no left hand turns). But it's really hard to keep my mind on the rule book, especially when a route becomes familiar.

I switch to pictures and just enjoy the scenery going by.

One day, I was out driving and I went through a very busy intersection. Against a red light. I didn't notice the light. I was too busy admiring the pictures of hanging flower baskets that were being added to my memories of "hanging flower baskets" and when I heard the sound of thirty car horns and screeching tires, I absolutely froze and did nothing.

Continued on through the intersection.

A few cars ended up in the ditch, and a few more on the wrong side of the road, but no one was injured. That was ten years ago. I never drove again. I still have the problem when I ride my bicycle, which is why I mostly stick to bike paths, but I have to remind myself to think about road rules when I approach intersections or ride short distances on the road.

I'm a terrible driver. I know that. Lots of other people are, too. Probably for the exact same reason. They stop paying attention to the rules and let their minds wander. Some of that wandering likely includes just admiring the scenery. So I doubt "thinking in pictures" is all that uncommon.

All of this leads me to believe that "high-functioning Asperger's" is basically just bullshit. Easily distracted, creative, eccentric, able to become deeply absorbed into topics (like hanging flower baskets rather than red lights) – those are all fairly common traits.

So why pathologize them? We used to be able to accept the socially eccentric with little problem, but now we need some sort of "diagnosis" and drug-taking or behavioral therapy regime to deal with what used to be considered "normal human variation".

I started reading around about Asperger's and the following two facts kept leaping out at me:

Most people diagnosed with this "illness" are men

Asperger's is highly correlated with scientific or mathematical genius

Indeed, Simon Baron-Cohen, one of the world's leading autism researchers, points to several of the world's greatest minds as meeting all the diagnostic criteria for Asperger's Syndrome.

Newton

Mozart

Einstein

Darwin

Curie

Bartok

Godel

Other famous people who meet the diagnostic criteria for Asperger's include:

Samuel Beckett (1906-1989, winner of Nobel Prize in literature in 1969, playwright, poet, novelist, left-handed cricket player)

Richard Borcherds (b. 1959, diagnosed with Asperger Syndrome, winner of Fields Medal 1998, professor of mathematics)

Paul Dirac (1902-1984, winner of Nobel Prize in physics in 1933)

Paul Erdos (1913-1996, winner of Wolf Prize in mathematics 1983/4)

Sir William Rowan Hamilton (1805-1865, mathematician, physicist, astronomer, polyglot, and child prodigy)

Keith Joseph (CH, PC) (1918-1994, British conservative politician)

Enoch Powell (MBE) (1912-1998, real name John Enoch Powell, controversial right-wing British politician)

Bertrand Russell (1872-1970, philosopher, winner of Nobel Prize in literature in 1950)

William Shockley (1910-1989, winner of Nobel Prize in physics in 1956, co-inventor of the transistor, Silicon Valley pioneer, professor, advocate of eugenics, sperm donor with the Repository For Germinal Choice)

Vernon L. Smith (b.1927, diagnosed with Asperger syndrome, winner of Nobel Prize in economics in 2002)

William Butler Yeats (1865 -1939, winner of Nobel Prize in literature in 1923, poet, dramatist)

With the exception of Marie Curie, they are ALL men.

Is Asperger's just a code word for male genius?

Why do we need to turn male genius into a disease? What could be the reason for that? Why would we want such a self-destructive diagnosis? I have a few theories. First, I think it's not ideologically palatable to acknowledge that men exhibit greater genius than women. And note that I use "genius", not intelligence.

Men and women may be more or less equally intelligent ON AVERAGE, but men far outnumber women when it comes to genius. Even when women DO exhibit genius, it is rarely attuned to scientific or mathematical pursuits.

If we can't objectively, quantitatively deny that there are more men than women in the highest echelons of human intelligence, then let's call those men "brain-damaged" in some way. Yes, men might be more capable of genius, but since they are violating the core ideological precept of perfect equality, they must be damaged in some way the rest of us are not.

Well, if Einstein's brain was damaged, can someone please damage mine in the same way? I'll take it!

Secondly, I think the fact that we have structured the formal education system to reflect what girls are good at, and how (most) girls like to behave, we prefer to pathologize exceptionally smart and capable boys rather than address the fact that we are closing down the possibilities for the very best and brightest of humanity to bring their obsessions and interests to fruition.

Because so many of those best and brightest happen to be boys. Boys that act nothing like girls, and indeed, even like most other boys. Their energy and focus and unwillingness to sit still and apply glitter is all diagnosed as "illness".

And they are drugged to high fucking heaven rather than celebrated, and encouraged and channeled.

What in the hell are we doing?

A boy named Albert who could barely add and thought school pretty much sucked, who wore flowered slippers and a bathrobe to work, with his hair all crazy nuts all over the place, was obsessed with thinking about time.

How does it work?

He wrote a paper about it, submitted it to a physics journal and the Theory of Relativity was born. If Albert had had the misfortune of being born today, he would have been subjected to intense behavioral therapy to curb his obsessive interests, he would have been drilled relentlessly and endlessly until his mind learned to add, he would have been hauled down to HR for dress code violations and some matronly bitch from the secretarial pool would have told him to cut his hair.

Unless he had a mother like Temple Grandin's, who protected her strange daughter fiercely and made certain she had the opportunities to pursue her unusual interests all the way through college to the doctoral level.

As a culture, we need to seriously question why we are diagnosing smart boys as neurologically damaged, and more importantly, we need to rally the parents of these children to cherish them, protect them, teach them what they lack and love them unconditionally for who and what they are.

Drugs are bad, after all. Just say no!

Lots of love,

JB

Hanna Rosin says we are witnessing the end of men! Oh yeah? How about we look at the facts?

Let's get Hanna's motivations clear right from the get-go, shall we? Hanna Rosin is not interested in equality. She is interested in dominance. Female dominance. Nothing more, and nothing less. From the author's own website:

"I come from a long line of matriarchs, women who either ruled over their husbands, or ran away from them. My mother is an intimidating figure. She has always served as the neighborhood watchdog, taking on bullies and running the co-op board with an iron fist. If you met her, it would be obvious why I was open to possibility of female dominance, because she embodied it long before it became the defining trend of our era."

Hanna acknowledges that female dominance is a central part of her understanding of how the world works, and that female dominance has become the defining trend of our era. Well, kudos to Hanna for at least being honest.

Hanna has been on a crusade to prove female dominance for some time now. In her original article, published at the Atlantic, she mused that "[f]or years, women's progress has been cast as a struggle for equality. But what if equality isn't the end point? What if modern, postindustrial society is simply better suited to women?".

What if female dominance is inevitable?

Her recent article at Time Magazine lays out five reasons men are slated to be the oppressed sex – five ways in which men are complete and utter failures:

> Men are failing in the workplace
>
> The traditional household is vanishing
>
> Men are increasingly subjected to violence from female partners
>
> Working and middle-class fathers have become non-existent
>
> Men have become feminized

Let's take these one by one.

Men are failing in the workplace?

And what workplace would that be? The one that keeps our infrastructure up and running?

Statistically speaking, 100% of power plant operators, distributors and dispatchers are men.

91% of the nation's electrical engineers are men.

97.6% of electrical power line installers and maintenance workers are men.

95.5% of water and liquid waste treatment plant and system operators are men.

95.9% of aircraft pilots and flight engineers are men.

98.4% of aircraft mechanics and service technicians are men.

91.9% of computer network architects, who design and implement all our computer based communications systems are men.

94.2% of radio and telecommunications equipment installers and repair technicians are men.

93.4% of garbage collectors are men.

78.2% of all workers in production, transportation and material moving occupations are men

82.4% of all industrial production managers are men

97.5% of all extraction workers, providing the raw materials to run our economy are men

Transportation, energy, communications, water treatment, resource extraction and waste management. Those are the things that provide us with a little something called civilization as we know it, and they are overwhelmingly provided by men.

While it is true that the manufacturing sector has taken a hit in recent years, the United States remains the world's largest manufacturer, with a 2009 industrial output of $2.33 trillion. Its manufacturing output is greater than Germany, France, India and Brazil combined.

70% of that total workforce is male.

Primary metals manufacturing? 85.6% men.

Apparel manufacturing? 68.3% women.

So ladies in manufacturing are basically just sewing clothes?

How shocking! How surprising! How very housewifely!

What are the ladies doing in the workforce anyways? Most common job categories for women in 2010?

> Secretaries (96.8% women)
> Nurses (92% women)
> Primary and elementary school teachers (81.9% women)
> Cashiers (74.4% women)
> Nursing aides (88.5% women)
> Retail sales (51.9% women)
> Retail sales managers (44.1% women)
> Waitresses (71.6% women)
> Maids (89.9% women)

Oh ladies. Thunderous applause. Doing all the same work in the paid market that you used to do at home. Progress!

Well, maybe the future will be different!

The top ten industries by annual average employment growth between 2Q09 and 2Q13:

> Information Services
> Support Activities for Mining

Educational Support Services
Technical and Trades Schools
Oil and Gas Extraction
Computer Systems Design
Management and Technical Consulting Services
Other Schools and Instruction
Ambulatory Healthcare Services
Employment Services

Educational support services? Maybe. Ambulatory healthcare and employment services? Okay. Sure. Women will dominate! But IT? Computer systems design? Mining support? Oil and gas extraction?

Ahahahahahahahahahaha!

Yeah. Right.

Hanna Rosin, you are full of shit. Women aren't excelling in the workplace. They are doing all the same housewifely jobs they've always done.

The traditional household is failing?

Gee, I wonder why? Women are out in the workforce doing their housewife gig, neglecting their children and partners and are deeply, deeply unhappy as a result.

They file most divorce proceedings, have more mental health problems and express greater dissatisfaction with their lives.

But let's blame men for that, shall we, Hanna? What women need is to be more dominant. To rule with an iron fist. Oh, except that women in traditional marriages are much happier.

Men are increasingly subject to violence from female partners?

It's just sickening that Hanna sees this as a good thing. There is no question that it's true, but how on earth can it ever be a net positive? Hanna links violence to women's sexual confidence, which is deeply disturbing in and of itself.

Women are becoming more sexually confident, and something Camille Paglia has been waiting for, more aggressive and violent in both good ways and bad.

What Hanna is not taking into account is that women get away with hitting partners because the men are taking it. For now. How long does she expect that state of affairs to last?

Suzanne Venker puts it nicely:

> *It is a dangerous thing to create a society of angry men. Feminists have no idea what a can of worms they've created — and what it's about to do to our nation.*

Working and middle class fathers are becoming non-existent?

Again, it's just sickening that Hanna thinks millions of children being raised without fathers is proof that women are dominant and men are obsolete. Children raised by single mothers do poorly on every imaginable scale. They have more emotional problems, experience more stress, are more likely to grow up poor, they have lower educational achievements and experience way more behavioral problems than children who grow up with married parents. Depression, suicide, drug abuse, jail and psychiatric medications are all more common in populations of children raised by single mothers.

The absence of fathers from the home is proof that women are stupid, heartless and profoundly unconcerned with their children's well-being. If that's dominance, I'll pass, thanks.

Men are becoming feminized? Which men?

64% of men do not wear any fragrance of any kind. Only 23% of men wear cologne daily. And cologne is hardly some arty-farty invention of middle class ladies.

80% of household spending is controlled by women. That 20% leftover is being used by men to "feminize" themselves? Bullshit.

Top Ten Things Women Enjoy Buying:

Handbags
Shoes
Summer dresses
Concert tickets
Jeans
Jewellery
Little black dress
Chocolates
Underwear
Beauty products

Top Ten Things Men Enjoy Buying:

Watches
Spirits
Apple Gadgets
Televisions and A/V equipment
Gifts
Dates and relationships
Life experiences
Sports
Gambling
Cars

It's interesting that the lady list has only two things that could ostensibly be shared with a partner (concert tickets, chocolates), while the men's list contains almost ALL shareable items. The preference for gambling, cars and sports doesn't suggest the sissification of men to me.

Keep dreaming, Hanna. Men are becoming the gentle kittens you would like them to be? Don't be fooled. Just because men can be and are very often gentle, kind and giving to women doesn't mean they will always be that way.

Here's an idea for you: let's claim that men are obsolete and worthless, like a map of a flat earth or a woolly mammoth snare, completely ignore the fact that they run the entire economy and make possible every service industry by doing the hard, shitty work, slap the shit out of them at home, take their children from them and then call them sissies.

How long do you think it will take before you discover that men are not only far from obsolete, they are faster, bigger, smarter and stronger than you?

How long will it take before they decide they have had quite enough of your shit?

How long, Hanna, can you live without water, power, communications, transportation or sewage treatment?

Obsolete?

I don't think so.

Obviously people want social calm, but if you do not let clever and ingenious people participate, there must be some dormant volcano that will erupt, sooner or later.

Lech Walesa

Hanna and her ilk think the revolution will be the triumph of feminism and the utter domination of women.

I wouldn't count on it.

Not for one second.

Lots of love,

JB

How do civilizations commit suicide? By elevating women at the expense of men. It doesn't have to be this way.

Oh dear. Camille Paglia is back in the news, pointing out some icky truths that make feminists stamp their feet and pout, as icky truths tend to do.

In a three hour interview, Paglia points out just what we're getting wrong, culturally.

"The diminished status of the military means that the cultural elite has no military experience – no explicit training in analysis, strategy, defense, offence, subterfuge – any of the tactics that permit an understanding of how to face down evil and triumph."

This leads to the idea that everyone is basically nice and if we're nice, they'll be nice right back. North Korea: just be nice and everything will be okie-dokie. How's that working out, Jang Song Thaek?

"These people don't think in military ways, so there's this illusion out there that people are basically nice, people are basically kind, if we're just nice and benevolent to everyone they'll be nice too. They literally don't have any sense of evil or criminality."

Women in particular are oblivious to the dangers of the world, and insist that they have every right to put themselves in vulnerable situations and when bad things happen, they cannot and must not be held responsible for that:

"I believe that every person, male and female, needs to be in a protective mode at all times of alertness to potential danger. The world is full of potential attacks, potential disasters." She calls it "street-smart feminism."

Men are neutered, essentially from birth, and taught that their energy and desire to interact physically with the world is a mental disorder that requires medication. "Sit quietly and color, boys, and please don't build projectiles with your crayons".

"Primary-school education is a crock, basically. It's oppressive to anyone with physical energy, especially guys," she says, pointing to the most obvious example: the way many schools have cut recess. "They're making a toxic environment for boys. Primary education does everything in its power to turn boys into neuters."

Primary school teachers, who tend to have backgrounds in the Barista of Arts academic tradition (degrees in reading, dancing, feeling, etc.) dislike teaching hard facts and quantitative skills (math is hard, Barbie!), and instead focus on "female values" such as sensitivity, cooperation and socialization. And it doesn't get better in higher education, either.

"This PC gender politics thing—the way gender is being taught in the universities—in a very anti-male way, it's all about neutralization of maleness." The result: Upper-middle-class men who are "intimidated" and "can't say anything. . . . They understand the agenda." In other words: They avoid goring certain sacred cows by *"never telling the truth to women"* about sex, and by keeping *"raunchy"* thoughts and sexual fantasies to themselves and their laptops."

The loss of the manufacturing base has stripped men of role models, leaving only the sports arena where traditional masculine virtues are openly celebrated. Being faster, stronger, smarter and more relentless than the opposition is a undeniable good. Of course, there are plenty of arenas (tech development, finance, high level corporate management) where men are as competitive and ruthless as ever, but the difference is that we only celebrate the sports heroes. Corporate heroes make the ladies feel a bit queasy, and they only like the soft, gentle ones. Bill Gates and his geeky ways are okay. Mark Pincus, not so much.

Pincus obsessively tracks analytics for all staff, sets harsh deadlines, and aggressively pushes his employees to meet them.

And how is that working out for Pincus?

"The data pipeline allows Zynga to fine-tune its games to optimize engagement, helping the company attract some 270 million unique users each month, many through Facebook. The four-year-old Zynga, which has emerged as the Web's largest social game company, recorded $828.9 million in revenue in the first nine months of 2011, more than double the period a year earlier. It is also the rare Internet start-up that is profitable, earning $121 million since the start of 2010."

Oh well then. Let's strangle that puppy on the doorstep. What could go wrong?

Paglia notes that it's not just men and boys who suffer when the demonization of men and masculinity becomes culturally *de rigeur*. She throws a bone out to the rich, white ladies, too, because we all know that no one has cornered the market on suffering quite like rich, white ladies.

Women, particularly elite upper-middle-class women, have become "clones" condemned to "Pilates for the next 30 years," Ms. Paglia says. "Our culture doesn't allow women to know how to be womanly," adding that online pornography is increasingly the only place where men and women in our sexless culture tap into "primal energy" in a way they can't in real life.

A lifetime of low-fat yogurt, Pilates and porn. Gosh, the tears are welling up here. It's so heart-rending. Poor, poor elite white ladies. That's just terrible.

Whatever can we do?

Paglia has a few ideas:

A key part of the remedy, she believes, is a "revalorization" of traditional male trades—the ones that allow women's studies professors to drive to work (roads), take the elevator to their office (construction), read in the library (electricity), and go to gender-neutral restrooms (plumbing).

Indeed. We've argued that exhaustively. Let's stop proclaiming men obsolete and start recognizing that our entire economy and civilization depends on men continuing to believe that their role is to provide and protect, even in the face of a culture that actively denies them basic human rights, such as reproductive freedom, equal treatment under the law and the right to genital integrity. The ingratitude of feminists is staggering, and Paglia is not shy about pointing it out, either, although she does frame it in terms of women only. Well, Paglia does call herself a "feminist", so that doesn't really come as a surprise.

In her view, these ideological excesses bear much of the blame for the current cultural decline. She calls out activists like Gloria Steinem, Naomi Wolf and Susan Faludi for pushing a version of feminism that says gender is nothing more than a social construct, and groups like the National Organization for Women for making abortion the singular women's issue.

By denying the role of nature in women's lives, she argues, leading feminists created a "denatured, antiseptic" movement that "protected their bourgeois lifestyle" and falsely promised that women could "have it all." And by impugning women who chose to forgo careers to stay at home with children, feminists turned off many who might have happily joined their ranks.

Well, this stay at home mother would never have joined their ranks in a million years, largely owing to the fact that feminism outright lies to women and actively attempts to deny women what they most desire: a life with children and family. A movement that has at its heart the destruction of women's most deeply held desires does not come across as "pro-woman" to me.

"I want every 14-year-old girl . . . to be told: You better start thinking what do you want in life. If you just want a career and no children you don't have much to worry about. If, however, you are thinking you'd like to have children some day you should start thinking about when do you want to have them. Early or late? To have them early means you are going to make a career sacrifice, but you're going to have more energy and less risks. Both the pros and the cons should be presented."

Paglia's prescription for how to "fix" feminism includes expanding membership to stay at home moms and focusing on true injustices by tackling matters like rape in India and honor killings in the Muslim world.

That's nice. But it won't "fix" feminism. Feminism, which continues to trumpet that gender is a mere social construct and that the lack of female engineers and computer programmers is due to the fact that boys are mean, cannot be fixed.

Paglia is absolutely correct that in neutering the masculine, we are destroying our civilization. But the solution is not more or better feminism. We can take all the things we have learned from this disastrous cultural experiment and apply them to create a world of true diversity and equality.

The first step is to recognize that women have been elevated at the expense of men, a situation that was observed a long time ago.

Bringing the cultural conversation back to equality is the first step, and where we are right now. We cannot effect any change until the need for change is acknowledged. And then what?

Here are three strategies that could be put in place to dramatically reverse the decline we are all facing together:

1. Full reproductive rights for men

When men have full reproductive rights, and cannot be forced into fatherhood (as women cannot be forced into motherhood) a few dramatic changes will take place. The era of the babymama will essentially evaporate overnight. When men are given the same rights as women to choose fatherhood, all the incentives to trap men and extract maximum resources without consequence will be eliminated. The only men who will have child support orders enforced against them will be those men who have legally agreed, in writing, to father children with a particular woman.

We used to call that "marriage". We still can, but I see no reason why any sort of legal agreement to parenthood should not be enforceable. And marriage itself is not a sufficient condition in which to enforce parenthood. Couples who intend to be childless need to specify that legally. Every child must be wanted by both parents. Every individual reserves the right to parent alone, but when that gargantuan task becomes even more difficult, we will see the rates of single motherhood collapse.

Men are grossly exploited by child support laws, and ending that is a matter of keystrokes. Change the legislation and give men and women equal reproductive rights.

2. Separate school streams

Schools should fall into two categories: those that emphasize qualitative skills with only a slight focus on quantitative, and those geared towards developing quantitative skills, with a correspondingly lesser focus on the qualitative.

In reality, boys will skew quant, and girls will skew qual, but there is no need to force anyone into any particular pathway. Boys who wish to study art and poetry and psychology will be permitted to do so and we will vigorously protect them from having their masculinity questioned or derided. Girls who wish to study robotics and calculus will be permitted to do so and we will vigorously protect them from having their femininity questioned or derided.

Creating a stream of schools, from primary onwards, focused on developing analytical, mathematical, hard skills will bring men back into the teaching profession in droves, because they tend to be the ones who have those skills. At the secondary stage, the schools can split further into skilled trades and advanced analytics, both quant and qual. Quant schools would feed programs in masonry, plumbing, carpentry on the skilled trades side, and STEM on the advanced analytics side. Qual schools would stream into hairdressing, childcare worker, food preparation on the skilled trades side and all the liberal arts on the advanced analytics.

People should be free to change streams according to their own desires and talents.

This is not a physically hard system to imagine. Germany runs an educational system that already does most of this in practice.

The opposition is entirely political and comes mostly from feminists, who cannot stand that the skills gap between men and women will be stark indeed when polytechs and vocational schools stand alongside liberal arts schools in the same numbers. And to be clear, this is not an argument that women are incapable of developing quantitative skills. Perhaps they are, or perhaps it is merely a complete lack of interest: either way the outcome is the same. It's mostly men who pursue quantitative occupations and skills.

3. Financial incentives to encourage parents to care for their own children

The practice of allowing families to deduct child care expenses as a tax credit needs to end immediately.

The correct incentive is to allow families to income split as long as one parent is at home fulltime with children. A single earner paying income tax on $50 000 will pay more tax than two individuals earning $25 000. Same income, lower tax burden. Effectively, one parent should be able to pay the other parent for their services. This not only incentivizes families to care for their own children, it offers a prestige and acknowledgement of the value of childrearing, something that is sorely missing in our culture.

Whether mommy or daddy stays home does not matter. The legal right to pay your partner for the work they do at home should be enshrined in law. Canada is slowly moving to make that a reality, but not fast enough.

Again, it is a simple matter of keystrokes to make this law. The short term loss in revenue will be made up for by having a nation of citizens who understand what responsibility and obligation actually means, by seeing that a lived reality in their own lives, and who are growing up without the negative effects in social development that arise when children are parceled out to daycare institutions.

It's really not that hard to reverse our decline. The first two strategies require a close focus on the rights of boys and men in particular, while subtracting nothing from women. Give men the same right to choose parenthood that women already have, and provide boys with schools that match their strengths, whatever those might be, while not excluding girls in any way.

If we can get those first two right, the third one will become a saner, more reasonable choice for men. It will restore reciprocity and interdependence to marriage, replacing the competitiveness and selfishness (mostly on the part of women) that currently reigns.

Paglia is right to highlight that we are in condition critical culturally, but her suggestion that a more inclusive feminism will light the way to salvation is ludicrous at best.

Focusing on the rights of boys and men is the way out of this mess. The good news is that this is not a zero sum game: enshrining the rights of men does not mean women will lose some of their rights.

The bad news is that women will have to surrender some unfair advantages.

They will no longer control men's incomes by controlling reproductive choices.

They will no longer exclude men from appropriate training and education by eliminating male interests or attributes.

They will no longer control poor men and women by exploiting them for cheap domestic labor.

And they will gain some important advantages, too.

If women stay home to care for their own children, which were born in legal agreement with the father, they will be rewarded with an income, as agreed to by both parents.

If they choose to work, they can legally pay their partners to care for their children

It's win-win.

And begins here. The MHRM.

We're not just an advocacy group. We're a suicide prevention group.

And we intend to save our whole world.

Let us go forth with fear and courage and rage to save the world.

Grace Paley

And so we shall.

Lots of love,

JB

#GamerGate is fundamentally a fight for men, for masculinity and for male spaces.

Allum Bokhari has a great article up at Breitbart, reflecting on a year of #GamerGate, the culture war that taught a younger generation why political action matters, and why resisting the "Thought Police", as Vox Day calls them, is so important. Bokhari has collected reflections from the following prominent #GGers:

Adam Baldwin
Adrian Chmielarz
Chloe Price
Ben Southwood
Andrea Castillo
Nick Flor
Dean Cain
Ashe Schow
Nick Robalik
Michael Koretzky
Lynn Walsh
Ed Morrissey
Gavin McInnes
James Delingpole
Jennifer Dawe
Elissa Shevinsky
Lauren Southern
Brandon Morse
Ian Miles Cheong
Sargon of Akkad

Jennifer Bharaj
Gwen Knight
Mark Ceb
Jess Dryden
Brendan McLeod
Eve Park
Milo Yiannopoulos
Oliver Campbell
Ethan Ralph
Mundane Matt

30 #GGers, 11 of them women. Of the 11 women, 4 are commenters on the broader issues and not directly involved in gaming itself. So 21% of the women are proper gamers. There was lots of excitement in the media when a survey revealed that 52% of all gamers were women, but that study is pretty much bullshit, because it includes middle aged women playing on mobile devices.

Candy Crush is not 'gaming'. Neither is Alphabetty, although I'm on Level 146 – Spread the Cheese! Gaming involves a console, and controllers and generally first person action, shooting or beating the crap out of people and things. Call of Duty, Assassins Creed, Halo, Gears of War, Grand Theft Auto. Those are the games and players #GamerGate is talking about.

Those games are played mostly by men. And that's fine, but it is disingenuous to pretend that the attack on gaming is anything but an attack on men, masculinity and male spaces. What #GG does demonstrate is that men are welcoming of women who genuinely share their interests, and will welcome real players into their spaces, as long as those women are respectful of that space. And in gaming, you show respect by playing the game. And playing it well.

Tits or GTFO is an admittedly crass and vulgar saying that originated in male spaces online to check the authenticity of women in those spaces. The idea is that if you are going to join a board discussing strategies in Gears of War, you better know how to play Gears of War. Women who show up just to enjoy male attention would be prompted to show their breasts, in a very derogatory, mocking manner. It wasn't about objectifying or sexualizing women, it was about calling out attention whores. And the impulse is by no means exclusive to gaming. Feminists routinely call out male allies who are spouting talking points for the purposes of getting laid. It's an ingroup/outgroup thing that virtually all humans participate in, in some form or another.

The language of gamers can be startling to the uninitiated, for sure. Gamers are fond of using words like faggot, retard, hoe, and the n-word, and they are extremely inventive at coining gratuitous neologisms by combining words in new and imaginative ways. Urban Dictionary contains a wealth of these words, for those interested. This language is the target of a great deal of criticism, and held up as evidence that gamers are homophobic, misogynist, transphobic, racist, fat-shamers, whatever –phobic have you, but that criticism demonstrates a very weak understanding of how language evolves and works. Not too long ago, moron, imbecile and idiot were medical diagnoses. They are now just common words to describe stupid people. Retard and faggot are undergoing the same linguistic transition, from referring to something very specific, to a more general word category. The opposition to the word faggot is particularly interesting because the word "gay" only recently evolved to mean "male homosexual", and is now rarely used to mean "effervescently happy". I'm quite certain if you described the flapper era as the Gay 20s, a significant number of people under the age of 30 would have no idea what the hell you were talking about.

I fully admit that the n-word makes me very, very uncomfortable, and I dislike hearing anyone use it, but I also understand the word is changing and evolving, too. According to one of the definitions at Urban Dictionary:

As my friend James says, "As a white man, I don't get to use the n-word, but I do get to say "thank you for your assistance, Officer". Not exactly a fair trade, but not one I'm going to complain about. My point here is that the accusations of racism, misogyny, bigotry leveled against gamers that are based on jargon and colloquial uses of words others deems offensive is completely wrong. A gamer calling another gamer a faggot is not a homophobic slur in the context of that community. And honestly, those accusations are only leveled as a form of red herring: they are banal objections, because people who oppose #GG know they cannot openly say what the real problem is: they hate men.

Gamers are mostly men, games tend to follow narrative trajectories and feature actions that express masculinity and the gaming world is a place where mostly men gather to have fun and talk shit about each other. Gamers welcome women who share their interests – they welcome everyone who just wants to play. #GamerGate is a pushback against the feminist/SJW mission to define men and masculinity as toxic and to destroy spaces where men gather, without the direct supervision of the Thought Police. I think this column at Reason is dead right: feminists and SJWs have no experience with adulthood, and demand that authority figures step in and supervise what other adults do. There's a delicious irony in their appeal to authority: if you are appealing to law enforcement, politicians, game developers and the heads of large corporations, you are appealing largely to the authority of men.

Establishing the complete authority of men over everyone else. Hmmmm. Isn't there a word for that?

PATRIARCHY!

It's actually pretty hilarious: smash the patriarchy by making sure that an elite group of men (and a few women) have the power to control what other people do on their own time! Yay! Brilliant!

Fucktards.

#GG is a cultural movement that resists the demonization of men. #GG resists a culture that portrays masculinity and male interests as wrong, bad and evil. It is a movement that rejects the assertion that men are just broken women. Men and women from all over the world, from all walks of life, from the entire political spectrum, have united under a single banner to refuse to engage in the sexist, feminist SJW project to declare half of humanity toxic.

And if you're gonna pick a fight, gamers are not really a wise group to attack. When it comes to the relentless pursuit of victory, dedication to the task at hand and complete devotion to the mission, people who have spent several thousand hours playing Call of Duty are gonna kick your ass ten ways to Sunday.

I don't play first person shooter games (because they're really fucking hard!), but I will join in the chorus of gamers around the world who refuse to hate men, masculinity or male space. Happy Anniversary, #GamerGate. Achievement unlocked:

VICTORY!

Lots of love,

JB

When the world goes to hell, it's men who die to save others. Remembering the first responders of 9/11

Of the 2977 people killed on September 11th, 2001, 414 were NYC emergency personnel who responded to the attack. 341 firefighters, 60 police officers, 8 EMTs and 3 court officers.

Two of those responders were women. The other 412 were men.

Glance through any newspaper or magazine, browse the web, listen to the radio, watch television and you will be bombarded with the message that men are bad. They are rapists and murderers and wife-beaters and misogynists who delight in hurting women and take every opportunity to do so. That is the story feminism concocted about men and they have been horrifyingly successful in disseminating it widely. Men are treated with suspicion and often outright hatred, and the only reason for that is ironic - because we are more or less living in one of the safest and most secure places on Earth.

Detonate a bomb or crash some planes into buildings, and it becomes very, very clear that what stands between us and abject horror is men. Men are the ones who rush into the smoke and flames and falling debris. Men are the ones who put their own lives on the line to save others. Men are the ones who die.

On this day I want to remember the men who died evacuating the World Trade Center, and making what could have been a death toll in the tens of thousands considerably lower. They were sons, husbands, fathers, brothers – they were brave men who did their jobs and gave their lives in that service.

They were not rapists or murderers or child abusers or sex offenders or incompetent bumbling idiots or any other negative, hateful stereotype we see and hear about men.

They were men. Just normal men.

Today is a day to remember the men who died, and to turn to all the men around us who are alive and say two simple words:

Thank you.

Thank you for your need to protect others. Thank you for your strength and courage and bravery. Thank you for taking risks. Thank you for being afraid and still doing what needs to be done. Thank you for facing danger. Thank you for being selfless.

Thank you for being a man.

Thank you.

Lots of love,

JB

Attention men struggling with mental illness: man up you whiny suckholes!

Oh, Hugo, you've really outdone your bootlicking little self this time. Have the girls let you in the clubhouse yet? No? Seriously, Hugo, you need to find some boys to play with. In a resoundingly depressing, and disgustingly opportunistic piece at Jezebel, Hugo links the sad shootings of children to one of the ugliest portraits of young men you'll read in the media this year[12].

So according to Hugo, there is a problem in America with young white men getting the shaft and falling drastically behind in achievement and status when compared to their female counterparts. Score one for NO SHIT SHERLOCK. The problem is NOT that an entire generation of young men are being chucked under the ideological bus, but rather that they are REACTING to this treatment by picking up guns and shooting children. Because, hey, that's what men do, right?

So much *facepalm*. Let's talk about the accusation that it is WHITE men in particular who are prone to pick up guns and shoot people in mass killings. The question is not "is the shooter white", but what PROPORTION of mass killings are carried out by white men relative to their presence in the general population? Seems like the folks at Virginia Tech might know something about WHITE men going nuts and shooting up innocent bystanders, as long as by WHITE, you mean KOREAN. There are some other folks in DC that lived through a round of snipers who also might contest the fact that mass murderers are lonely white guys.

Why the race-baiting? Well, men of color have LEGITIMATE reasons to complain that their chances in life might be blighted by the circumstances of their birth (80% to single mothers), their economic status (poor), an educational system geared to ensure they fail, a culture that reviles them and a justice system that is more willing to detain them for years for crimes other folks get away with. And those ARE legitimate complaints. To be clear, I am not making EXCUSES for criminality amongst any group, but I am suggesting life circumstances offer some sort of EXPLANATION. It is still up to every adult to take responsibility for their own actions, full stop.

Hugo's article is designed to cast white men as whiny suckholes who can't man up to circumstances, and who have NO LEGITIMATE complaints to make. He goes even further, suggesting that young white men are not just angry about a school system designed to fail them, the complete demonization of masculinity and manhood and the annihilation of employment prospects for men in particular, but they are specifically angry at WOMEN who benefit from the New World Order. And you know what, probably a lot of them ARE. For bloody good reason.

Here's where Hugo outdoes himself: he cites an article that claims as long as we continue to fuck over young men, we will continue to have mass killings of children and other innocent bystanders – indeed, those sorts of killings should INCREASE because patriarchy. Also masculinity.

Think about that. According to Hugo, picking up an automatic weapon loaded with flesh shattering bullets and killing six year olds is part of what makes you a MAN. As long as you are going to define yourself as MANLY, you will have to accept that you are willing and able to shoot children.

Hugo is deliberately perpetuating the most destructive portrait of masculinity that he can, in order to justify why he rejects it so resoundingly and to ingratiate himself with a movement that despises men while claiming to love them. Hugo doesn't consider himself particularly manly, therefore he is exempt from his horrifying concept of what constitutes masculinity. He acknowledges that men are getting a shitty deal in the current climate and then insists that the only response open to them is to pick up a gun and shoot children.

Because according to Hugo, that is what masculinity IS. The Sandy Hook shooter was not a mentally disturbed person with a severe personality disorder, raised by a wingnut Armageddonist mother who provided him with wickedly effective weapons and ammunition, raised in broken family with a father he

---

[12] http://jezebel.com/5970262/poor-pitiful-dudes-why-you-should-defer-to-men-with-post+patriarchal-depression

hadn't seen in years – no, none of that mattered. He wasn't in desperate need of psychological help, he was just a MAN and killing children in a brutal bloodbath is simply what men DO.

The willful ugliness of Hugo's concept of what men are and what they do is not just outrageous, it's profoundly, disturbingly sad. Inside his insistence that men are angry, unstable violent brutes hides a wretched reality: men who ARE struggling with mental health issues, who DO have unresolved, deeply troubling feelings and thoughts are told that there is no help for them. There is nothing they can do to assuage the loneliness and pain and despair of their lives. Indeed, if they reach out for help, they are just whiny assholes who can't handle the END OF MEN and the rise of women.

The Christmas season is almost upon us, and across every western, feminized country, there will be countless thousands of men who will sit out the day alone, deprived of their children and families, grappling with isolation and desolation. The vast, sweeping majority of them will face their demons alone, swallow their anger and hate and the injustice of their lives, try to hang on and hope for the future and carry the faces of their children in their hearts.

They will find the courage and strength and stamina to carry on. To persevere, to face the future unafraid, to remain the Captain of their own souls. And for men who find that the burden is too much to bear, that your strength has failed you, that you cannot go on, ignore hateful assholes like Hugo. There IS help, and there is nothing unmanly about asking for it. A man who staggers is still a man. And somewhere, there is a shoulder for you to lean on until your strength is back.

Courage, strength, stamina, perseverance and always, always love for your children. For children everywhere. That is a man.

Lots of love,

JB

You don't need to care about men to care about men's rights. You just need to be fucking human!

Here's an interesting study out of Baylor University in Texas[13].

Researchers set up two groups of people with some "resources". Let's imagine those resources are M&Ms. The first group got together and had to decide how much of their resources to donate to other people, and a few "planted" participants led the giving round: they gave around 65% of their M&Ms away. What did the other people in the group do? They followed suit, and also gave around 65% of their M&Ms away.

A second group did the same thing, except that the planted participants only gave 25% of their M&Ms away. What did the other participants do? Yep, they followed suit and gave 25% of their M&Ms away.

Now here is where the study gets interesting: all the participants were given M&Ms and asked to make an anonymous donation that no one else would be able to scrutinize or know about. The participants in the group who gave away 65% of their M&Ms continued to do so, even though their contributions were anonymous. Same for the participants who gave away 25%. Even with no one looking, they held onto the group norms and were cheap-ass M&M donators.

---

[13] http://www.baylor.edu/mediacommunications/news.php?action=story&story=127023

Why did they do this? The researchers at Baylor asked all the participants, after the experiment was over, to fill out surveys exploring their attachment to the group and how they felt about the other group members and themselves. And it turns out that adhering to group norms, no matter what that norm is, makes people feel happy and contented and accepted and powerfully attached to their own group.

Even if an individual participant felt that giving away 25% of your M&Ms was a pretty stingy thing to do, they went ahead and violated their own internal sense of right and wrong for the pleasure of feeling that they belonged to a group and adhered to the norms of that group.

What does this have to do with men's rights? It's a pretty strong indicator that what the movement needs right now is to get people to feel part of a group, even if the ideas the group promotes are unpopular, unpleasant or unfamiliar. Feminism benefits hugely from this tendency to go along with the group, even when the norms of the group are demonstrably, objectively destructive and deeply hypocritical.

The feeling of "wanting to belong" is simply human, and humans will attach themselves to a group to achieve that, without considering the implications. It's a rare man or woman who can stand up and challenge the herd.

The past 20 years have seen the challengers take up the gauntlet and bring the issue of human rights for men into the mainstream conversation. It's now time for the rest of us to start expanding the group and welcoming members who might not even understand the conversation, but who want to belong.

We can do that by articulating, very clearly, what some basic human rights for men should be:

The right to bodily integrity

No person, male or female, should have a part of their body cut away without their full and informed consent. That's an inalienable human right. No one's imaginary friend gets any say in this. Mutilating infant genitals is part of the dark ages and we have no room in our society for that kind of medieval cruelty.

The idea that is it a criminal act to cut a girl's genitals, an act of despicable immorality, but acceptable to cut a boy's genitals plays into an incredibly damaging stereotype: that males, from birth, can be subjected to pain and torture and they must accept this as part of their existence. Male feelings can be ignored, overridden, denied and eradicated. Little boys are disposable. They can be hurt with impunity and their only choice is to suck it up and accept their fate.

Wrong. Circumcision of infants – ALL INFANTS – must be abolished immediately. This is ground zero in the human rights movement for men, and even people who can't accept any other precept of a human right's movement for men can get behind that sentiment.

They will join the group and quite likely begin to understand and identify with the entire movement, lending support, just to belong.

It's a start, and one that should be exploited fully.

Planned Parenthood

Men deserve the right to absolve themselves morally, ethically, legally and financially of all responsibility towards children they did not intend and do not want, just as women can. A woman can abort a child, surrender it to authorities under safe haven laws or place it for adoption, absolving herself of any further obligations. Men should have the same right.

Assumed Custody

When a marriage or partnership breaks down, men should have the same rights as women to custody of the children. Automatic 50% and any other arrangement must be agreed to in advance or supported with evidence for why one or the other parent should not have 50% custody.

Children have a right to be cared for by BOTH their mothers and fathers.

There are many more basic rights (healthcare, social services, disproportionate sentencing in criminal courts) that are also on the table, for the very good reason that men are being punished or denied vital services BECAUSE they are men, and expected to just "man-up" and deal with their shit in a way that women aren't.

But the first three items are pretty much no-brainers. They open a dialogue with people who might not otherwise identify, or who even actively resist the idea that men need some basic human rights protections.

Group affiliation is a powerful motivator. Time to hand out some M&Ms. Just a few at a time.

That's all it takes.

Lots of love,

JB

Of course you can blame the victim. Who else are you going to blame?

Do you have diabetes? Is that because you're 200 pounds overweight and you maintain your heft with a steady diet of donuts, hotdogs and big gulp sodas?

Gosh, that's too bad. It's not your fault, though, sweetie. A nefarious plot between corn producers, the government and convenience store owners caused you to walk by that bag of unsalted almonds and bypass the bottle of water and head straight for the squeezy cheese and nachos. Nothing you can do about that.

There, there.

We can't blame the victim, now, can we?

Did you grab your boyfriend's phone and hit him in the face with your shoes and then he beat the shit out of you?

Not your fault. We're not blaming the victim.

Did you get shit-faced at a football party and chase after some star players and then pass out and get treated like a little tramp?

That was completely unpredictable and you cannot be held responsible. No victim blaming, people!

Victim-blaming is MEAN! It's an expression of privilege and an advantageous position in a hierarchy of power and it must never be used to further wound or injure people who have, by definition, already been hurt: that's what VICTIM means.

Unacceptable.

Are you a working class male suffering from depression and a sense that your life has no meaning or value or direction? Did you deal with your crippling sense of dislocation and detachment by putting a gun to your head and pulling the trigger?

Oh. Well, in that case, it IS your fault. You're the sort of victim we CAN blame.

Congratulations.

This is actually very upsetting.

Public policy needs to respond urgently to the problems that men and boys create and the problems that they experience, according to a new report by the Coalition on Men and Boys. This must take place alongside efforts to improve the position and status of women.

Taken from a report called Men, Suicide and Society: Why Disadvantaged Men in Mid-life Die by Suicide[14].

The report links men's suicide rate to masculinity and identifies that as a problem. Masculinity, or the idea of "manliness" is a destructive force in society that must be eradicated, thereby "solving" the male suicide problem. If men could just stop being men, they wouldn't feel the need to kill themselves.

More accurately, they wouldn't be so good at it.

While men commit suicide more often, women ATTEMPT suicide in greater numbers. Once again, men are better at identifying a problem, isolating a solution, and carrying through. Part of that has to do with the fact that women attempt suicide as a cry for help. When the weight of their lives becomes too great to bear, they cry out for help.

Save me, please.

I am in no way suggesting that women do not feel the same kind of despair or pain or emotional agony as men, but rather that they respond to that by seeking help in the form of "attempted suicide". Women surrender themselves to the idea that their lives are out of control and they cannot manage anymore, and they take actions to ensure that someone will notice their pain and intervene.

Men take a completely different approach.

They identify a problem: my life has become unbearable.

They isolate a solution: suicide.

They carry it out.

In the case of suicide, the results are maddeningly, saddeningly tragic. The fact that so many suicides occur amongst veterans is even more heartrending. More men have died by suicide than combat in the recent

---

[14] http://www.samaritans.org/sites/default/files/kcfinder/files/press/Men%20Suicide%20and%20Society%20Research%20Report%2020151112.pdf

conflict in the Middle East. Soldiers, who risked their lives to carry out our government's mandates (whether we agree with that mandate or not), who went at OUR BIDDING, return to confront pain so profound, they take their own lives.

This is a crisis not in masculinity, but in health care. Self-inflicted gunshots are a major and almost always lethal threat to men's health. The idea that we should address this crisis by identifying masculinity as a problem is laughably, tragically stupid.

Men identify a problem, isolate a solution and carry through. With resounding and incontrovertible success, in most cases. Every single piece of technology, every tool, every device, every object or service we have in our modern world is a result of someone identifying a problem, isolating a solution and carrying through.

Those "someones" are almost always men.

Seeing masculinity as a threat, and something that needs to be undermined is a strategy guaranteed to take us back to the dark ages. It's nihilism, pure and simple. The death of our culture.

The correct strategy to address the tragedy of male suicide is to intervene at the point that a "problem" is identified. Men who see themselves, their lives, their value, their contribution, their intrinsic worth as a human being as a "problem" ARE NOT HELPED by ideologies that define them as, yes, a problem.

I truly, deeply wonder if the researchers who wrote the report on male suicide are just blindingly stupid, or if they really do want men to die? Most suicides occur amongst middle-aged, white working class men, the group hardest hit by dramatic changes in our economies and culture. Their jobs have been outsourced, their families have disintegrated, their livelihoods have disappeared and their ability to get the job done is no longer the machine that drives our society.

They're not particularly useful, are they?

Oh, but they're good at one thing: dying.

I usually try to end my posts with some smart-ass comment that mocks whatever it is I'm talking about, but today I just can't do that.

All I really want to do is cry. I wish I could find every man sitting in a room with a loaded gun, wondering if anyone would even notice if he pulled the trigger and tell him:

I would. I would notice. Please don't. The problem is not you. The problem is not that you're a man. The problem is a world that has decided you're useless. A world that exists BECAUSE of men, finding solutions to problems. It's what men do. They solve problems.

Don't solve this problem. Not this way.

Please don't.

Lots of love,

JB

Feminism

Now that we've established that men aren't really the terrible, violent, toxic, horrible monsters the media wants you to believe they are (but you knew that already), let's put on our hip-waders and begin to muck our way through the ugliness of modern feminism.

Once upon a time, I would have called myself a feminist, as perhaps many of you do right now. I thought feminism was about equality, about affording women the opportunity to do the things they wanted and were qualified to do, and then sitting back and letting women make their choices. If women wanted to be stay-at-home moms, then so be it. If women wanted to be corporate raiders, so be it. If women had the guts, strength, dedication and drive to be Navy SEALS, so be it.

Let them try.

Let no one stop women from trying simply because they were women.

But that isn't what feminism is, anymore. It's about equality of outcome. It's about, ironically, defining everything men do as inherently superior to everything women do, and then insisting that standards be lowered, paths be cleared, quotas be instituted so that women can appear, at least superficially, to be equal to men.

Feminism is profoundly, deeply misogynist, in the true sense of the word. Feminism hates women, femininity and women's natural desires. What women want out of life is seen as inferior to what men want. If men work killer hours, then women have to work killer hours, too. Feminists unquestioningly accept that whatever men do, it's better, and if you don't want those things as a woman, there is something wrong with you.

It would almost be funny, if it were not so tragic. By uncritically accepting men's view of the world as superior, feminism has created the very thing it seeks to dismantle: male supremacy. Men never asked to have their interests and approaches to life elevated above women. Feminism demanded it. Few men scoff at women who spend their lives raising happy, healthy children, in loving communities where everyone cares for everyone else. I have never had a man ask me "what I do all day".

They know.

Feminism has been the worst thing in modern memory to happen to women. And to men. And especially to children.

Let's investigate why femin**isn't**.

The moment I knew feminism was a crock of shit

When I originally started university, I enrolled in the Sociology of Work and Industry specialization, thinking that I would complete a degree that would give me some sort of qualifications for employment. I wanted to get a head start on my program, so I took my first course during summer school and it took me all of twelve weeks to figure out that a professor's job is pretty much the best one you could possibly have. Professors have more or less complete control over how and when and what they work on, and they are free to follow their own interests. I watched with complete envy as professors strolled into class late, gave lackadaisical lectures, rambled on about their own ideas and then went to the pub with us to grab a few beers and discuss some esoteric bullshit in further detail.

Going to university was a revelation for me. Suddenly, pointing out in exquisite detail exactly why people were stupid and their arguments were retarded was not some awkward social flaw, it was the key to getting those participation marks! Explaining in graphic detail why other's people's ideas were ludicrous was called an essay! Being all judgy and bitchy was the entire point!

Needless to say, I loved it.

True story: I once made a girl cry in class by calling her stupid (not in that exact word, of course). For one of my electives, I took Women in Christianity (hey – bird course!) and some little chicky thing got up to explain the virgin birth as an example of parthenogenesis. Basically, that means self-fertilization. An ovum develops into an embryo without sperm, commonly occurring in insects and plants. Leaving aside the fact that insects and plants ARE NOT HUMANS, obviously the offspring would have to be genetically identical to the parent. Where would any new genetic information come from? So not five minutes into what was supposed to be a 30 minute presentation, I put up my hand and said, "Wait! Are you saying Jesus was a WOMAN"?

She thought about that for two seconds, realized her entire argument was a colossal piece of shit and burst into tears.

Yeah, I'm a bitch. And kind of judgy, too.

I knew that I would never leave the university. I would go on take graduate work, then post-graduate work and snag me an office of my own. I became very good friends with an untenured history professor who cemented my resolve to become a professor. She had to "work" quite hard, but her thesis was on farm girls and what they actually did, and to me, spending hours in the library pouring over agricultural records didn't seem much like work at all.

It seemed like heaven.

FarmGirl's thesis was eventually published as a book (earning her tenure) and she is now compiling a historical record of the evolution of the butter churn. For well over $100 000/year. What a great fucking job. FarmGirl encouraged me to choose something that really interested me, and so after careful consideration, I decided that sitting on my ass watching movies for the rest of my life seemed like an excellent use of my time and intellect. So I left sociology for the Department of Film Theory, and so began my journey deep into the heart of feminism.

Naively, I thought a degree in Film Theory would involve film and theory. Little did I know that the theory was a rather specific one: men suck and women are awesome. AKA feminism. Well, okay. I was just a teenager myself, having walked away from a marriage proposal from an awesome guy because I was suspicious that being married and having children might ruin my life – that's what all the ladies around me were saying. "Don't do it! You have your whole life in front of you! Don't throw it away on a man, even if he is kind of fantastic".

So down the rabbit hole I went. My first "theory" was written by Laura Mulvey, called "Visual and Other Pleasures". The theory is that when men look first in a film, that gaze is controlling (bastards!) and turns women into objects (assholes!) and then when women DO look first, they get punished (misogynists!). We watched an Alfred Hitchcock film and then sat about railing about what dicks men are. Sadly, the class was overwhelming male, and I wonder what has happened to those men? Sitting through class after class, learning that men are cruel and useless and stupid.

Throughout the four long years of my indoctrination, I was always a bit nervous and embarrassed and dare I say ashamed of the things I was learning. I have three brothers, and going home for Thanksgiving and Christmas and summer holidays was always a stark reminder that my life was filled with men and they were nothing like the men I was learning to fear and hate at school. There was always something a bit off with all the theories. It wasn't until my fourth year, when I confronted Moniqe Wittig that the bulb suddenly blared into full spectrum light.

Essentially, Wittig's argument is that only lesbians are truly women and that only lesbians experience true freedom. Taking as a starting point the idea that freedom is central to the definition of humanity, Wittig is basically arguing for the end of the human race. If the only way to experience freedom is to be a lesbian, men are instantly irrelevant. Without men, there are no children. Without children, there is no future. It's PD James and the End of Men.

That's when I knew the whole theory was just a giant crock of shit. My last essay was "Feminism as Nihilism" and I think I made the professor cry, but you know what? Fuck her. Fuck all of them. Fuck their ugly theories and their hatred of men and their cavalier attitudes towards the flesh and blood men who sat in front of them taking notes on their own extinction. Fuck my whole four years of useless squabbling and arguing and pointless pedantic pedagogy.

I left university and decided to go to work. And with a degree in Film Theory – yeah, that worked out well. I know how to make awesome lattes and Frappuccinos. Thanks feminism!

So we know what happens next: I go to MBA school and walk away with an MRS and every day I breathe a sigh of relief that I escaped a life of endless whining and complaining and imagining myself a victim and railing over at Jezebel about what a bunch of fuckers men are!

In retrospect, I should have married that lovely boy when I was 19. I should have done dishes for a decade and thought about my future and what I wanted and why.

I'm very lucky that things worked out for me so beautifully. For many women, that isn't the case. They bought the "men suck, women are awesome" theory of reality and find themselves living lives they hate with men they don't respect and children they never see. How sad.

And how splendid is the irony that in just a few short years, I WILL be a professor? In the Faculty of Business. The one faculty where women's studies majors fear to tread. We try to limit our bullshit to currency swaps and derivatives pricing.

One thing that strikes me, looking back at four years of Catherine McKinnon, Andrea Dworkin, Luce Irigaray, Germaine Greer and Kate Millet.

Why are all these bitches so ugly?

Could be a theory there.

Lots of love,

JB

Jessica Valenti admits she is obsessed with what men think of her

"At the end of the day, I care very little whether other women wear makeup. Some women love it, some hate it, and some of us feel conflicted about it. But many of us find it a necessity because very few women are immune to beauty standards - myself included. I rarely (okay, never) leave the house without at least some blush and mascara on. But I have no illusions as to why the thought of going bare-faced makes me so uncomfortable: it's the sexism jealous competition with other women that I can't get over, stupid."

I have to laugh at this new column by Jessica Valenti[15] in which she practically spits jealous venom over poor Miranda Lambert and her "flawless, shining beauty". Oh dear, really Jess? Of course, it's men's fault that women wear make-up. It couldn't be insecure women competing relentlessly with other women for sexual attention from men, right? There's a reason a lot of lesbians don't wear make-up, sweetie pie. Jess won't leave her house without her whore paint!

"I rarely (okay, never) leave the house without at least some blush and mascara on."

Think you might be overestimating random men's sexual interest in you, Jess, and definitely overestimating the power of blush and mascara. I rarely leave the house in anything BUT my natural state – sunscreen is a must, but make-up? Yeah, generally not. I could look prettier on a day-to-day basis by wearing make-up, it's just not a priority.

Who cares?

I'm not competing with other women for the sexual attention of men. I'm married, you see, and have already won the man I wanted. YouTube is a totally different story, because in that situation I AM trying to be eye-candy because it makes the message more palatable, and that's not sexism, it's human nature. All humans are attracted to pretty, sparkly things. We all have some residual magpie genes, apparently. But women are not content to simply admire an attractive woman. Virtually 100% of women will aggress against a woman who presents as sexually attractive. Men don't make them do this. The relentless competition for men's attention makes them do this. I have no study to back it up, but I would guess most men would love to see an end to the jealous girl bullshit drama that so many women engage in.

It's boring and extremely unproductive.

There's nothing radical about having the confidence and self-esteem to leave the house without cosmetics. There is indeed something radical about understanding that maintaining a normal body weight, basic grooming (comb your hair, brush your teeth, etc. – the same stuff men do) and a cheerful demeanor makes almost all women attractive.

Feminists don't understand this? What a surprise.

Next time you leave the house, Jess, try some Spanx and a smile.

That's all you need. It's all any woman needs.

Lots of love,

JB

Jessica Valenti coughs up a ball of full retard

[15] http://www.theguardian.com/commentisfree/2015/apr/24/miranda-lambert-no-make-up-radical-act-being-yourself

Remember When Jessica Valenti proudly tweeted her "I Bathe In Male Tears", and how I promised to make Jess rue the day she paraded around like the stupid, fat, heartless bitch that she is? The day has come. Poor Jess had to activate both her brain cells to explain how wearing a hateful shirt doesn't mean she hates men, and she does that by .... wait for it ..... explaining why it's okay that she hates men.

Yep, she went full retard.

Let's take a look.

One of the most common derisive taunts thrown at feminists – and one of the oldest – is "manhater".

Gee, I wonder why?

It's been around since the days of suffrage, and still gets used today, though its a pretty anodyne insult.

Hating men is so lulzy. It's no big deal. Like saying you hate cockroaches. Who doesn't amirite? Nothing to cause offense. It's just hate, lololol.

Also, *it's

Most feminists, like me, shun the label and work to convince people that despite the stereotypes feminists absolutely, without a doubt, do not hate men.

Oh, like this, for example? Is this how you show you don't hate men?

> I feel that man-hating is an honorable and viable political act, that the oppressed have a right to class-hatred against the class that is oppressing them.
>
> **Robin Morgan**

But so what if we did?

Engage the retard drive.

It's not that I recommend hating men or think it a particularly wise use of one's time, but to each her own.

Cool. I suppose you're good with people hating Blacks, gays, Jews, poor people, illegal immigrants and Muslims, too, because to each her own, amrite?

Straight white men still hold the majority of political, economic and social power in the world, and everyone else struggles to make their lives work with less.

A small number of men (relative to the population) are elected by a group of mostly women voters. Sounds like patriarchy to me! And is everyone struggling Jess? Really? Seems to me your last big issue was wrapping the "goddamn clusterfuck" Christmas presents.

So if the worst thing that happens to a man is that a woman doesn't like him ...well, he has it pretty damn good. It's not as if we're living in some sort of Wicker Man-inspired dystopia, after all.

Yeah! Especially all those homeless men! And the ones with prostate cancer! And the ones working life-threatening jobs! And the ones in jail, facing longer, harsher punishment for no reason other than the fact that they are men! And the ones denied custody of their children! And the ones getting the crap beat out of them by women! And the rape victims! And the ones struggling in classrooms that punish them for being male! All those guys can shut the hell up because y'all have it pretty good and Jess does not hate men, do you understand?

Besides, when women hate men, we hurt their feelings.

Jody Arias would like a word.

So would the senior editorial staff at Jezebel, 40% of whom admit to physically attacking and hurting their male partners. So would the five million men who were victims of domestic violence in 2011. Seems like women are more than capable of hurting more than feelings, or do you not think women are human, Jess? Are we not capable of the full range of human responses, emotions and reactions?

When men hate women, they kill us: mass shootings have been attributed to misogyny, and sexual and domestic violence against women is often fuelled by a hatred for women.

Attributed by whom? By feminists? Gee, they have no vested interest in portraying men as monsters who kill women, all the while ignoring men who are victims of female violence.

What was that about not hating men again?

That's why it's so hard to take seriously any claims that "misandry" is a tremendous problem – they're based on the idea that merely insulting men is similar to the life-threatening misogyny women face worldwide.

Boys failing en masse at schools that punish them for being boys, massive incarceration of poor men and men of color, an incredulous suicide rate, underfunded health care worldwide, used as cannon fodder in wars – yeah, misandry doesn't hurt men at all. The boys murdered by Boko Harem would talk to you about that, except they all had their throats slit, while their sisters were allowed to live.

(Most recently, Newsday writer Cathy Young argued that men being called "mansplainers" or rape apologists is akin to the rape and death threats that women get online.)

What she actually said was "a Pew Research Center study last year found that online threats of physical violence are more often directed at men, and both sexes are equally likely to report experiencing "sustained harassment" on the Internet."

Nice try, though.

But a younger generation of feminists has embraced what Slate writer Amanda Hess calls "ironic misandry". Hess wrote last year that the rise in popularity of "male tears" mugs and man-hating inspired shirts and crafts serves as a sort of fuck-you to the constant barrage of harassment that feminists often face: "On its most basic level, ironic misandry functions like a stuck-out tongue pointed at a playground bully."

Men attempting to speak on issues that affect them is not harassment. You are asked to defend an ideology that literally opposes equality, that lies to women, that infantilizes women, that celebrates genocidal racists, and when asked to offer a defense you run crying to moderators that you are being harassed.

Who is the bully again?

Guardian contributor Jess Zimmerman – and self-proclaimed "misandrist witch" – told Hess: "It's inhabiting the most exaggerated, implausible distortion of your position, in order to show that it's ridiculous."

Except that when the actions of feminists are taken into account, it's not the extreme position. It's the norm. You just don't like being called on it.

In other words, calling ourselves misandrists is both a way of reappropriating one of the most common insults feminists weather, and a way to blow off some steam after a long day of fighting the same battles we did 30 years ago. And honestly, if feminists really hated men we'd probably come up with a better way to hurt them than funny t-shirts that insist that their tears are delicious. (Men may have some very sensitive parts, but even the manhating-est among us doesn't go around kicking them willy-nilly.)

No, it's a way of attempting to deflect legitimate criticism. If your best defense against hatred is "I don't kick random men in the balls", you may want to rethink your position.

Despite all the fun-loving, internet-in-joke misandry, the vast majority of women and feminists do not hate men. Many of us might hate bad men: the sexists, misogynists and all-around jerks.

Your hatred prevents men from choosing parenthood. Your hatred prevents men from seeing their children. Your hatred prevents government services from assisting men and boys in any way. Your hatred demands men put themselves in harm's way to protect you. Your hatred demands men cater to your every irrational demand and if you don't think that harms men, you do not understand what harm means.

But our hatred is just a feeling, and not something that can impact men in any meaningful or oppressive way.

This hatred is not ironic. It encourages the world to continue to ignore the suffering of men and boys. You will be held accountable for that, Jessica.

Men who claim to be genuinely worried about man-hating or "misandry" are grasping at straws, and searching for a victim status that simply doesn't exist. Guys are still doing pretty well, so let us have our "man-hating" fun while you go on ruling the world.

Let you have you man-hating fun? I don't think so.

But keep one eye open. (Just kidding ... sort of.)

Try it.

I dare you.

Lots of love,

JB

It makes me laugh when feminists love Jane Austen because I'm pretty sure she would spit on them. Politely, of course.

This year marks the 200th anniversary of the publication of the greatest novel ever written in the English language – *Pride and Prejudice*. If you have never read this book, you need to drop what you're doing right now and grab a copy. You don't even need to pay for it - The Gutenburg Press has a version you can have right now!

It's in the public domain! It's free! And it's utterly magnificent, from the first sentence to the last.

> *It is a truth universally acknowledged, that a single man possessed of a good fortune must be in want of a wife.*

Naturally, Jezebel has a piece celebrating the undeniable achievement that is *Pride and Prejudice*. They venerate this most illustrious author and hold her up as an example of female genius (and god knows there is a shortage of that to be had). Here is a triumph worth celebrating!

Oh wait. Nope. That's not what Jezebel is doing at all[16]. "Why," writes sneery Katie Baker, "are women so obsessed with Jane Austen?" I mean after all, all she wrote about was love and marriage, and really, *Pride and Prejudice* isn't much different than *Twilight* or *Fifty Shades of Grey*. Well, other than the complete absence of whips and vampires, that is, but let's not get fussy. For god's sake Katie, the entire POINT of *Northanger Abbey* is to mock the ridiculousness of gothic romance novels! Have you even read Austen?

Katie goes on to say that she prefers the Bronte's dramatic love affairs, and honestly, I'm not surprised. Catherine is a whiny, spoiled, petulant whore who marries for money and Heathcliff is a vindictive, self-absorbed asshole. There's the dream feminist marriage right there.

There seems to be two critical responses from feminists about Jane Austen:

She wrote about love and marriage and the importance of family and therefore she sucks

She never married, had no children and wrote books instead, therefore she's awesome

Let's take these apart, shall we?

Jane wrote about love, absolutely. She promoted a version of marriage that was centered on companionship, respect, mutual admiration and above all, love.

Elizabeth Bennet, the heroine of *Pride and Prejudice*, muses to her beloved sister Jane, that since Jane is quite the prettiest of all the five Bennet girls, it will fall to her to raise the family's fortunes by marrying well, and she advises Jane to take care to fall in love with a rich man. Only the deepest love will compel Elizabeth to marriage.

---

[16] http://jezebel.com/5979033/is-jane-austen-so-popular-because-her-books-are-kinda-just-highbrow-twilight

Jane has no love at all for ambitious women who seek out husbands solely for what they can provide. Isabella Thorpe tries to nail Captain Tilney AND James Morland in *Northanger Abbey* and gets a bitter comeuppance for her whorish little ways. In *Mansfield Park*, Mary Crawford, who expresses delight that the eldest son might die and therefore leave the family's fortune to Edmund, whom she is hunting, gets a brutal beat down, too. And Jane has no sympathy for male fortune-hunters, either. In *Sense and Sensibility*, the grasping, faithless Willoughby is left with a wife whom he hates and a broken heart, all because he ditched Marianne Dashwood in favor of Sophia Grey with her fortune made in trade.

Certainly, Jane was writing inside a particular class structure, and that is reflected in her writing, but her insistence that women choose husbands based on love and mutual affection and respect is most decidedly anti-feminist. Women are NOT encouraged to pursue wealth or status or power. Jane denounces those values completely. The only acceptable moral relationship between men and women must be based on love, and I suspect this is what pisses writers like Katie off so badly. The idea that the love for a man should govern a woman's choices in life. Not her own comforts, not her need for a roof over her head, not her desire to be perceived as successful and accomplished and strategic.

Love.

In every novel, the heroines face obstacles to their love, but it always triumphs in the end. The one thing that Jane does so well is create a believable happiness. Anne and Frederick, Fanny and Edmund, Eleanor and Edward, Elizabeth and Fitzwilliam, Catherine and Henry, Emma and George – they all end up in relationships that are just so believably happy. You close the book, and you can imagine how the rest of their lives will play out.

That is a direct result of accurately portraying love and respect and compatibility. Jane's men and women do not COMPETE with one another. They complement one another, and find their joy in doing so.

Now, let's take on the second banner feminists tend to wave for our lovely Jane: Jane and her sister Cassandra rejected marriage and children in favor of pursuing literary ambitions and material wealth in the form of royalties from publication.

Screw men and children! I want money! Show me the money!

Said Jane Austen NEVER.

Jane did, in fact, accept and then subsequently reject a proposal of marriage from a man named Harris Bigg-Wither. He had a whole pack of sisters whom Jane loved dearly, and was heir to a very respectable farm and Jane would have lived a life of great comfort and ease. We will never know her exact reason for declining Harris, but if her books are to be taken as evidence, it was because she did not love him.

Tom LeFroy was the man she DID love. Jane wanted to marry Tom, but his family would not allow it. It broke her heart. Jane didn't reject marriage and family and children – she was actually incredibly close to many of her nieces and nephews and thoroughly enjoyed their company.

Jane was not permitted to marry the man she loved, and it appears that she never met another man she could love as much as Tom. There is a bit of a mystery about a man she met in Lyme much later in her life, but as Cassandra destroyed most of Jane's letters, we will never know. Perhaps she did meet another whom she could love. Either way, Jane did not reject love or marriage. It was denied to her by forces beyond her control, and she never recovered.

As for Cassandra, she also accepted a proposal of marriage, but her Tom (Tom Fowle) died in the West Indies before they could marry. Her Tom had gone to make his fortune, but perished of yellow fever, leaving Cassandra a modest amount of money and a thoroughly broken heart. Cassandra's grief over losing Tom is largely thought to have inspired the quiet dignity of Eleanor Dashwood in *Sense and Sensibility*.

So you see, neither of the Austen sisters rejected love or marriage and it was not possible to reject any subsequent children, nor is there any evidence that either of them were in any way opposed to the idea of having children. Jane was dismayed to hear of friends and family members having twelve children, but in *Northanger Abbey* she declares the Morlands, with their ten children, a fine family, so clearly she wasn't of the mind that having a lot of children is automatically a horrible thing.

Jane Austen is, and always will be, my favorite author in any language. Her characters have a grace and dignity and liveliness and cheerfulness that inspires me daily. In many ways, Jane has been a more important influence on me than any living person. She taught me what a happy life looks like, what kinds of mistakes to avoid, how to deal with overpowering emotions in a mature and principled way (you don't need to impose your every feeling on those around you) and most of all, she taught me that the only thing that matters in life is love.

Here's to you, Jane! Happy anniversary - 200 years and you're still fabulous!

Lots of love,

JB

Babies? We don't need no stinking babies! The genius of Amanda Marcotte. Again.

There are two kinds of dumb in this world: bag of hammers dumb, and Amanda Marcotte. She's a blogger at Slate Magazine's Double XX feature, and she has really outdone herself this time[17].

America Is Doomed Unless Women Start Having More Babies.

Hmm. Really? That's interesting. I know we can blame men for ALMOST EVERYTHING, but declining fertility, too? For fuck's sake, men, would you please start having babies? What, you think women should do everything? Sorry lads, we're too busy working on oil rigs and flunking out of STEM courses to have babies.

Who needs babies, anyways?

Oh, just, you know, the ENTIRE WORLD. I could be wrong, and correct me if you think so, but I believe babies actually grow into adults and without them, WE HAVE NO SOCIETY.

"Ever since it became less socially acceptable to argue openly that women—at least white, middle-class women—owe it to men to curtail our professional ambitions in favor of a life as our husbands' support staff, conservatives started to panic about declining birth rates."

Ladies, you must not curtail your professional ambitions. And what are those professional ambitions? Oh yeah, to work as SUPPORT STAFF for someone who is NOT your husband.

---

[17] http://www.slate.com/blogs/xx_factor/2013/02/04/america_s_declining_fertility_rate_it_is_not_up_to_the_female_reproductive.html

Yay, ladies! Don't be support staff for the man you love! Go and do it for someone else.

Ok, that's just one job. I hear you. What are the other jobs women tend to do[18]?

> Teachers
> Nurses
> Retail sales clerks
> Home health care workers
> Cooks
> Waitresses
> Maids
> Childcare workers

So, let's see. Women found being a housewife so terribly dull and dreary and oppressive that they flocked to the labor market to teach children their alphabet, tend to the sick, fold clothes, care for the elderly, cook food, fetch food, clean house and take care of small children. And that's just all the ladies who couldn't find a cushy job organizing a man's professional life.

Organizing, tending, fetching, wiping noses and asses, cooking and cleaning.

Wow. Those are some pretty big ambitions. Kinda makes you wonder, doesn't it? If it's not the actual JOB that women dislike, since they clearly don't mind doing those things for OTHER people, what is it that women didn't like?

We'll get to that. For now, let's go back to our favorite little retard, Amanda.

And don't give me any crap about using the word "retard". Retard DOES NOT mean someone with Down Syndrome any more than gay means "effervescently happy" or computer means "someone who does calculations". Language evolves. It's called semantic change, and it's WHAT language IS.

"To save America, women, especially those aforementioned pesky middle-class, white women, are going to have to start having more babies at a younger age, the argument goes. That this demand means that women will end up curtailing their ambitions and moving into the support-staff role is simply a coincidence, of course. Nothing to see here."

Uhm, Amanda? WOMEN HAVE NEVER LEFT THEIR SUPPORT STAFF ROLE. That is what they do, by and large. Women are not building airplanes or crafting bridges or curing cancer or designing new technologies or searching for the Higgs-Boson. They are SUPPORT STAFF for the MEN who are building airplanes and crafting bridges and curing cancer and designing new technologies and searching for the Higgs-Boson (it's not a done deal, yet folks!).

And those are the ambitious ones. The rest of them are fetching and carrying food and sorting out shit on shelves or scanning things across a bar-code reader (designed by men!) or taking care of children, the sick or the elderly.

Your outliers don't mean shit. Look at the facts. The doors have been thrown open to women for decades, and most of them are still housewives.

They're just not at home.

---

[18] http://jobs.aol.com/articles/2010/07/27/where-women-work/

"If women don't want to have more children, then instead of abandoning women's equality as a goal, we should rework our economic system so it doesn't rely on a steadily growing population to function."

WOMEN'S EQUALITY? Equal to what? Because it sure as hell isn't men.

Where is our Mozart?

Where is our Galileo?

Where is our Hawking?

Where is our Mersenne?

Oh, wait, I know. She's busy getting an order of wings ready.

Let's rework our economic system, shall we?

First of all, ladies, stop going to college. Seriously. Just stop. Most of what you study is complete and utter bullshit (film theory degree here). You don't need an exhaustive knowledge of the Sonnets of the Portuguese to be a secretary. You need to know your alphabet, how to tell time and the days of the week.

Secondly, get out of the labor market during your reproductive years. Stop taking care of other people's children and parents and husbands and go take care of your own. You can get to filing shit alphabetically AFTER you have made your contribution to society by raising stable, happy, healthy children and supporting a man who is probably out there doing something useful.

Those two things combined would have quite an impact. First of all, the labor market would contract dramatically and wages for men would rise correspondingly, allowing them to support a wife and young family. Funding that is currently being poured into Children's Literature and Urban Anthropology would go instead to the STEM fields, where all the real innovation and work is done. By men, of course. Social spending by the government would decline as women contribute more to the care of children and the elderly. Federal tax revenues would stay about the same, because the fact is that while there are MORE jobs in the current labor market, there is not more MONEY. The money would shift to men, and they would pay tax as usual on that income. If anything, reduced need for social spending would lower the government's outlay, giving them MORE money to spend on defence and debt repayment and infrastructure.

So why don't women want to do this?

Because it would make them dependent on a man during their reproductive years. They would need to rely on a man for income, and if you are going to rely on a man, you will have to give him something in return for that. His own children, first of all. Oh my. Well that will require fidelity, won't it? #sorrysluts

If he is heading out into the labor market every day, earning a wage for all of you, you will have to accommodate the stresses and anxieties that entails. How do you do that?

Be nice. Cook. Clean. Take of the children. Teach them manners and how to read and how to count. Take care of your parents. His and yours. Keep the house organized. Fold clothes. Book your appointments and needs around his schedule. Watch your finances. Don't spend too much money.

In other words, do all the jobs that women do in the labor market. Secretary, teacher, retail sales clerk, home care worker, nurse, waitress, cook and maid.

But don't do it for money. Do it for love. Love for your husband, love for your children, love for your parents, love for your country. The alternative is to do everything for yourself. Your own goals (be a secretary!), your own ambitions (fetch people food!), your own fulfilment (fold clothes at the Gap!), your own actualization (I never see my children!).

There is plenty of time to get to being a secretary or a waitress or a teacher. Children are only young for a short period of time. The real problem with people like Amanda is that she has uncritically accepted a male timeline for achieving what she defines as "equality". Go to college, repay horrendous loans, build a "career" (if you can call being a secretary a career) – all during a woman's reproductive years. The result is obvious: no babies.

All to avoid being dependant on a man for a few years. Amanda is probably one of those feminists who would claim that she "loves men". And yet, she's terrified of them. She has bought, hook line and sinker, the idea that men are abusive power-mongers who will oppress and mistreat their dependent wives and children without remorse or hesitation. And she is hell-bent on making sure other women believe that, too.

And we all pay for that. Dearly. The consequences will be stark when we have failed to produce the next generation. The most important thing we lose is love. Feminism has destroyed the family, destroyed the love between men and women and destroyed the love between parents and children.

How very sad.

True love, and true happiness comes from loving another person. For most of us, the greatest love we will ever know will be for our children.

Who needs babies? We all do. Without them, we have nothing.

There is only one happiness in this life, to love and be loved.

George Sand

Lots of love,

JB

Feminism is a voice that speaks for all women. As long as you're white. And rich. And you work outside the home. The rest of you bitches can step off.

So the beautiful ladies of Jezebel are at it again today[19], all in a gleeful lather that fewer and fewer girls express a desire to make caring for their families a priority, and that the labor market definition of an egalitarian relationship seems to have triumphed in the mind of the young.

They start by mocking all the dumb twats whose work doesn't include sitting in a cubicle sorting out the marketing strategy for OPI nail polish, which, as we all know, is an incredibly important social issue.

You see, for the Jezzie crowd, the only thing that counts as work is stuff you do in exchange for cash. All you folks volunteering for your favorite causes? That's not work, and it contributes nothing. All you folks taking care of either younger or the older generation because they are your family and you love them? Nope. Sit down, you're not working. None of that counts. All you folks with hobbies? Nah. That isn't work either.

[19] http://jezebel.com/5979665/holy-crap-is-feminism-actually-working-and-changing-the-world

Oh wait, now. If you are taking care of the older or younger generation, and they are not related to you, and you are doing it for COLD HARD CASH, well, that IS work. If your hobby is quilting and you do it for fun THAT'S NOT WORK, but if you work in a quilting factory and someone pays you, ok. You get a pass.

My point here is that no matter how much Jezebel and their ilk like to shriek that women (and increasingly men) who are at home, taking care of their families AREN'T WORKING, that work still needs to get done.

So who does it? Who cooks the food, washes the dishes, cleans the house, sorts out the laundry, does the gardening, raises the children, takes care of the elderly, walks the dog and every other thing that needs to get done?

Well, looky here[20].

Here's the summary: *women of color*.

All the nice white feminist ladies abandoned their homes and children and husbands and rushed pell-mell into the labor market, and then paid all the brown-skinned ladies money to do the work for them.

Isn't that nice of them?

And the lovely white lady feminists wonder why black women don't identify with them?

Feminists are celebrating two triumphs:

One, that they have succeeded in convincing young women and men that a woman's value can only be measured in labor market achievements. Honestly, this more a triumph of late capitalism, which has ensured that the major proceeds of capital go to shareholders and not workers, creating a situation in which women work for survival, and not because they want to. The rush of women into the labor market COMBINED with the supremacy of the shareholder has seen real wages stagnate, and the family wage has all but disappeared unless you are very well off.

Most women wake up to the lies of feminism too late. It's not until they have children that they realize they have not made the choices in life that allow them to make a choice! Most women WANT to be at home with their small children. In the UK, the number is 75%! Only one out of four women with small children who are working are doing it because they want to. The other three have been sold a pack of lies and they have guilt and shame and despair to show for it.

And that's something to celebrate?

The second triumph of feminism is to shove all the work of caring for a family off onto women of color. It's mostly white women who benefit from feminism, as scant as those benefits are. Earning a family wage is tough enough for a white family. For black families it has become nigh unto impossible, because their labor force participation is limited to doing all the work white ladies don't care to do, for very little money. Combine that with a cultural narrative that celebrates single motherhood as empowering and beneficial, and dismisses the importance of fathering, and you end up with a whole lot of black women who have no decent chance for success in the labor market at all.

Feminism hasn't been a triumph for women of color at all. It's been a disaster.

---

[20] http://factfinder2.census.gov/bkmk/table/1.0/en/EEO/10_5YR/EEOALL4W

The solution to this mess isn't more of the same. When is it ever? What we need is to start telling the truth to young men and women about how they will feel when they have small children to care for. We need to start telling the truth about just how fulfilling it will be to sit in a cubicle while your baby is being raised by someone else. We need to tell the truth about what impact it will have on men's ability to support a family when women move into high-status and high paying jobs. We need to give the younger generation a clear picture of the consequences of their actions.

And then let them choose. Yes, women should have the right to have any occupation they like, and they have the right to pay someone else to do all their hard work of raising a family. Men have the right to choose women based on how much she earns. Go right ahead. The reality is that most women WON'T choose to value themselves for how much they can earn in the labor market. The ones who are in the labor force are deeply, despairingly unhappy. "Opting out", which is another way of saying "become a housewife" has become the new dream.

It doesn't have to be a dream. It can become a reality. All it takes is a little dose of the truth. You won't find that truth in the mouths of feminists. Time for a game change.

The sooner, the better.

Lots of love,

JB

Jezebel solves the problem of women's inequality! It's about bloody time.

As we all know, we are currently living through a cultural crisis in which women are demonstrably coming up short against male achievements and are thus still not equal to men. This is obviously a huge problem, particularly in terms of the eventual and inevitable triumph of feminism, a theory that insists men and women ARE completely and absolutely equal in every measurable term, except for those terms in which we are not, but ....

Shhhhh

Those terms don't count anyways. Pipe down, lads. The ladies are speaking now.

Jezebel has an excellent suggestion for how ladies can actively counter the obviously blatant lie that we are NOT equal to men: humanities degrees are to be severely restricted, the school system is to be revamped to focus on science and mathematics and girls are to undergo rigorous training in all STEM fields and start going head to head with men on the basis of intellect and intelligence.

Put your tits away, girls. It's time to start getting serious about inventing, producing and creating useful shit that benefits all of humanity. Enough with your fucking nail polish and urban anthropology and filing papers alphabetically.

We're going to Mars, ladies! Who wants to sign up for the cold fusion team?

Oh shit.

Wrong article.

In actual fact, Jezebel thinks that the way forward to women's equality lies in teaching women to ....

Wait for it….

It's pretty good….

FART MORE.

I know, I know. You're thinking, "Judgy Bitch, you've got to be fucking kidding me!"

Nope. Not kidding[21].

To not let women fart is to not let them be fully human. To be free to fart it up with the menfolk is a sign of acceptance, not disintegrating social norms. And the feeling that women need to hide their farts is all part of the intense, building pressure to wax, pamper, perfume, and mask the realities of our own humanness. It's all part of a system that shames us into feeling, yet again, like how we actually are is never, ever, ever as sweet-smelling as it should be. It's enough to shame the most bulletproof secure among us into holding in a lifetime's worth of farts just to fit in.

You know, I think I've really been doing this human thing wrong. I've been operating under the basic premise that to be human is to acknowledge the presence of other people in my world, and to behave in a way that suggests I believe them to have some basic entitlements to respect and courtesy, which oddly includes the right to NOT have to breathe in sulfuric gases that have just escaped my ass!

Goodness me! Well, that was a giant fail. Turns out I should have been ripping giant stinky ones the whole time, because anything less is a denial of my basic HUMANITY.

Of course, we all know that MEN fart wherever and whenever they please. Meeting the President? Let 'er rip! Conference with the boss? Start with a Bronx cheer. Chatting up a chick at the bar? Impress her by dropping the cabbage bomb.

Yep. Men everywhere, farting at all times. Hanging out with men is like living in an open sewer. I love the smell of ass gas in the elevator!

I'm seriously not sure what to make of this kind of advice. Young women are growing up in a culture that tells them it's okay to be fat, dress like a slut, not give a shit about how they look, not care about what men think EVEN IF THEY HAPPEN TO LIKE MEN AND WANT A RELATIONSHIP WITH ONE, and now this: feel free to fart as an expression of your basic humanity.

Do I really have to explain what is wrong with this advice? One doesn't deliberately fart in front of other people because it is rude, it is gross, it is disrespectful, it is crass, it is deeply unpleasant and it suggests that you do NOT give one fuck about other people.

Charming. To the lady above, I hope you love being single, too.

Just the sort of advice women need MORE of: care less about other people.

You know, I realize that passing wind is a perfectly natural bodily function, but so is taking a dump. That doesn't mean I should do it in public and impose the accompanying aromas on other people because fuck them anyways.

---

[21] http://jezebel.com/5984630/all-the-flatulent-ladies-farts-are-the-great-equalizers

This is Tracy Moore, the lady who wrote the article at Jezebel. Try not to get on an elevator with her. She might feel the need to prove she is human.

I have a feeling that might really stink.

Lots of love,

JB

Attention feminists: please stop being so sexy and start being more shrieky and angry!

Here's an interesting article from the Guardian written by the effervescently happy Ellie Mae O'Hagan[22]:

Apparently, there are some sexy, cool feminists out there and they are wrecking the fun for all the screechy, withered shrews who are accustomed to having the ear of the media.

You see, feminism has undergone a change in recent years, from the earnest whining of Betty Freidan about the crushing oppression she, and other middle-class ladies endured in their carpeted bungalows stocked with every modern convenience to a raunchier, more aggressive sort of feminism, personified by the lovely ladies of *Sex and the City*.

I will confess that I have only seen a few episodes of that show, and they all left me with a bit of a bad taste. That red-headed one, who is a lawyer, is just a massive cunt, the blonde one is a whore, the curly haired one is a shallow gold-digging bore and the mousy one is just, well, mousy. I thought all those ladies sucked. I'll take Ripley any day.

"Get away from her, you bitch!"

There has recently been a media kerfuffle over two of Ellie's Strong Sexy Feminists™ going after Taylor Swift, who dares to dress modestly, chase after boys, sing about getting her heart broken and who yearns for love and marriage and children.

Oh, Taylor, you silly girl. You've got it all wrong. Boys don't matter. Don't you know that girls run the world? You shouldn't be lying on the cold hard ground, sweetie. You should be crushing him against a wall in your Cadillac.

Amy Poehler and Tina Fey are a couple of strong, sexy feminists, and they personify what feminism has come to mean rather perfectly. These ladies don't undermine feminism: they are the embodiment of it.

Let's go back to Ellie's article, wherein she writes:

"In my mind, if being sexy and funny are the two cornerstones of a new feminist movement, we may as well all pack up and go home now. At its core, feminism should be angry. It should be angry because women are still being taken for a ride. Like the women in The Feminine Mystique, we are being sold a lie of equality in a society where the odds are politically, socially and economically stacked against us.

Feminism's most basic function should be to emphasise that sexism is not an accident, but an inevitable consequence of a society structured to favour men. Jokes about vaginas and reassurances that we won't

---

[22] http://www.guardian.co.uk/commentisfree/2013/feb/26/feminists-sexy-funny-anger-changes-world

have to give up lipstick are not enough. To put it bluntly, a new feminism should not be afraid to piss people off."

On that last note, success is yours honey! You've certainly managed to piss me off.

Let's take this apart, shall we?

A society structured to favor men.

And which men would those be? The ones who are behind their peers in academic achievement before they are even FIVE YEARS OLD? Or the ones who commit suicide at a rate double that of the social average? Maybe you mean the men who are ten times more likely to go to prison than the social average, mostly for non-violent, drug-related crimes? You must mean the men who have seen their jobs evaporate and their livelihoods disappear and their social usefulness eradicated.

Fortunately, some men still have jobs, because their jobs are shitty and dangerous and dirty and obviously, they adore living in a society structured to make sure their lives are the ones that can be thrown away in a mine explosion. Well, the ones who aren't drafted into the military to die as cannon fodder, either by poverty or legislative decree.

You know which men benefit from the social structure? Rich white men. Who tend to have WIVES.

And daughters.

I've said it before, but I think it's worth saying again: PATRIARCHY IS NOT THE SAME THING AS ARISTOCRACY.

The majority of the men in the world have been, and continue to be, slaves working for a rich class of men AND women who have been ever willing to exploit their labor and ingenuity and raw brute strength for their own gains.

The odds are politically, socially and economically stacked against us (women)

Bitch, are you crazy? The entire political system is rigged to ensure that politicians must chase after women's votes, which is not a bad thing in and of itself, except that the media has convinced women there is a "war" against them, and that they should vote, not with their economic interests in mind, but with their cultural interests. Yeah, socially, the rich, white world just sucks for women. Oh, the injustice of being able to jail men for poor decisions made while drunk! The terrible burden of being able to force a man into parenting and paying for a child he did not intend and does not want.

Economically, women are just screwed.

They earn more university degrees than men (albeit in useless subjects like Film Theory), have the option of staying home with their small children, paid for either by a husband or by the state, and they continue to push for the right to be paid on par with men, even though men tend to work harder, work longer hours, acquire more training and spend more time doing socially productive and useful things.

A new feminism should not be afraid to piss people off.

Oh honey.

Your new feminism is indeed pissing people off. Maybe not the people you intend, though. There is a growing group of men and women alike who are getting sick and fucking tired of feminism's screechy, jackassed whinging and who have had just about enough of this shit.

I hate Sex and the City. I think slutwalks are basically a bunch of stupid, ugly whores using the occasion as an excuse to prance around in their underwear. Look at me! Look how edgy I am! Check out my tits! I think single mothers are selfish slags who don't give one shit about their children. I think Betty Freidan can kiss my pampered ass. I think hiring poor women to raise your children is the height of feminist hypocrisy.

And mostly, I think Amy Poehler and Tina Fey can go fuck themselves. Two rich white ladies who stand in their halos of wealth and privilege and honestly argue that women are oppressed and in need of more benefits, opportunities and advantages, paid for by men, of course. All the while mocking young women who reject the feminist narrative in favor of something a little more human. That is what feminism has become. Women so blind to their own privilege that they honestly believe they are getting screwed while all men, everywhere, are benefiting somehow.

In Bossypants, Tina writes:

"It is an impressively arrogant move to conclude that just because you don't like something, it is empirically not good. I don't like Chinese food, but I don't write articles trying to prove it doesn't exist."

Indeed, Tina.

Welcome to the New World Order. Women are starting to get angry again.

You might be surprised to find out just what we're angry about. Hang on to your rich, white asses, bitches. This ride could get nasty. And never forget that we're fighting not just for men, but alongside them.

That tends to be a lethal combination.

Lots of love,

JB

How to spend a ton of money being a "woman" and still be a shrill bitch at the same time.

Jezebel has certainly been a treasure trove of gobsmacking nuttiness this week! In a new post, the infallibly sensible Tracy Moore (she's one who farts a lot) does a cost benefit analysis on being a woman and it's the usual *facepalm* level of idiocy one has come to expect from ol' Jez!

So, apparently, it costs MONEY to be a woman. Here's all the things ladies must cash up for:

Hair
Makeup
Clothing
Shoes
Therapy
Weight management

To a total of $849 000 over the course of a lifetime! The average woman spends $65 A WEEK on cosmetics! Holy fucking Christ! I spend maybe $65 a YEAR on cosmetics and I like Lancome!

As we know, men (who typically have short hair that must be cut much more frequently) do not spend money grooming all the various hair on their bodies. Most dudes do not wear make-up, so yeah, I'll give her a pass on that one, although Mr. JB has quite the post-shave skin care regime going on. Men do not spend money on clothing or shoes. They do not spend money on stress relieving activities like video games, nor do they spend money taking care of their bodies and maintaining their weights.

Okay, okay. Tracy is simply pointing out that women typically spend MORE money than men on these items.

Because patriarchy. They HAVE TO. It's all part of the system of oppression. Ladies are FORCED to own 30 pairs of shoes and 200 separate items of clothing and to spend $65 a week on makeup (Jesus that blows my mind). They have NO CHOICE IN THE MATTER. The shoe gestapo is well known for randomly bursting into lady homes and taking a shoe inventory and god help the gal who doesn't own her requisite 30 pairs.

This is the kind of shit that drives me completely insane when I read Western women complaining about their lot in life.

Here we have a system, set up to benefit WOMEN, with completely voluntary participation and women start screaming because there is a cost associated with taking full advantage of that system. Grooming, hair, makeup, clothing, weight management are all things that women can use to emphasize their sexual attractiveness and then parlay that into some material benefits, should they so choose.

No one is REQUIRED to wear make-up or do their hair up fancy every day. Bullshit. There are BENEFITS associated with doing so, but it always comes down to personal choice. And along with benefits, there are COSTS!

And always, there is this unwritten assumption that men don't have to do these things. Do the writers have any idea how much razor blades for men cost? Have they ever imagined what it's like to get up every day and have to shave and wear a suit and tie? The number one aspect of physical appearance that affects men's income isn't even one they can control: HEIGHT.

Oh, the injustice of it! Ladies be crying.

And just in case you were thinking that feminism represents the interests of all women, take a good look at their whining over self-imposed sartorial sanctions: $6 000 a year spent on clothing.

$6 000!

Are you fucking kidding me? Oh, hello rich white lady working as a secretary in an office somewhere. Plenty of folks don't have $6 000 a year to spend on FOOD, never mind the latest taffeta shrug from Zara.

Personally, I'm surprised the costs associated with mental health aren't higher, since these women are all clearly batshit insane. Apparently, self-help books aren't particularly effective. Thank god for the blogosphere, eh?

It comes down to this: women want to have all the benefits associated with being feminine, they want the right to NOT ACTUALLY BE FEMININE, and they don't want to pay for that. Yeah, that seems reasonable. I want all the benefits of an education, but I don't want to actually become educated and I would like there to be no cost associated with my lack of education.

The reality is that most of these women have completely lost the ability to compete on the basis of femininity, which is, to be certain, a powerful force that can be harnessed and exploited for tremendous gains, and THERE IS NOTHING WRONG WITH THAT. Men and women alike respond to a man's height, just as men and women alike respond to a woman's beauty, which is far more than just what she looks like.

True beauty involves some basic attention to your physical appearance, but it doesn't have to cost a lot. Don't be fat. There's 95% of your beauty problem solved right there. Don't want to fuss with your hair? Grow it out. A chignon requires a few bobby pins and a trim once or twice a year.

Don't care to spend a great deal of money on clothes? Buy classics. That's WHY they're called classics! They don't need to be replaced. My professional wardrobe, which I have not worn in over ten years, is hanging in my closest and is still perfectly acceptable for wear because it consists of classic clothing that never goes out of style. And yes, three kids and ten years later, I still fit in every single piece.

But the most important aspect of beauty, which happens to be A) FREE and B) apparently elusive is to have a cheerful heart and a genuine sense of care and concern for the people who surround you. Beauty is about how you interact with the world and the people in it. Be kind, be generous, be thoughtful, be considerate, be gracious, be giving.

In other words, be feminine. Be a woman. It won't cost you anything and you might just find you gain far more than you could ever imagine. And you'll probably save a shit ton of money on self-help books, too.

Lots of love,

JB

There are more male nurses than ever. Highly specialized, technically qualified male nurses, who get paid more than female nurses because SEXISM!

I don't know why this kind of stupidity continues to amaze me, but it does.

Jezebel is running a piece[23] talking about how men are now moving into nursing, and typically, they are kicking the ladies asses in terms of salary. Average female nurses earn $51 100 while their male counterparts earn $60 700.

Cue the screaming morons!

Here's a comment at Jezebel from *concretewalls*, although *concretebrains* might be more accurate:

> I don't understand. Do employers sit down and look at names and dock pay if they are female? HOW DOES THIS HAPPEN? I mean the thought process would have to be right from the start. "Oh, Suzy started today, since she has a vagina, she is therefore not going to do work as well as someone with a penis, therefore she will only make 31.25 an hour instead of 32 an hour." I mean....how the fuck are employers getting away with this? HELP ME UNDERSTAND. I'm raging all the time about this. It's like, the most dumb shit EVER to me. I will never understand how this happens or why.

OK, *concretewalls*, let me explain it to you.

You see, there are different kinds of nursing. They all start out as RNs, and they all have the option to continue their training into highly technical specializations. A certified registered nurse anesthetist (CRNA),

[23] http://www.guardian.co.uk/commentisfree/2013/feb/26/feminists-sexy-funny-anger-changes-world

for example, requires years of additional training, which is then reflected in salary. CRNA's easily make $100 000/year and more!

Nurse Practitioners also require several years of additional training, and that certification results in higher earnings, too. Same goes for clinical nurse specialists. More training, more experience, more money.

Guess where male nurses are?

Male nurses make up 9% of the nursing population, and 41% of the CRNA population.

Take a job, pretty much any job, add complex technical specifications that take years to master, advanced training that requires years to complete, increased responsibilities and a correspondingly high salary, and abracadabra! You will begin to attract men.

There is no barrier to women proceeding through the CRNA specialization process and capturing those +$100K/year salaries.

They just don't.

You will hear it repeated over and over again in the media that there is a wage gap between men and women and that women continue to get paid less than their male counterparts. AND THAT IS TRUE.

Big fucking deal. The real question is why? Female doctors get paid less than male doctors. Why? They cluster in family medicine and not pediatric cardiology. They work fewer hours. They take years off to have children. The wage gap exists because men and women make different choices about how much time to dedicate to their jobs and how much more training they are willing to acquire.

It's the absolute height of hypocrisy for women to demand the right to compete with men head to head in every arena, and then cry like whiny suckholes when the men kick their asses.

That's not sexism, ladies. That's life.

It's what happens when you try to play with the boys.

You lose.

Get used to it.

Lots of love,

JB

Men: stand up for yourselves and we WILL hate you. The new feminist war cry!

Okay, this is going to be a long one, but it's an important one that needs to be taken apart. Let's all hold hands and pray that Lindy West learns to be a little more concise in the future, but for now, we just gotta wade through the sewage filled swamp of her mind.

Ready? As always, Lindy is *in italics*.

If I Admit That 'Hating Men' Is a Thing, Will You Stop Turning It Into a Self-Fulfilling Prophecy?[24]

Lindy West

Okay, so maybe you are a man. Maybe you haven't had the easiest ride in life—maybe you grew up in poverty; you've experienced death, neglect, and despair; you hate your job, your car, your body. Maybe somebody (or multiple somebodies) pulverized your heart, or maybe you've never even been loved enough to know what a broken heart feels like. Maybe shit started out unfair and became irreparable and you never deserved any of this. Maybe everything looks fine on paper, but you're just unhappy and you don't know why. These are human problems and other human beings feel for you very deeply. It is hard to be a human. I am so sorry.

Maybe? Maybe you haven't had the easiest life? Maybe you grew up in poverty? Maybe you've experienced death, neglect, despair?

Almost certainly. That is the fucking reality for almost everybody alive. The vast majority of men and women, even in the wealthiest countries on the planet are a mass of disposable humanity.

#clueless

#whiteladyproblems

That top 1% of the population, comprised of both men and women? Yeah, that's the ruling elite. Power and wealth and control is concentrated in the top, and the rest scrape by the best they can. The traditional word for that sort of social organization is aristocracy.

Patriarchy and aristocracy are not the same thing. One is rule by men. The other is rule by elite. Try to keep them straight.

However.

Here goes the hamster.

Though it is a seductive scapegoat (I understand why it attracts you), none of these terrible, painful problems in your life were caused by the spectre of "misandry." You can rest easy about that, I promise! In fact, the most powerful proponent of misandry in modern internet discourse is you — specifically, your dogged insistence that misandry is a genuine, systemic, oppressive force on par with misogyny. This is specious, it hurts women, and it is hurting you. Most feminists don't hate men, as a group (we hate the system that disproportionately favors men at the expense of women), but — congratulations! — we are starting to hate you. You, the person. Your obsession with misandry has turned misandry into a self-fulfilling prophecy. (I mean, sort of. Hating individual men is not the same as hating all men. But more on that in a minute.) Are you happy now? Is this what you wanted? Feminism is, in essence, a social justice movement— it wants to take the side of the alienated and the marginalized, and that includes alienated and marginalized men. Please stop turning us against you.

Quaking in your boots a bit, Lindy? You should be. Declaring openly that you hate an entire group of individuals for daring to speak is a dangerous precedent to set. The fact that you are starting to hate men (and women) for noting that there are actually are systemic forces that discriminate against men in favor of women is really just expressing that you fear them.

~~You should.~~
---
[24] http://jezebel.com/5992479/if-i-admit-that-hating-men-is-a-thing-will-you-stop-turning-it-into-a-self+fulfilling-prophecy

It is nearly impossible to address problems facing women—especially problems in which men are even tangentially culpable—without comments sections devolving into cries of "misandry!" from men and replies of "misandry isn't real" from women. Feminists are tired of this endless, fruitless turd-pong: hollow "conversation" built on willful miscommunication, bouncing back and forth, back and forth, until both sides throw up their hands and bolt. Maybe you are tired of this too. We seem to be having some very deep misunderstandings on this point, so let's unpack it. I promise not to yell.

Oh, but that's the problem, isn't it? We won't throw up our hands and bolt. We're here, and we intend to speak, and calling what we have to say "fruitless turd-pong" may satisfy some deeply immature, let's chuck rocks at boys resentment down in the depths of your sour little heart, but it still won't make us bolt.

Part One: Why Feminism Has "Fem" in the Name, or, Why Can't We All Just Be Humanists?

I wish, more than anything, that I could just be a "humanist." Oh, man, that would be amazing! Because that would mean that we lived in a magical world where all humans were born on equal footing, and maybe I could live in a house shaped like a big mushroom and birds would help me get dressed or something. Humanism is a gorgeous dream, and something to strive for. In fact, it is the exact thing that feminism is striving for right now (and has been working on for decades)! Yay, feminism!

We don't live in a magical world where all humans are born on an equal footing. We live in a democracy where all humans have equal (theoretically) access to the power to control the state through the power of the vote, regardless of the circumstances of their birth. Both men and women have the power to vote.

The single greatest influence on how successful (or not) a person will be in their lifetime is how successful (or not) their parents are.

That is true for BOTH men and women. There's that aristocracy problem rearing its ugly little head again. Addressing the concentration of wealth and the restrictions on social mobility in what is supposed to be a meritocracy requires us to focus on human rights, and not just women's rights.

Because those things affect humans, and not just women.

Unfortunately, the reason that "fem" is a part of the word "feminism" is that the world is not, currently, an equal, safe, and just place for women (and other groups as well—in its idealized form, intersectional feminism seeks to correct all those imbalances). To remove the gendered implications of the term is to deny that those imbalances exist, and you can't make problems disappear just by changing "feminism" to "humanism" and declaring the world healed. That won't work.

Nope. It won't. But by using the term "humanism", you explicitly acknowledge that the world isn't an equal, safe or just place for some humans, who happen to be both men and women, and that the problems of ALL those individuals matter. Not just the women.

Think of it like this. Imagine you're reading a Dr. Seuss book about a bunch of beasts living on an island. There are two kinds of beasts: Fleetches and Flootches. (Stick with me here! I love you!) Though the two are functionally identical in terms of intellect and general competence, Fleetches are in charge of pretty much everything.

If Fleetches are men and Flootches are women, then they are not functionally identical in terms of intellect and general competence.

The Fleetches are physically stronger than the Flootches.

The Fleetches are more likely to be of higher intelligence.

The Fleetches have a greater tendency to take risks and pursue rewards.

The Fleetches tend to cluster in occupations that invent, create and deliver tangible technologies and tools that collectively drive our entire society forward.

Stronger, smarter, more willing to take risks and occupied in technologically sophisticated pursuits. That is why the Fleetches are in charge of pretty much everything. **Because they are qualified to do so.**

I'm just going to cut the rest of Lindy's stupid metaphor because there is no point pursuing an argument that is based on the idea that men and women are functionally identical. They're not and no amount of screaming at the heavens is going to change that.

It's a nice example of the contradictory logic of feminism: let's observe that men are better than women in lots of ways, and then insist that there is some imaginary force that keeps women from being equal to men. As opposed to assuming that women are different from men and that our skills and abilities and contributions are equally valuable. Men set the bar at heights they can reach, and when women can't quite reach that high, the bar gets lowered because equality? Reining in male accomplishment just so women can feel "equal" is stupid. It denies that women have a very specific contribution to make and it slows down our entire trajectory of progress and innovation.

Back to Lindy.

Part Two: Why Claiming that Sexism Isn't Real Is a Sexist Thing to Say

We live in a world of measurable, glaring inequalities. Look at politicians, CEOs, film directors, law enforcement officers, comedians, tech professionals, executive chefs, mathematicians, and on and on and on—these fields are dominated by men. (And, in many cases, white men.) To claim that there is no systemic inequality keeping women and minorities out of those jobs is to claim that men (people like you) are just naturally better. If there is no social structure favoring men, then it stands to reason that men simply work harder and/or are more skilled in nearly every high-level specialized field.

Correct. They are.

Men work longer hours.

Men acquire greater, and much more highly specialized skills.

Even in traditionally female occupations (like nursing – see above), men acquire greater specializations, earn more money and work longer hours.

God, facts just suck, don't they?

It's fine (though discouraging) if you legitimately believe that, but you need to own up to the fact that that is a self-serving and bigoted point of view. If you do not consider yourself a bigot, then kindly get on board with those of us who are trying to proactively correct inequalities. It is not enough to be neutral and tacitly benefit from inequality while others are left behind through no fault of their own. Anti-sexism, anti-racism, anti-homophobia, anti-transphobia—that's where we're at now. Catch up or own your prejudice.

By others, we assume Lindy means women? Because choosing a college major is usually done with a gun to your head? The entire school system is rigged to benefit girls, specifically, and women enroll in college in much greater numbers than men, but they take utterly fucking useless degrees that confer no skills other than the ability to perpetually imagine oneself a victim in need of succor.

The demonization of little boys in the school system and the utter failure of society to address the needs of boys as they proceed through a system designed to benefit girls is an excellent example of sexism. You want to talk about being left behind through no fault of your own? Let's talk little boys in public education.

Part Three: Why People Being Shitty to You Is Not the Same as You Being Systematically Disenfranchised

There might be a lot of women in your life who are mean to you, but that's just women not liking you personally. Women are allowed to not like you personally, just like you are allowed to not like us personally. It's not misandry, it's mis-Kevin-dry. Or, you know, whoever you are. It is not built into our culture or codified into law, and you can rest assured that most women you encounter are not harboring secret, latent, gendered prejudices against Kevins that could cost you a job or an apartment or your physical sanctity. That doesn't mean that there aren't isolated incidents wherein mean women hurt men on purpose. But it is not a systemic problem that results in the mass disenfranchisement of men.

I'm assuming that by "disenfranchised, Lindy means "downtrodden" and not "denied the right to vote", but she opens a nice little can of revealing worms. Turns out there is a large group of people who are, in fact, disenfranchised: felons.

91% of whom are male[25].

74% of whom were non-white males.

And men are far more likely to receive a conviction for a felony than women.

Black men, in particular are sentenced more harshly.

And even when women are convicted of crimes, they receive preferential sentencing.

Yeah, no systemic problem here, and certainly not one that results in disenfranchisement.

There are some really shitty things about being a man. You are 100% right on that. You are held up to unreasonable expectations about your body and your career and your ability/desire to conform to traditional modes of masculinity (just like women are with traditional femininity), and that is absolutely oppressive.

One of the unreasonable expectations, apparently, is to have intact genitals and to be protected from mutilation, just like girls are.

There are radical feminists and deeply wounded women and women who just don't have the patience for diplomacy anymore who absolutely hate you because of your gender. (However, for whatever it's worth, I do not personally know a single woman like that.) That is an unpleasant situation to be in—especially when you also feel like you're being blamed for the seemingly distant problems of people you've never met and towards whom you feel no particular animus.

---

[25] http://bjs.gov/content/pub/ascii/vfluc.txt

Deeply wounded women who openly hate men? Let's offer the poor ducks some support, shall we? Create a safe space where they can express their rage and anger and sense of helplessness.

Deeply wounded men who openly hate women? Well fuck you, MRA[26]s.

The difference is, though, that the radfem community on Tumblr does not currently hold the reins of power in every country on earth (even in nations with female heads of state, the political and economic power structures are still dominated by men). You do, abstractly. No, you don't have the ability or the responsibility to fix those imbalances single-handedly, but refusing to acknowledge that power structure is a slap in the face to people actively disadvantaged by it every day of their lives. You might not benefit from patriarchy in any measurable way—on an individual level your life might actually be much, much worse than mine—but the fact is that certain disadvantages are absent from your experience (and, likely, invisible to you) because of your gender.

Why do men control the reins of power over political and economic structures? Because women don't want them! When women DO express political ambition, they are MORE likely to be elected than their male counterparts. There is absolutely zero systemic bias against women in political power. Women are not elected to the senate and the congress and the Oval Office because they DO NOT RUN FOR THOSE OFFICES.

The same is true for the "glass ceiling". Women do not run the corporations or organizations of the world because, for the most part, THEY AREN'T INTERESTED. In Australia, women who DO reach the top of the corporate ladder have almost universally suffered some deep trauma in their childhood, and their career ambitions are a reaction to that trauma.

Maybe you're saying, "Hey, but my life wasn't fair either. I've had to struggle." I know it wasn't. I know you have. But that's not how fairness works. If you present fairness as the goal—that some day everything will be "fair" for everyone—you're slipping into an unrealistic fantasy land. Life already isn't fair, because of coincidence and circumstance and the DNA you were born with, and we all have to accept the hands we're dealt and live within that reality. But life doesn't have to be additionally unfair because of imposed systems of disenfranchisement that only affect certain groups. We can fight against that.

Oh, preach it, sister! That's exactly right!

Oh wait. You mean only when life is additionally unfair to women.

Oops, my bad.

Feminism isn't about striving for individual fairness, on a life-by-life basis—it's about fighting against a systematic removal of opportunity that infringes on women's basic freedoms. If a woman and a man have equal potential in a field, they should have an equal opportunity to achieve success in that field.

Agreed. And when men and women DO have equal potential in a field, they DO have an equal opportunity for success. Provided they work the same hours, acquire the same advanced training, dedicate the same resources, men and women achieve at equal measures of success.

Let's look at medicine, for example. Women are now enrolled in medical school in equal numbers to men. And what do they do with their qualifications? They decline advanced specializations and work as family physicians, mostly part time. Basically, they write prescriptions for painkillers and antibiotics and as soon as

---

[26] http://jezebel.com/5967923/fuck-you-mras

a perplexing problem crops up, they refer it on to a specialist man. That's why female doctors make less money than male ones: they work fewer hours in less technically qualified specializations.

It's not that we want the least qualified women to be handed everything just because they're women. It's that we want all women to have the same opportunities as all men to fulfill (or fail to fulfill, on their own inherent merits) their potential. If a particular woman is underqualified for a particular job, fine. That isn't sexism. But she shouldn't have to be systematically set up, from birth, to be underqualified for all jobs (except for jobs that reinforce traditional femininity, obv).

That's not sexism. It's biology. And evolution. Women prefer caretaking jobs. They are naturally more nurturing than men. They have been designed by nature to be so.

Men's greater abilities at spatial orientation and women's greater abilities at speech and communication are present at birth. There is no socialization aspect involved. It's simple biology.

Part Four: A List of "Men's Rights" Issues That Feminism Is Already Working On

Let's go all the way back to this:

In fact, the most powerful proponent of misandry in modern internet discourse is you — specifically, your dogged insistence that misandry is a genuine, systemic, oppressive force on par with misogyny. This is specious, it hurts women, and it is hurting you.

The entire point of this article is that there is NO genuine, systemic, oppressive force working against men.

Now watch the hamster dance.

The next section claims exactly the opposite: there IS a genuine, systemic, oppressive force working against men, and that force is the PATRIARCHY! And what is the greatest foe of the PATRIARCHY? Why, that would be FEMINISM, of course.

So all you men who are NOT oppressed by any genuine, systemic force working against men, except all of you who ARE oppressed by a genuine, systemic force, come and join hands with FEMINISM.

We're here to rescue you. Let's see what that rescue will look like.

Feminists do not want you to lose custody of your children. The assumption that women are naturally better caregivers is part of patriarchy.

Widespread feminist support of single mother families and the insistence that the state offer generous benefits to single mothers is BY DEFINITION denying men custody of their children. If men were custodial parents, either solely, or in unison with the child's mother SHE WOULDN'T BE A SINGLE MOTHER.

Feminists do not like commercials in which bumbling dads mess up the laundry and competent wives have to bustle in and fix it. The assumption that women are naturally better housekeepers is part of patriarchy.

They do, however, like ads that portray domestic violence as being something only men do to women. The assumption that men are violent and women are victims is totally understandable, right?

Feminists do not want you to have to make alimony payments. Alimony is set up to combat the fact that women have been historically expected to prioritize domestic duties over professional goals, thus minimizing their earning potential if their "traditional" marriages end. The assumption that wives should make babies instead of money is part of patriarchy.

But they will rail against divorce lawyers who specialize in making sure that men get treated fairly in divorce proceedings[27].

Feminists do not want anyone to get raped in prison. Permissiveness and jokes about prison rape are part of rape culture, which is part of patriarchy.

But they will demand that juvenile offenders be sentenced to adult facilities, where, hopefully, they will get raped[28].

Feminists do not want anyone to be falsely accused of rape. False rape accusations discredit rape victims, which reinforces rape culture, which is part of patriarchy.

They do, however, support the right of women to claim state benefits on the basis of rape without actually having to prove the accusation. There should be an automatic assumption of guilt. Against the man, of course.

Feminists do not want you to be lonely and we do not hate "nice guys." The idea that certain people are inherently more valuable than other people because of superficial physical attributes is part of patriarchy.

Except for all the nice guys on OKCupid[29]. Those guys suck and are worth hating.

Feminists do not want you to have to pay for dinner. We want the opportunity to achieve financial success on par with men in any field we choose (and are qualified for), and the fact that we currently don't is part of patriarchy. The idea that men should coddle and provide for women, and/or purchase their affections in romantic contexts, is condescending and damaging and part of patriarchy.

But we fully expect you to offer to pay for dinner. That's just being a gentleman. It's up to us to decide how the check gets split, if at all. The person who proposes the date should be the one who pays. And who is required to propose the date? Oh yeah. That would be men.

Feminists do not want you to be maimed or killed in industrial accidents, or toil in coal mines while we do cushy secretarial work and various yarn-themed activities. The fact that women have long been shut out of dangerous industrial jobs (by men, by the way) is part of patriarchy.

But don't ask us to lift any heavy bags when we're pregnant, even if that is part of our job[30]. That's not fair! Get some guy to do it for us!

---

[27] http://jezebel.com/5928162/bros-before-hos-a-new-breed-of-divorce-lawyer

[28] http://jezebel.com/5991944/what-lies-ahead-for-the-steubenville-rapists

[29] http://jezebel.com/5969737/meet-the-so+called-nice-guys-of-okcupid

[30] http://jezebel.com/5992775/pregnant-hospital-worker-forced-to-take-unpaid-leave-because-she-couldnt-lift-50+pound-bags-of-trash

Feminists do not want you to commit suicide. Any pressures and expectations that lower the quality of life of any gender are part of patriarchy. The fact that depression is characterized as an effeminate weakness, making men less likely to seek treatment, is part of patriarchy.

Unless you're a white man, of course[31]. In that case, your depression is definitely worth mocking and deriding and ignoring.

Feminists do not want you to be viewed with suspicion when you take your child to the park (men frequently insist that this is a serious issue, so I will take them at their word). The assumption that men are insatiable sexual animals, combined with the idea that it's unnatural for men to care for children, is part of patriarchy.

But they will question your masculinity and declare a "creepy" factor should you happen to like My Little Pony.

Feminists do not want you to be drafted and then die in a war while we stay home and iron stuff. The idea that women are too weak to fight or too delicate to function in a military setting is part of patriarchy.

But they're not down with drafting the ladies[32]. Mostly because rape.

Feminists do not want women to escape prosecution on legitimate domestic violence charges, nor do we want men to be ridiculed for being raped or abused. The idea that women are naturally gentle and compliant and that victimhood is inherently feminine is part of patriarchy.

Except for all those times when women were naturally gentle and compliant and forgot to tell someone they were actually being raped[33].

Probably the most ridiculous account of "rape" you will ever read. But it WAS rape, because gentle and compliant by nature, dontcha know?

Feminists hate patriarchy. We do not hate you.

I'll just quote from the opening paragraph:

— we are starting to hate you. You, the person.

If you really care about those issues as passionately as you say you do, you should be thanking feminists, because feminism is a social movement actively dedicated to dismantling every single one of them. The fact that you blame feminists—your allies—for problems against which they have been struggling for decades suggests that supporting men isn't nearly as important to you as resenting women. We care about your problems a lot. Could you try caring about ours?

If you really care about those issues as passionately as you say you do, you should be thanking men's rights activists, because the men's human rights movement is a social movement actively dedicated to

[31] http://jezebel.com/5970262/poor-pitiful-dudes-why-you-should-defer-to-men-with-post+patriarchal-depression

[32] http://jezebel.com/5986756/the-lady+draft-may-be-in-our-future

[33] http://jezebel.com/5964359/when-will-we-stop-pretending-that-college-athletes-cant-be-rapists

dismantling every single one of them. The fact that you blame men —your allies—for problems against which they have been struggling for decades suggests that supporting women isn't nearly as important to you as resenting men. We care about your problems a lot. Could you try caring about ours?

Part Five: I'm Sorry That You Are in Pain, But Please Stop Taking It Out on Women

It's not easy to swallow your own privilege—to admit that you're a Fleetch—but once you do, it's addictive. It feels good to open up to perspectives that are foreign to you, accept your complicity in this shitty system, and work on making the world better for everyone instead of just defending your territory. It's something I had to do as a privileged white woman, and something I still have to work on every day, because it's right. That doesn't make me (or you) a bad person—it makes me an extremely lucky person who was born into a white body in a great family in a vibrant, liberal city in a powerful, wealthy country that implicitly values white bodies over all other bodies. The least I can do is acknowledge the arbitrariness of that luck, and work to tear down the obstacles facing those who are disenfranchised by the insidious fetishization of whiteness. Blanket defensiveness isn't going to get any of us anywhere.

Work on making the world better for everyone instead of just defending your territory.

Exactly, Lindy.

To all the men who have had shitty lives and mistake that pain for "misandry": I totally get it. Humans are not such complicated creatures. All we want is to feel like we're valued, like we deserve to exist. And I'm sorry if you haven't found that so far in your life. But it's not women's fault, it's not my fault, and it's certainly not feminism's fault. The thing is, you're not really that different from the women you rail against so passionately in these comment threads—the women who are trying to carve out some space and assert their value in a world of powerful men. Plenty of women know exactly what it feels like to be pushed to the fringe of society, to be rejected so many times that you eventually reject yourself. That alienation is a big part of what feminism is fighting against. A lot of those women would be on your side, if you would just let them instead of insisting that they're the villains. It's better over here, and we have room for you. So stop trying to convince us that we hate you and I promise we'll start liking you a whole lot more.

Nice try at sucking up, Lindy.

Newsflash, bitch: **I don't give a fuck whether you like me or not**, and neither does anyone else fighting for men's basic human rights. Because human rights are a goal worth pursuing whether you benefit directly from them or not. And if you are human, then guess what?

YOU DO!

The fact that you even wrote this article means that the voices are beginning to penetrate. You hear us. And you're afraid.

Good. You should be.

We're coming. And we don't care if you like it.

Lots of love,

JB

Bitter old feminist is bitter and old.

Janet Street Porter[34]. Oh this woman is just delightful. Let's take her apart, shall we?

When these brain-dead bimbos finally grow up, they'll realise we need the F-word (that's feminism) more than ever

Let's talk about the F-word. Many young women today regard feminism as a dirty word, a cause they say has no relevance to their own lives.

To my generation, that's a real cause for concern — whatever happened to the notion of sisterhood?

Which sisterhood would that be, Janet? The one that thinks calling OTHER WOMEN brain-dead bimbos is an expression of solidarity? Pass, thanks.

In a recession, women ought to be united, looking out for each other, being supportive — especially when huge numbers of us are being laid off, ordered to work fewer hours and having our benefits cut.

That would explain why the recession is called the mancession. Because most manufacturing and construction jobs, the hardest hit segments of the economy, were held by women, right? And the obvious solution to gender inequality is to band together on the basis of gender, even if you do think I'm a brain-dead bimbo. Riiiiiiight. Good plan.

Worse, a distressing number of modern girls think you get on in life by looking good, not because of what's between your ears — celebrity culture promotes the notion that it's perfectly acceptable to judge other females on first impressions.

Because bimbo is a term that suggests deeply nuanced thought?

The world of The Only Way Is Essex and the Kardashians, of fake tans, Rihanna, Tamara Ecclestone and Katie Price focuses to an unhealthy degree on the external packaging we should strive for in order to attract the opposite sex and be successful at work.

These brain-dead creeps tottering around in crippling shoes and body-con frocks, with frozen faces, a mane of hair extensions, false nails and thick eyelashes should be thanking my generation for what we achieved, not treating us as embarrassing pariahs!

Awww. That's so sweet, the way you support other women and don't judge them by their appearances. What's the matter, bitch? Jealous?

Back in the Sixties, we campaigned for equal pay, better childcare and our rightful place in the boardrooms of Britain. With the long-awaited Labour victory in 1997, more women than ever took their places in the Commons — and posed for that (fateful, as it turned out) Blair's Babes picture with Tony, who looked like the cat who got the cream.

Well, sweetie, if you managed to do equal work, you might have a shot at equal pay. And how nice that you decided a child's mother isn't the best person to care for that child. No one has a "right" to a position in a boardroom. You have to earn that, doll.

Since that day, when we thought we stood at the beginning of a new era (ha ha), feminism has gradually waned in popularity, along with the number of women in power.

[34] http://www.dailymail.co.uk/femail/article-2291204/Janet-Street-Porter-When-brain-dead-bimbos-finally-grow-theyll-realise-need-F-word-thats-feminism-ever.html

Gosh, with women like you representing the movement, I can't figure out why that might be?

Which is why I want to send out this message to young women — feminism is nothing to be ashamed of. We still have so much to fight for.

We? Oh, are you talking to me? So sorry. I was busy being a brain dead creepy bimbo. It takes up so much of time, you see.

Don't expect politicians to be supportive — they've turned out to be our worst enemies.

In spite of David Cameron's pleas that he 'understands' women, an increasing number of female voters are unimpressed — they've seen his government cut legal aid and child benefit.

Goddammit, David! Don't you understand that we are OWED child benefits and legal aid? Do you seriously expect me to use my own money to pursue my false rape charge?

Where's free childcare? Why isn't there a quota to get women fairly represented in the boardrooms of the top UK companies — bizarre when we wield the most purchasing power?

Yeah, seriously. Why should I have to care for my own children? That's stupid. And why should I have to EARN a position at the boardroom table. That kind of bullshit is for MEN. I want a fucking quota for women! Right now!

Cameron has admitted his wife Sam is unhappy with his failure to promote women (fewer of us than ever in the Cabinet), but he needs to keep his fellow MPs happy, and rank-and-file Tories are not exactly female-friendly.

As for the Lib Dems, embarrassing revelations about Lord Rennard and alleged sexual harassment of young female party workers reinforce the message that Westminster is a boys' club.

Is Sam equally unhappy at the fact that very few women have any interest in political leadership, and even fewer are in any way qualified to lead?

Politics, in spite of Blair's Babes, remains a macho environment — and a recent report entitled Sex And Power 2013: Who Runs Britain? reckons the UK has fallen 37 places internationally since 2001 to joint 60th in the world when it comes to women at the top in public life — the law, the city, the civil service, parliament and education.

You do know that being macho is not the same thing as being a man, right? No more so than being a woman makes you feminine. You can go look in a mirror if that comes as a surprise to you.

Only one in five MPs is female.

And in every race, there was a female candidate, right? No? Well then, how is it you expect women to be elected when they DON'T RUN? Perhaps you need to review how elections actually work.

That's why feminism is still relevant today — we haven't even won round one of the battle for true equality.

Except the one about being allowed to kill any man's baby should said baby be inconvenient. Except the one about being able to force a man to pay for a child he does not want and did not intend. Except the one about being the presumed custodial parent in divorce proceedings. Except the one where the entire education system is skewed to reflect women's natural skills and interests.

Oh wait. That isn't equality either, is it? Well, okay. I'll give you that. You haven't won any rounds in the battle for equality. Supremacy? Yes. Equality? No.

New research indicates that today's young women think of themselves as 'empowered individuals', who claim they rarely encounter discrimination at work and are comfortable in their relationships with the opposite sex.

How dare they?!?! Comfortable with men? The slags! They don't experience discrimination? Those stupid whores. Empowered my ass. Empowered means every bad feeling you have must be blamed on men and if you aren't running smack into the patriarchy every day, you are just doing it wrong.

Many say feminist is a term that applies to lesbians and women who hate men.

Hmmm. Now why would that be?

I want to weep — are these women living in dreamland, brainwashed into thinking all's right in the world, when the reality is so different?

You know that philosophical conundrum where you can't tell if you're dreaming you're awake? Yeah, maybe Janet, it is YOU who is living in a dreamland and the brain dead bimbos are living in reality.

They are smug and self-satisfied, when they should be taking a long, hard look at the realities of life in modern Britain.

Fact: for older women, life has just got much tougher. Nearly 30,000 of us (three times the number of men) have to continue working in our 60s because of the rise in the pension age. Losing out on a pension we spent all their lives paying for, as well as paying tax on our wages. Talk about a double negative!

Call the waaaaahmbulance. Ladies have to work longer. No fair! Just because they live longer, on average, than men is no reason to ask them to work a bit longer. Life is too cruel. Oh, the injustice!

Fewer women than ever are married, and more are choosing not to have children. Those who do are increasingly starting a family later in life.

All of which indicates the growth of a 'me first' mentality, which may be admirable, as it means more independence, rewarding careers and sexual freedom, but I suspect many (younger) women forget that inevitably they will one day be old, needing care and support.

No, darling, I think it's YOU who forgot that. When you older feminists chucked out your husbands and aborted your babies, you gave new meaning to the "me first" mentality. And now that you have no men to love and no children, you're bitter and lonely. You made your bed, cupcake. Get ready to sleep in it.

They aren't bothering to save for that grim day, and credit card bills have never been higher.

In business, many have decided that rather than try to struggle to the top of a male-dominated company, they will start their own businesses, where they set the rules — 90,000 did so in 2008.

Entrepreneurs who want flexible hours and more out of life than just the satisfaction of beating men, which is actually really hard to do. God they suck.

Good luck, but the route they have chosen is not only financially risky and demanding, but side-steps the big issue, the need to overhaul the UK's male-dominated leadership culture.

Why is this a need, again? Men have created and built and invented and improved on every modern convenience and technology and tool we have at our disposal. Seems to me that male-dominated leadership is doing great!

Why are those in power so frightened of giving women (the majority of the population, at 51 per cent) an equal number of seats at the table?

Why do women think they should be GIVEN a seat at the table? You know how men get to the table? THEY EARN IT BY WORKING HARD. Want a seat? Get your ass in gear and earn it then.

Why should change be 'gradual'? There are 30 million women in the UK, and yet two-thirds of all public appointments go to men.

How many of those 30 million women are qualified to do anything other than clean up after or care for other people? No one forces women to be secretaries and nurses and teachers. They CHOOSE those jobs. Housewives for other people.

And what kind of women do these men choose to work with? Researchers have found that bosses, faced with two equally qualified candidates, are more likely to choose the one they find attractive or even secretly fancy.

No!?! Shocked I tell you! The fact that men are valued for their height is immaterial, right? Because with a trip to the hair salon and some time at the gym, you can totally alter your height? I'd say the advantage here goes to women.

Look at the online abuse heaped on respected academic and broadcaster Mary Beard after she appeared on Question Time — it won't all have come from men. This woman has the effrontery to have grey hair and characterful teeth — hardly a crime.

Nope. Not a crime at all. Of course, having nice teeth and pigmented hair isn't a crime either, Janet.

I'm sure many young women secretly thought Mary should get her act together and smarten up — in their eyes, we should 'make the most of ourselves'.

Oh hell, no. You're so lovely just as you are. Why on earth should you change? You're perfect!

Futurologist Ian Pearson wrote a recent essay for the International Longevity Centre claiming that in the past women united against men (ie back in the Sixties) — but these days women are divided into groups, each fighting for their own special interests. Pretty versus plain, young versus old. Skilled versus unskilled. Either way, older women are being ignored.

Well, except for the pretty, skilled old women. They seem to be doing just fine.

Social networking means younger women can easily network with others who share their interests and lifestyles — many have less sympathy for an older generation.

Gosh, why it's almost like there's some kind of ..... sisterhood! And all the old, bitter bitches who call women bimbos and brain dead and judge them by their appearances are being left out. It's a mystery, folks! Like the origins of the universe. So difficult to cipher.

Young women have benefited at work and risen up to managerial roles and decent pay (even outstripping men in some professions in their late 20s and early 30s), whereas women in their 50s tend to work in lower grades, earning far less than men of the same age.

Well, maybe that's because men in their 50s choose to acquire some actual skills, which combined with their experience, makes them very valuable. That's children's literature degree will only get so much mileage.

To many young women, the old are the enemy, or the problem they don't want to think about.

Only when the old are bitter hags shrieking insults at them. They seriously have better things to do than listen to moany feminists call them bimbos.

Look at the outcry over the lack of older women on television — there's hardly been a groundswell of support from any of the young females who dominate prime-time television.

Ah, so there you have it. Young women dominate. Those bitches. It's fine to dominate MEN, but they shouldn't be kicking the big girl's butts.

Discrimination is something you only care about when it happens to you. By the time today's young women reach later life, who will pay for their care (and the number of women in residential homes far outstrips men) and look after them?

The fact that you haven't saved enough money to pay for your own care is not DISCRIMINATION, dearie. It's stupid financial planning. Your future is YOUR responsibility.

When they discover their state pensions are pitiful, they have no savings and they can't heat their homes or buy food, perhaps they might stop and consider how very different life might have been if the sisterhood had stuck together and fought for equal representation.

Ok, now I'm lost. The sisterhood was going after rich pensions, lots of cash, free heat and food – and that was to be paid for by whom, again? And are men getting these things, too?

Methinks the lady doth protest too much.

You know which ladies will have all those things? The ones who got married and stayed married. The ones who fell in love with a man, pledged their lives to him, had children, launched them the from nest and then grew old together. The ones who walked through life with a man at their side.

At the end of the day, your sisters don't matter. Your husband does.

Oh snap!

Lots of love,

JB

There never was a patriarchy, and there isn't one now

A reader named Sherlock sent me a link to an article, written by a woman named Susan Carol Rogers, called **Female Forms of Power and the Myth of Male Dominance: A Model of Female/Male Interaction in Peasant Society**[35].

It's a fairly long slog, at 29 pages, but I'm going to give you the quick and dirty summary.

Susan starts by noting that anthropology as a discipline makes a couple of sweeping generalizations and assumptions that directly affects how they understand and investigate power and authority. Anthropologists typically assume that the only forms of power that matter are those that are codified and formalized: things like rules and laws and positions in political institutions. There is no room in their observations for informal power. The mayor has power. The mayor's wife has none.

This focus on only formal aspects of power and authority makes it seem as if male dominance is virtually universal across human societies. To make matters even more complicated, both men and women behave as if men are dominant, when in reality, the situation is much more nuanced.

Susan writes, "although peasant males monopolize positions of authority and are shown public deference by women, thus superficially appearing to be dominant, they wield relatively little real power" (p.728).

In the peasant societies Susan explores, women control a major portion of the resources and make most of the decisions regarding how those resources are used, in effect, wielding the greater power.

Why would they do that? Why act like men have all the power, when in reality, it's women who have most of it?

This is the absolute kicker in Susan's article. She gets this 100% right, if you ask me. She starts by defining a myth as a belief that one can see is factually untrue. Take the idea that black men have bigger penis sizes than any other racial group. It's a myth that's been repeated so often, even black MEN, who are most likely to have seen a black penis (their own, for starters) tend to believe it. But it's not true. It's part of a racist narrative to define black men as animals, and it has its roots in the history of American slavery.

We're going to come back to that idea, and talk about how myths can be productive, but also incredibly destructive when society no longer perceives the myth as a myth.

In the groups that Susan is looking at, neither men nor women believe the myth that men are dominant, but both men and women behave as if that is, in fact, true.

Why?

Both groups want to think of themselves as having distinct advantages, values and prestige relative to one another, and they want those attributes to be distributed fairly, and in such a way that neither group feels like they're getting the shaft. They want to seem like "winners" to one another. Furthermore, both men and women see themselves as mutually dependent upon one another, which, when you come right down to the very basic reality of reproduction is absolutely, unequivocally true.

Technology, driven by the dominant ideology of female supremacy, is working furiously to eliminate men from the reproductive process, creating embryos that are genetically identical to the mother, by triggering a process called parthenogenesis. The end of genetic diversity. How clever. And how sad is it that most of the specialists working in human fertility are actually male? Working to eradicate themselves.

---

[35] http://www.faculty.fairfield.edu/dcrawford/rogers.pdf

Let's get back to Susan. She observes that men and women in peasant societies understand perfectly that they are dependent upon one another, and seek to create a social structure that makes both men and women feel valued and that they are being treated respectfully and fairly.

What resources do women control?

In peasant societies, the key unit of economic and social production is the nuclear family. Husband, wife, children, and perhaps extended members of the family in the form of grandparents. Jill Dubisch, also trying to evaluate the power that women hold in peasant societies, came up with four criteria to evaluate how evenly power is distributed between husbands and wives:

How respectfully did the spouses treat one another, both privately and publicly?

How often or much did the spouses interfere with one another's domains?

How were family resources allocated?

How were decisions regarding plans for children made?

Here is an example of how that works: in Greek villages, women control all the family finances, because they take principal responsibility for producing the food/goods that will be sold at the local market. The women make the bread, churn the butter, weave the cloth, collect the eggs, raise the goats, make the cheese, etc. They attend the markets, set the prices, and collect the payment.

So far, they are the primary drivers of the family's prosperity and comfort. A man without a hard-working wife like this is well and truly fucked. This kind of scenario has been in effect since the beginning of written culture.

One of the my favorite passages from the Bible is Proverbs 31, commonly called, the Virtuous Woman. And because I am an atheist, I absolutely want scripture read at my funeral! I also want to be buried in my Star Trek uniform, but that's another story.

> Who can find a virtuous woman? for her price is far above rubies.
> The heart of her husband safely trusts in her, so that he shall have no need of spoil.
> She will do him good and not evil all the days of her life.
> She seeks wool, and flax, and works willingly with her hands.
> She is like the merchants' ships; she brings her food from afar.
> She rises also while it is yet night, and gives meat to her household, and a portion to her maidens.
> She considers a field, and buys it: with the fruit of her hands she plants a vineyard.
> She girds her loins with strength, and strengthens her arms.
> She perceives that her merchandise is good: her candle goes not out by night.
> She lays her hands to the spindle, and her hands hold the distaff.
> She stretches out her hand to the poor; yea, she reaches forth her hands to the needy.
> She is not afraid of the snow for her household: for all her household are clothed with scarlet.
> She makes herself coverings of tapestry; her clothing is silk and purple.
> Her husband is known in the gates, when he sits among the elders of the land.
> She makes fine linen, and sells it; and delivers girdles unto the merchant.
> Strength and honour are her clothing; and she shall rejoice in time to come.
> She opens her mouth with wisdom; and in her tongue is the law of kindness.
> She looks well to the ways of her household, and eats not the bread of idleness.
> Her children arise up, and call her blessed; her husband also, and he praises her.

> *Many daughters have done virtuously, but you excel beyond them all.*
> *Favour is deceitful, and beauty is vain: but a woman that fears the Lord, she shall be praised.*
> *Give her of the fruit of her hands; and let her own works praise her in the gates.*
>
> **Proverbs 31: 10-31**

Let her own works praise her in the gates. So lovely.

Look carefully at what our virtuous woman's husband is doing. He praises her, basks in how her hard work improves his reputation and he sits with the elders.

Now, the typical feminist response to this is wahhhhhh... look at how hard that poor woman works...wahhhhh... her husband just sits on his ass doing nothing.... wahhhhh... she's so abused and exploited....

Which ignore two realities completely: first of all, this woman and her family are clearly very affluent. Not everyone is. That's life. The only thing that matters is that any family that works hard has a CHANCE to be affluent. She may consider a field and decide to plant an olive grove, but you can be damn sure she ain't out in the fields doing the work herself.

Who does the backbreaking labor in peasant society, or any society for that matter?

Yeah, that would be men. Generally poor men, struggling to get a foot on the ladder and pull their whole family up.

Secondly, the affluent men are not sitting on their asses doing nothing: they are creating the political and social structures that make it possible for their economies to work. They set the terms of economic exchange, they mediate disputes, they enact laws and enforce them.

In other words, they formalize power and authority and create the political context that governs how the whole society works. And when ONLY the formal structures of power are examined, they appear to be completely and utterly dominant.

But they're not. So Virtuous spends the day managing her male workforce out toiling in the olive grove, she gets the new linen ready for market, she makes sure her maidens and children are taken care of, she packs up a basket for the local poor folks, she does all the work her day requires.

Then Mr. Virtuous comes home, cracks her in the face for backtalk, takes her money, decides he doesn't like what the kids are up to, complains about her new tapestry and then demands dinner?

My fucking ass he does.

But that's what the myth of patriarchy wants us to believe, isn't it? That men are exploitive and abusive and violent and controlling and they hold all the reins of power and won't hesitate to use them to harm and confine and limit the lives of women. Their wives, their sisters, their daughters, their mothers.

And in doing so, destroy the whole society.

The only solution to this terrible problem of male abusiveness and exploitation is to take all the public, formal power away from them while still retaining all the control over family resources. That's feminism in a nutshell. Remove men from power, while still maintaining all of women's traditional power.

Abortion laws, reproductive rights (for women only), the rise of single motherhood, divorce, custody and division of property laws are all ways to enshrine women's absolute control over family resources. And all the while, women are exhorted to "lean in", fight for more power and influence and control of formal power structures.

More women in corporate board rooms.

More women in government.

More women in the judiciary.

More women at the top of every formal power structure we have.

Traditional peasant societies could see that women produced and controlled most of the actual, finite resources in society, including the labor of less affluent men. And they could see how that might make men feel a bit vulnerable and defensive. Who wants to be treated like a utility? Like oxen, good for labor and then the soup pot?

So both men and women agreed to allow men to control most of the formal power structures, none of which can exist without the labor of women and poor men. And to make certain that both men and women felt equally valued and appreciated, they created a myth of male dominance, all the while knowing that the true balance of power swayed heavily in favor of women.

Everybody understood that the idea of male dominance was a MYTH. A story designed to engender respect and mutual prosperity. And for thousands of years, it worked perfectly.

In traditional families like my own, that myth is alive and well. Technically, Mr. JB has all the power. The formal power. He earns all the money, and he handles all the bills. He makes all the financial decisions, without input or interference from me. I am completely dependent upon him for survival. And when his Boss calls up and asks if Mr.JB can take on an extra project, the first thing he says is, "I'll have to check with the boss".

That would be me.

Because at the end of the day, if I'm not happy, and I don't feel respected or valued or appreciated, his life is going to be very unpleasant. And it works both ways. Can he take on the extra project? Does he want to? How important is this to him? Will it make him happy? That's how I make my decision.

That's how we make decisions together.

Remember the whole myth of the black male penis thing? I'm going to link to a post at The Good Men Project[36], although I generally don't like that site. It's worth a read because the writer talks about the origins of that particular myth and how it has come to harm black men in particular.

It harms them because the myth is no longer seen as a myth, but as an incontrovertible truth.

And that's what happened with the myth of male dominance. At some point our culture has forgotten that this is a STORY, with a very commendable purpose: it's a story that assures mutual respect and admiration.

---

[36] http://goodmenproject.com/featured-content/the-good-life-average-size-for-a-black-man-penis-size-myths-racism-and-the-patriarchy/

A group of angry women decided that shutting women out of formal power structures was a problem that needed to be fixed.

And you know, fair enough. Okay. Let's get more women into formal power structures, even though they show little inclination or desire to be there.

BUT, in exchange for that access, women will have to give up access to traditional female power structures.

And that isn't happening. Women want both male and female powers. Preferably ALL the power. The right to control men by controlling the most precious resource any culture has: children, and the right to hold the reins of formal, institutionalized power that governs all our lives.

That reduces men, and poor men in particular, to mere social utilities, with little value and correspondingly little respect. And that is just what is happening. Men are belittled in the media and their concerns scoffed.

The rates at which they take their own lives are ignored, or worse, they get blamed for the very real despair of knowing you are nothing but a tool, easily discarded when your usefulness has run its course.

Feminists continually point to the fact that men continue to dominate formal power structures as evidence for patriarchy. Their suggested redress is to wrest formal power from men and give it to women, while still holding on to their own traditional advantages and informal powers.

We have a word to describe the society that will eventually evolve if such an effort is successful. It's not patriarchy.

It's matriarchy.

It's quite an impressive inversion, isn't it? When feminists use the word "patriarchy" what they are opposing is respect and the equal attribution of power and control between the sexes. When feminists identify the "patriarchy" as a problem, they are in effect saying that valuing the contributions of men and women equally, and in a way that is designed to make both men and women feel as if they are being treated fairly is a problem.

The reality is that power skews to women. That's easy to ignore or even outright deny, because that power is informal. The balance is restored when formal power rests in the hands of men. And despite 70 years of shrieking and protesting and gnashing of teeth, formal power DOES reside mostly in the hands of men.

Patriarchy has never existed in the form that feminism insists. And it has never been the problem.

On the contrary. It's the solution.

Let's bring back patriarchy. And let our own works praise us in the gates.

Lots of love,

JB

The real face of domestic terrorism? Radical white feminists. It's not about equality and they're not afraid to say it.

Well ain't this just a little peach of an article? Here is Louise Pennington, writing for the HuffPo UK version[37].

You're gonna need some brain bleach after this one.

I have always been a feminist. It is a label I chose for myself as a teenager, back before girl power was invented and when New Kids on the Block were cool.

Louise, Louise, Louise. You give new meaning to the phrase "start as you mean to go on". Honeypie, you CANNOT have "always been a feminist" if it is a label you chose as a teenager, unless your mother had the longest pregnancy in the history of the universe and gestated you for 13 years.

At some point in your sad little existence, you were a human. Just like the rest of us. You probably understood that humans are all different from one another, some with talents and abilities that others do not share and that despite these differences, we were all equal.

My original feminism was about equality: women were equal to men and all we needed was the laws to force misogynists to stop being misogynists.

There. You see? Equality.

Here's where you go off the rails, lovey. Women are equal as human beings. We are not equal to men. And until your wrap your little mind around that, you will never understand how to "solve" the problem of inequality.

An apple is equal to an apple. It is not equal to an orange, although they are both fruits. An Austin mini Cooper is equal to an Austin Mini Cooper. It is not equal to a Peterbilt, although they are both vehicles and both can be used to transport apples and oranges from one place to another.

See how that works? You are confusing equity with equality. Equity has to do with fairness, and equality is more about measurement. Equality is removing gendered sports from the Olympics. You wanna run? Run bitch. You won't win a single race.

Equity is about making sure that men and women have equal opportunities to run against competitors of equal skill.

That's why there are ladies out there with gold medals. If the competition was thrown wide open, there would be no women athletes at all.

On average, men are stronger than women. They're faster, smarter, and more willing to take risks. Deal with it. Screaming that it isn't true because it violates your sense of equality only means you need to take another look at your world and pick a different word.

Also, the earth is not flat and there be no dragons.

The older I get, the more I believe that 'equality' is nothing more than a smokescreen to prevent the true liberation of women. Equality before the law means nothing when violence is endemic; when women are most likely to live in poverty; when no one bothers to actually enforce the existing equality legislation. I grew up in an area of Canada where misogyny, race and class should have been impossible to miss but I did. We grew up with serious cases of cognitive dissonance; where hyper-masculinity was the norm and feminism

[37] http://www.huffingtonpost.co.uk/louise-pennington/radical-feminism_b_3169754.html

didn't exist. It was a great place to learn that as a middle class white woman my chances of being a victim of sexual violence were a lot lower than Aboriginal women but that was seen as normal, not something to be upset about. I may have labelled myself a feminist but I wasn't a real feminist.

Let's take these points one by one, shall we?

Violence is endemic. Really? Did you mean violence against women? Or just violence in general?

You are, of course, aware that men are far more likely to be the victims of violent assault?

In 2010, males (9.5 victimizations per 1,000 males) experienced violence by strangers at nearly twice the rate of females (4.7 per 1,000)[38].

They are also much more likely to be murdered and when the murderer is a SHE, she is more likely to pick a male victim than a female one.

Males are most often the victims and the perpetrators in homicides: males were more than nine times more likely than women to commit murder, and male and female offenders are more likely to target male than female victims.

And god help young black men. They are the most likely to be victimized of all. In 2005, 49% of all the people murdered in the US were black men. Almost half.

But you know what? This violence that you seem to think is endemic is actually not. Violent assaults and murders and crime overall has been declining for decades. The scary world you think you live in? It doesn't exist anywhere but in your mind.

Violent crime has declined to rates not seen for forty years[39].

Did I mention that the earth is not flat?

Let's look at poverty rates now. Women are NOT more likely to live in poverty. The poverty rates for men and women are fairly equally distributed.

You are likely basing that statement on research like this:

In 2010, the gender distribution of people in poverty was

45% of people in poverty were male; males accounted for 49% of the total population

55% of the people in poverty were female; females accounted for 51% of the total population

The poverty rate by gender were

14.0% for males

16.2% for females

According to 2010 US Census, the population hit 308,745,538.

[38] http://bjs.gov/content/pub/press/vvcs9310pr.cfm

[39] http://www.wanttoknow.info/g/violent_crime_rates_reduction

49% of those people are male: 151,285,314

51% of those people are female: 157, 460, 224

So 25,508,556 women and 21,179,943 men live in poverty.

Those numbers leave out a few important variables:

Women live longer than men

The prisoner population is not included in the count of men who live in poverty

The homeless population is not included in the count of men who live in poverty

Let's account for those variables. The male prisoner population in 2010 was 1,499,573. That brings our count of men living in poverty to 22,679,516[40].

The estimated homeless population in 2012 is 633,782, 62% of whom are men. Add another 392,944 to the count for men, bringing us up to 23,072,460[41].

Life expectancy for men is 76 years and for women it's 81 years. So when Think Progress reports that women over 75 are three times more likely to be living in poverty as men it's because THE MEN ARE DEAD ALREADY.

The gross number of men and women living in poverty is more or less equal (23 million vs 25.5 million), but that doesn't take into account the fact that women live, on average, five years longer than men. While there are more numbers of women living in poverty (because there are more women than men), the RISK of ending up in poverty is actually higher for males.

Although poverty increased for all race-gender groups (except for nonwhite males in their 60s and nonwhite females in their 20s, 50s, and 60s), the largest increases occurred for white males as a whole and for nonwhite males in their 30s, 40s and 50s.

So this scary world full of poor ladies eating cat food out of a tin? That world doesn't exist either.

No one bothers to enforce existing equality legislation? You mean legislation like forcing corporate boards to hire women?

Or legislation eradicating gender from language?

Or legislation creating human rights and equality tribunals and offices?

We spend a shit ton of taxpayer money enforcing these kind of stupid laws in the name of equality. Mostly because someone, at some point, thought a mouthy broad like you had something important to say.

Don't worry. That oversight will be corrected. Just give us time.

I was a feminist who lacked any kind of analysis of women as a class. I didn't understand that feminism was a political theory. I knew I couldn't have gotten through university as a teenage single mother without

[40] http://bjs.gov/content/pub/pdf/p10.pdf

[41] http://homeless.samhsa.gov/ResourceFiles/hrc_factsheet.pdf

the benefit of a, still flawed, welfare system but I didn't realise just how privileged I was; even with a student loan debt that would make British students cry! It wasn't until the Canadian federal and provincial governments started slashing these programs that I started thinking about feminism as a political theory. I started self-defining as a socialist-feminist, but I still didn't think about women in terms of an oppressed class. Instead, I focused on the idea of class, in Marxist terms, as a barrier for 'some' women. I assumed that equal access to education and equality before the law would solve all women's problems.

Oh no! Did you lose all your special privileges? Well now. That sucks, doesn't it? It took the loss of your heavily subsidized education to get you to think about women as an oppressed class because student loan programs don't affect men, right? The welfare system doesn't have an impact on men, right? Those entitlements belong only to women, and the loss of them constitutes oppression?

I was wrong.

You got that right.

Feminism requires more than equality. It requires liberation. It requires the liberation of ALL women from male violence.

What "male violence?" What the fuck are you talking about?

Look at this article, just for illustration. Read the comments.

Have You Ever Beat Up A Boyfriend Because Uh We Have[42]

Seriously. ALL OF THESE WOMEN are "liberated from male violence" because the men they decided to beat up let them walk away. I'm guessing that pretty much every man Louise has ever met wanted to punch her in the big fat mouth, but they didn't. You're already liberated, sweetheart.

Until two years ago, I would have still identified as a socialist-feminist, although my awareness of the structural oppression of women was growing. The unrelenting misogyny and rape apologism on the left made me reconsider my political stance as did the creation of the Feminist/Women's Rights board on Mumsnet. The more I read on Mumsnet, the more radical my feminism became. I started reading Andrea Dworkin, Natasha Walters, Kate Millett, Susan Faludi, Susan Maushart, Ariel Levy, Gail Dines, Germaine Greer, and Audre Lorde. I learned about cultural femicide and I started reading only fiction books written by women: Isabel Allende, Alice Walker, Maya Angelou, Kate Mosse, Margaret Atwood, Kris Radish, Barbara Kingsolver, and Andrea Levy amongst many others. I started reading about women's lives and the power of real sisterhood.

Really? You're really going to say that? I refuse to read any book written by a man BECAUSE it was written by a man.

I refuse to read any book written by a Jew. Ew. Jews.

I refuse to read any book written by a black person. Ew. Black people.

I refuse to read any book written by a gay person. Ew. Gay people.

I refuse to read any book written by a fat person. Ew. Fat people.

[42] http://jezebel.com/294383/have-you-ever-beat-up-a-boyfriend-cause-uh-we-have

I refuse to read any book written by a .... man?

My feminism, both the definition and activism, has changed dramatically over the past 18 years. Now, I self-define as an anti-capitalist, pro-radical feminist as I believe that the source of women's oppression is male violence which is perpetuated by the structures of our capitalist economy. The Patriarchy may predate capitalism but we cannot destroy it without destroying capitalism too. I don't always feel a 'real feminist' or a 'good enough' feminist. All I know is that I am a feminist who truly believes that women have the power to liberate all women from male violence; that feminism is fundamentally about the power of sisterhood.

Oh good. You don't want to destroy our culture, but our economy, too. Excellent plan. Hope you know how to make a good fire and set a snare because without capitalism, you will be back living in the dark ages before you know it.

Communism: 150 million people dead

Socialism: 62 million people dead

Fascism: 70 million people dead

My feminist activism involves privileging women's voices over men's voices. I now only read books written by women. I try to get my main news from women's news sites and women journalists like Soraya Chemaly, Samira Ahmed, Bidisha, Helen Lewis, Bim Adewunmi, and Sarah Smith. I follow only women journalists on Twitter and Facebook. I support organisations which are placing women's experiences at the centre of public debate: Women Under Siege, The Everyday Sexism Project, and The Women's Room UK.

And there you have it. Not women equal to men. Women OVER men.

Could it be any more clear?

My feminism acknowledges the realities of intersectionality and, whilst I'm not perfect, I am more aware now of how disparate women's experiences are from one another. I still believe that women, as a political class, have the ability to liberate ourselves from the Capitalist-Patriarchy but I do so with the knowledge that I do not yet fully understand the full impact of the multiple oppressions in women's lives. My feminism is a journey. The destination is the full liberation of women but we are all on different paths and at different points. My feminism requires I listen to my sisters and support them in the ways they deem best. My feminism is women-centered.

Women at the center. Men at the margins.

Feminists have the power to change the world. It requires listening and respect but we have the power to save each other; after all the largest study on global violence against women has conclusively proved that feminists hold the key to positive change for women.

Feminism doesn't care what happens to men and boys. They are not interested in humanity. They are not interested in fairness. They are not interested in justice. They are not interested in peace. They are not interested in equality.

They want women at the center, women's voices and experiences privileged over all others and women saving each other.

We shall continue the jihad journey no matter how long the way, until the last breath and the last beat of the pulse - or until we see the Islamic Feminist state established.

Who said it? Abdullah Yusuf Azzam, mentor to Osama Bin Laden?

Or Louise Pennington?

Doesn't matter.

They're both terrorists.

And they aren't going to win.

Lots of love,

JB

Gang of female rapists abuse male prisoners and they are not even being charged! Oh, okay. That seems fair.

According to the Baltimore division of the FBI, 13 corrections officers are among the 25 people indicted on charges of racketeering and conspiring to possess and distribute illegal drugs. Apparently, some gang members had a nice little scam running inside the jail, aided and abetted by 13 female corrections officers. Four of those women became pregnant by the gang-leader and two of them had his name tattooed on some part of their body!

FBI release[43]

Gosh, there's so much to talk about here! Why are women working with male prisoner populations? Whose brilliant idea was that? Is this kind of stuff common? What was the motivation for the women to get involved with gang related activities inside the jail? How and when do you manage to have sex with a prisoner? How do the logistics of that work? And isn't sex with a prisoner technically rape? How can prisoners consent to sex?

Maryland is one of the leaders of the pack when it comes to defining sexual assault. In 2008, the state updated it's statues to include a provision for "withdrawal of consent", and naturally, it can only be used against men. Withdrawal of consent is when a woman consents to sex, and then at some point during penetration, decides she has changed her mind. If her partner does not immediately cease all activity and withdraw, he is guilty of rape.

Giving new meaning to the withdrawal method.

Wow. Sex in Maryland sounds like so much fun, doesn't it? The courts are basically policing sex down to each and every thrust. Guys, you need to stop after every stroke and check to see if consent is still in effect. Well, I guess that's one way to deal with lovers who rush the act.

Looking over the Maryland sexual assault laws, I came across this one:

2010 Maryland Code[44]

---

[43] http://www.fbi.gov/baltimore/press-releases/2013/thirteen-correctional-officers-among-25-black-guerilla-family-gang-members-and-associates-indicted-on-federal-racketeering-charges

[44] http://www.wcl.american.edu/modernamerican/documents/Huff.pdf

CRIMINAL LAW

TITLE 3 - OTHER CRIMES AGAINST THE PERSON

Subtitle 3 - Sexual Crimes

Section 3-314 - Sexual conduct between correctional or Department of Juvenile Services employee and inmate or confined child.

(a) Definitions.-

(1) In this section the following words have the meanings indicated.

(2) (i) "Correctional employee" means a:

1. correctional officer, as defined in § 8-201 of the Correctional Services Article; or

2. managing official or deputy managing official of a correctional facility.

(ii) "Correctional employee" includes a sheriff, warden, or other official who is appointed or employed to supervise a correctional facility.

(3) (i) "Inmate" has the meaning stated in § 1-101 of this article.

(ii) "Inmate" includes an individual confined in a community adult rehabilitation center.

(b) Prohibited - Correctional employee with inmate.-

(1) This subsection applies to:

(i) a correctional employee;

(ii) any other employee of the Department of Public Safety and Correctional Services or a correctional facility;

(iii) an employee of a contractor providing goods or services to the Department of Public Safety and Correctional Services or a correctional facility; and

(iv) any other individual working in a correctional facility, whether on a paid or volunteer basis.

(2) A person described in paragraph (1) of this subsection may not engage in sexual contact, vaginal intercourse, or a sexual act with an inmate.

Hmm. Well, that seems pretty clear. No fucking prisoners.

What is the punishment for violating the rules?

In New York state, corrections officers who have sex with inmates are charged with rape and professional misconduct. This lady corrections officer was arrested and charged when she was six months pregnant by an inmate. They would get busy while she was on shift, right in the cell block, apparently! Talk about cell block tango!

Yeah, just for one second, let's talk about the Cell Block Tango. If you're not familiar with the musical Chicago, here's the chorus:

> *He had it coming*
> *He had it coming*
> *He only had himself to blame*
> *If you'd have been there*
> *If you'd have seen it*
> *I betcha you would have done the same!*

Six lady murderers, all defending their actions. One guy snapped his gum in an irritating manner, so Liz killed him. Another guy accused his lovely wife of having an affair with the milkman, so she stabbed him. Six times. And on and on and on it goes.

It's a snappy little number. It's relevant to this discussion because it plays on the way we understand women and crime – even very serious crime like murder. Can you imagine six men dancing and singing and about how those bitches they murdered had it coming and only had themselves to blame? Would it seem charming and edgy all at the same time?

Not likely. They would come off as straight up psychopaths, and rightly so. But women are .... special? Even when they are unrepentant, remorseless murderers. Or rapists.

The law in Maryland is clear. The correctional officers who had sex with an inmate are rapists. They are guilty of rape. It does not matter, in a legal sense, whether that sex was consensual. Inmates cannot give consent, full stop.

And it's entirely possible that the sex was NOT consensual. The lady guards demanded sex, and the inmates complied because they had no realistic choice. It happens. Especially in juvenile facilities, it happens.

It's possible, but in this case, not particularly plausible. Technically, the ladies are rapists. But more likely, they are simply women who responded in a rather predictable way to the powerful swagger of an Alpha thug. The old "bad boys" story.

The appeal of the dominant male is what set in motion the entire shitstorm at the Maryland jail, and if we're going to continue to mix female guards with highly dangerous, dominant male prisoners, we'll see more of the same results.

Even so, even IF the sex was completely consensual, even IF the relationship between the guards and the gang members was predictable, even IF the guards and the gang members decide to get married and live happily ever after, the cold hard facts of the law state that the prisoners were raped.

So why aren't these women being charged with rape?

It's amusing in kind of a sickening way to watch the media try to give the ladies a pass[45]. Oh, gosh, they suffered from "low self-esteem". The prisoners "took advantage" of the poor dears.

---

[45] http://www.independent.co.uk/news/world/americas/baltimore-criminal-gang-took-advantage-of-female--prison-warders-8586749.html

Low self-esteem? They're having sex with prisoners! No shit they don't value themselves very highly. The prisoners took advantage of the guards? Are you shitting me?!? Who had the keys? Who was locked in a cage? Who had the upper hand?

Of course, when we try to talk about a couple of football players who fingered a drunk girl as suffering from self-esteem issues, the entire culture is an screaming uproar! Whatever "issues" the boys have or had, it doesn't matter! Lock them up! Throw away the keys!

This whole story is a perfect example of one of the most profound injustices boys and men face in Western society: they are held to much harsher, much sterner standards of the law than women are, for no reason other than the fact that they are men.

Justice is supposed to be blind. Rape is rape. Murder is murder. It shouldn't matter whether a man or a woman committed the crime.

Female corrections officers raped male inmates, under the law. They should be held accountable for those actions. Just as men are.

Equal or Special

Pick one

Lots of love,

JB

Feminists agree, at least in theory, that women MUST face the consequences of deciding to have sex.

First up, apologies to real, actual whores, who are experts in preventing pregnancies and STDs. If, after reading this post, you lads decide to never get within ten feet of a reproductively capable woman, always keep in mind that professional ladies are there, and they are fair! They know what they are doing, in every way that counts. Pleasure? Check. Pregnancy? Er, nope. STDs? Not likely. You'll need to hit up a group of middle aged swingers if you want one of those.

College girls will also deliver for you on the oozing dick front.

Do NOT be afraid to trust your average escort, gentlemen. Know why? Because they're PROFESSIONALS, that's why. Screw this Alpha - Beta shit. Be a John. Paying a fine beats 18 years of child support, no? I'm being a bit facetious, I know. The consequences can be much more severe, but it's worth checking just what they are in your particular jurisdiction and weigh those against the consequences of an unintended pregnancy with your local herd of ladies.

Let's start with a definition:

fem·i·nism

/ˈfeməˌnizəm/

Noun

The advocacy of women's rights on the grounds of political, social, and economic equality to men.

We'll keep that definition in mind as we go along.

In the New York Times this past week, Professor Laurie Schrage wants to know if forced fatherhood is a philosophically defensible position[46], given that reproductive autonomy and equality are such touchstone issues for feminism. Is it fair to force men to become fathers of children they do not want and did not intend when culturally, we have agreed, that it is unacceptable to force women into such a position?

If a man accidentally conceives a child with a woman, and does not want to raise the child with her, what are his choices? Surprisingly, he has few options in the United States. He can urge her to seek an abortion, but ultimately that decision is hers to make. Should she decide to continue the pregnancy and raise the child, and should she or our government attempt to establish him as the legal father, he can be stuck with years of child support payments.

The responses at the NYT to Schrage's question fall into three main camps:

1. We don't have complete and utter reproductive freedom for women, so none of this applies! Ladies are still not allowed to waltz into clinics and abort the day before they're due, so none of this applies anyways, lalalalalalala I can't hear you.

> StephWAtlanta
>
> *Don't think this issue can adequately be approached until all women have the right to end their pregnancy in a safe manner at a respectable facility. Until then discussing men's rights confuses the issue.*

2. If you don't want babies, don't have sex, you man-whores!

> CillasiNYC
>
> *Men have the ultimate control over pregnancy and fatherhood. They've always had it. Keep your sperm out of women's vaginas. Period. End of story. Historically, men have always been able to walk away from parental responsibility. Now they can't. Tough noogies. It's not forced anything. They just have to choose to be responsible a little earlier.*

3. If you consent to sex, you consent to all the possible outcomes of sex.

> CherylLake County, IL
>
> *"In consenting to sex, neither a man nor a woman gives consent to become a parent, just as in consenting to any activity, one does not consent to yield to all the accidental outcomes that might flow from that activity."*

I beg to disagree. That is EXACTLY what consenting to sex means.

You don't get on an airplane expecting it to crash, but you are giving implied consent to that possibility by stepping on the plane. It implies you are willing to accept the risk of undertaking that action. If you can't accept that risk, or the consequences are too great, you don't fly.

---

[46] http://opinionator.blogs.nytimes.com/2013/06/12/is-forced-fatherhood-fair/

When you have sex, you know that a pregnancy is a possible outcome, even with birth control. If you don't want to take that risk, you don't have sex! If you ignore that possibility, have sex and it results in a pregnancy, that's the chance you took.

Pretty much the exact arguments come up at Jezebel[47]:

> DuchessOfDorkUMeher Ahmad671L
>
> *IF YOU PUT YOUR PENIS IN A LADY THERE IS A CHANCE YOU MIGHT MAKE A BABY. THERE IS ALWAYS A CHANCE UNLESS YOU GET A VASECTOMY. IF YOU DON'T WANT TO TAKE THAT CHANCE, DON'T PUT YOUR PENIS IN A LADY.*
>
> *Thank you*

Let's take all this at face value. Okay, we agree 100%. If you have sex, you are required to face the consequences, no matter what your personal preferences.

Let's start with reproductive freedom. Women don't have unlimited, completely untrammeled rights to destroy the child within their body at whim. There are some very good reasons for that, but leaving all that aside, let's take a look at what opportunities men have to control the reproductive tissues of their own bodies.

In other words, male birth control. Men have basically two choices:

Condoms

Vasectomy

"With proper knowledge and application technique—and use at every act of intercourse—women whose partners use male condoms experience a 2% per-year pregnancy rate with perfect use and a 15% per-year pregnancy rate with typical use." (Wikipedia)

Look at that statement carefully. Even when we discuss men's birth control, men's bodies, men protecting themselves against the consequences of pregnancy, the whole argument is framed in terms of women. WTF? How fucking hard is it to write MEN using condoms have female partners who experience a 2% per-year pregnancy rate with perfect use and a 15% per-year pregnancy rate with typical use.

Vasectomy, which is a surgical procedure involving a scalpel applied to men's bodies (which birth control method for women involves a scalpel, again?), and which is only reversible at significant expense, still has a failure rate of 1 in 100!

So if a man doesn't care to have children with YOU, he should get sterilized and never have any children ever? Oh, right. That seems fair. How about we cut women's fallopian tubes? Perfectly reasonable measure, no?

The reality is that no matter how careful, no matter how responsible, no matter how diligent and conscientious a man is about birth control, failure is possible. If we are waiting for conditions to be absolutely perfect before we discuss a particular topic, we will wait forever.

---

[47] http://jezebel.com/forced-fatherhood-yeah-okay-whatever-513168822

And isn't that the point of argument one? I refuse to deal with this issue. No way. Not talking. I can't tackle the actual argument, so I'm just going to pretend you aren't here.

Preposterous. Fraught conversations still need to take place. Welcome to being a grown-up.

Argument number two is actually completely hilarious, and it stuns me that anyone, but feminists in particular, would give it a spin.

If you don't want a child, don't have sex?

Okie-dokie, whores. Turnabout is fair play. If men are REQUIRED by law to face the music, then so are you. And the argument that women's bodies are sacrosanct and pregnancy is asymmetrical is nothing more than sophistry. Turning over a significant portion of your income to a woman who may or may not use that income to provide for a child you did not intend and do not want has a dramatic impact on the well-being of the man required to make remittance, particularly when that man is already poor!

Indeed, Scrage quotes another Professor, Elizabeth Brake, who has precisely that point to make, and she chimed in at the NYT with the following comment:

> *Elizabeth BrakeTempe, AZNYT Pick*
>
> *My article, which Prof. Shrage cites, doesn't argue against legal child support but against one reason often given for it. The political point is that "a just law of child support ... must be responsive to the economic situation of individual fathers."*

Women who are pregnant unintentionally have a few choices to mitigate against the consequences of bearing a child: abortion, adoption, legal surrender. Women are permitted to end the potential child's life, and from 1973 to 2008, more than 50 million potential children were destroyed in the United States.

Unsurprisingly, the rate of adoption declined dramatically once abortion became a viable option. Nevertheless, in 2000, the US Census found that more than 2 million children were identified as "adopted".

Safe haven laws[48], which allow WOMEN to legally surrender all parental rights with no obligations and no subsequent responsibilities are in effect in all 50 states.

If we are going to have EQUAL reproductive rights for men and women, then all these options are EITHER available to BOTH men and women, or to NEITHER. How would that work, in practical application?

Men can't physically be pregnant. Are we going to allow men to force women to abort children on the basis of genetic relationship? That seems like a pretty scary proposition, although from a philosophical point of view, why not? If you are going to be held legally responsible for any humans containing your DNA, why should you not be able to force an abortion? It's your DNA. You own it. The Supreme Court recently ruled that human DNA cannot be patented. It belongs to the individual person, and if you do NOT consent to that DNA being deployed in the creation of another human, you should have the right to have the person terminated, within the limitations of the law, no?

Unfortunately, the potential human on the butcher's block is a combination of DNA, and there is an unavoidable King Solomon's dilemma. In the name of equality, neither the mother nor the father can unilaterally decide if the child lives or dies. That takes abortion as an option off the table, unless both DNA contributors consent.

---
[48] https://www.childwelfare.gov/systemwide/laws_policies/statutes/safehaven.pdf

So men cannot force women to abort, but neither can women abort a child the father wishes to keep. Fair is fair. If he can't force you to bear his biological offspring when you do not wish to, then you cannot destroy offspring for whom he is prepared to accept full responsibility.

Oh dear. That kind of equality sucks, now doesn't it. But remember ladies, if you don't want to have a baby, don't have sex, you sluts!

The same must be true for adoption: you cannot surrender a child for adoption without the father's consent. That is already technically true, but there is a way around that for women: don't identify the father.

In some cases, the women genuinely does NOT know the identity of the father. This is particularly true in cases of rape. But there is little point in making an exception for rape, since all that will happen is that women will claim they were raped. Unverifiable. A child cannot be aborted or adopted without the consent of the biological father, no matter what the circumstances of conception. Full stop.

Oh, boo hoo! This reproductive equality thing is looking worse and worse.

Needless to say, safe haven laws must apply equally to both men and women, as well. If a woman cannot identify the father, or does not have the consent of the father to surrender the baby, she is guilty of criminal abandonment and should face the full legal consequences of her actions.

Now here is where the argument gets interesting: safe haven laws are designed to keep women from strangling their newborns and tossing them in the trash.

Supporters of safe-haven laws claim that the laws save lives by encouraging parents to surrender infants safely instead of aborting, killing, or discarding them.

Cute that Wikipedia uses the word "parents", when they really mean "mothers".

Women who have a an actual, physical, living, breathing completely separate human being who DO NOT WANT THE RESPONSIBILITY of caring for that human being are entitled to surrender all legal obligations towards that human and simply walk away.

Accidents happen. Mistakes occur. Unintended consequences turn into little tiny people who are entitled to love and care and attention and life itself. And if women can't, or won't or don't want to meet the needs of this new little person THEY CREATED, they can walk away and never look back. Their biological ties to that person are irrelevant.

Men deserve the same right. Biology is irrelevant. Just as any pregnant woman has the right to terminate her legal responsibility for that child, men should have the right to terminate their own legal responsibility. The practical reality is not even that hard to envision. Any woman who finds herself pregnant needs to know that the father of the child has the right to disavow paternity in a legal context.

Do you accept responsibility for this child?

A woman must make her decision about whether or not to have the child based on the knowledge that her decision is hers, and ONLY hers. She does not have the right to unilaterally impose her will on any other adult, no matter what the biological relationship. The fact that she is pregnant does not make her special, and should not give her any special rights to inflict potentially ruinous consequences on a man who made the mistake of having sex with her. Not unless she'd care to face the same consequences.

Being a parent should be a choice. It's either compulsory for both, or elective for both.

Equal or special. Pick one.

Lots of love,

JB

Married to a feminist? Congratulations. By the way, your baby is really sad and your wife will never be happy.

Here is W. Bradford Wilcox, writing on the three biggest myths about marriage for The Atlantic[49].

What are the three biggest myths? Glad you asked.

Unequal
Unfair
Unhappy

Well now. We've left out a tiny little detail, haven't we W. Bradford?

Unequal for whom?

Unfair to whom?

Unhappy for whom?

Let's take a gander at W. Bradford's "analysis", shall we?

There is only one problem with the dour and dismal portrait of heterosexual marriage painted by Liza Mundy in this month's Atlantic cover story. It's wrong.

In her bleak rendering, contemporary marriage comes across as unequal, unfair, and unhappy to today's wives.

Oh, there we go! It's the ladies, pissing and moaning, yet again. You're shocked, right?

Wives are burdened with an unequal and unfair "second shift" of housework and childcare, husbands enjoy "free time" while their wives toil away at home, lingering gender inequalities in family life leave many wives banging "their heads on their desks in despair," and one poor woman cannot even have a second child because she does "everything" and her husband does nothing. Mundy also suggests that recent declines in women's happiness can be laid at the feet of "lingering inequity in male-female marriage."

Oh god, men just SUCK, don't they. Lazy fuckers, playing video games while their poor women slave themselves to the bone, doing housework and taking care of the children in between slamming their heads against their desks in despair and curtailing their fertility.

Let's take a look at the evidence.

---

[49] http://www.theatlantic.com/sexes/archive/2013/06/unequal-unfair-and-unhappy-the-3-biggest-myths-about-marriage-today/276468/

When you combine paid work with housework and childcare, it looks like it's MEN who are actually doing more work.

It's true that married mothers do more of the housework and childcare, but in most households this doesn't amount to an onerous burden for them. That's because most married mothers do not work full-time (43 percent work full-time) and do not wish to work full-time (just 23 percent wish to work full-time, a fact rarely mentioned in media accounts of work and family life).

Oh, there are some media outlets that will tackle the icky little truth that women don't really want to work. Just today, the Daily Mail wrote about the looming crisis in the UK's national healthcare system because all the lady doctors trained at great expense by the state and taxpayers simply do not wish to work[50].

I wonder how many hours the male applicants to medical school who were rejected in favor of female candidates were prepared to work? According to the American Medical News,

In 2011, 22% of male physicians and 44% of female physicians worked less than full time

And who are these men working less than fulltime?

Two of the fastest-growing physician demographics -- men near the end of their careers and women at the beginning or middle -- are the most likely to demand part-time or flexible work schedules, according to experts in physician recruitment.

Men at the end of their careers. Rather than simply quit, they work fewer hours as they slow down. A well-earned reward.

Okay, so we have established that in terms of work, marriages are indeed unequal. Men work more.

What about fairness?

The rough parity in total family work hours enjoyed by most couples, combined with the fact that most married mothers don't wish to work full-time, may explain why most husbands and wives judge their marriages to be fair. In fact, 73 percent of married fathers and 68 percent of married mothers reported that their marriage was fair, according to the 2010-2011 Survey of Marital Generosity.

That research[51] was conducted by some guy named Bradford Wilcox. Hmm. The name rings a bell.

Looks like women are more likely to consider their marriages unfair. Which women?

Mothers who work full-time.

The most notable exception to the positive marriage portrait I have painted here can be found among married couples with children where both spouses work full-time—the one group that featured prominently in the statistics cited by Mundy. In these marriages, there really is a "second shift" for many married mothers; wives in these marriages do about five hours more of total work per week and enjoy six hours less free time per week than their husbands, according to research by sociologist Suzanne Bianchi. Such marriages may indeed be more vulnerable to the kinds of tensions and unhappiness Mundy dwelled upon.

[50] http://www.dailymail.co.uk/news/article-2336235/Female-doctors-NHS-tremendous-burden-married-children-want-work-time.html

[51] http://generosityresearch.nd.edu/current-research-projects/foundation-of-marital-generosity/

Well, okay. How many hours does the husband work?

In the UK, the Office of National Statistics found that in families where both parents work full time, it is fathers who work more hours and get less sleep.

The new ONS survey shows that life is also extremely tough for fathers with young families, particularly those whose youngest children is under the age of four.

They sleep less, works more and do more "domestic" work than any other "type" of man, such as one with older children or one with no children.

A typical father whose youngest child is under four gets less than eight hours sleep a night and does more than three hours of domestic chores every day.

They are also working more than one hour a day longer than their male colleagues who do not have children.

We can take a guess at which men reported their marriages to be unfair – the ones married to a woman working full-time, but still likely fewer hours than her husband.

Now let's tackle happiness.

More men than women are happy with their marriages, despite working longer hours, on average, than their wives. Again, I would guess that the men and women who were the unhappiest were the ones trying to manage a family while both holding down full time jobs. The Pew Research Council[52] agrees:

Among mothers with children under age 18, married moms are happier overall than unmarried moms. Fully 43% of married mothers say they are very happy with their life these days; only 23% of unmarried mothers say the same. There is also a significant gap in happiness between working and non-working mothers: 45% of non-working mothers say they are very happy, compared with 31% of mothers who work either full or part time. When other factors (race, ethnicity, income and education) are taken into account, marriage is a significant predictor of a mother's happiness while employment status is not.

Unequal? Yep. Men work more hours than women.

Unfair? Only when the wife works full time.

Unhappy? Only when the wife works full time.

So what's the moral of this little story? Women are encouraged to believe that working full time will bring meaning and happiness and fulfillment. Lean In, says Sheryl Sandberg. And when they do, women are unhappy and feel they are being treated unfairly by their husbands.

What's the answer to that?

Divorce won't change how unhappy women are at all. Know why? Because it's not marriage that makes women unhappy.

It's working full time.

---

[52] http://www.pewsocialtrends.org/2013/03/14/modern-parenthood-roles-of-moms-and-dads-converge-as-they-balance-work-and-family/

Men aren't the cause of women's unhappiness. Women are, especially the ones trumpeting the lies about how full time employment is the only meaningful contribution a woman can make to the world. Mothers who work full time jobs spend just 19 minutes a day with their children.

That's a tragedy, for all of us.

It's time to start telling women the truth. Stop blaming men for your unhappiness. Take the blinders from your eyes and throw the chains away. Stop listening to the lies other women tell. Don't quit your marriage. Quit your job.

Equality is valuing husbands and wives for their differences. Fairness is understanding that when one person does the paid labor, the other person does the unpaid. Happiness is caring for your husband, being there for your children and loving them all.

Those are no myths.

Lots of love,

JB

Legal Parental Surrender is NOT morally equivalent to an abortion and no amount of bitchy sarcasm will make it so, Amanda Marcotte.

It was heartening to see the New York Times jump into the reproductive rights fray recently with their editorial questioning whether men actually have any. Answer: Nope. Not really.

If a man accidentally conceives a child with a woman, and does not want to raise the child with her, what are his choices? Surprisingly, he has few options in the United States. He can urge her to seek an abortion, but ultimately that decision is hers to make. Should she decide to continue the pregnancy and raise the child, and should she or our government attempt to establish him as the legal father, he can be stuck with years of child support payments.

Predictably, feminist website Jezebel responds with compassion and intelligence to a fairly complex conundrum that seems to be inherently biased against men[53].

Boo fucking hoo. At the end of the day, the only thing the government, and society, requires fathers to do is pay money, which is a hell of a lot easier than raising a child alone, as most mothers who have children out of wedlock are forced to do.

Mary Elizabeth Williams at Salon[54] is equally concerned when men's freedom to choose to be a parent is curtailed:

I have to laugh at her question, "Do men now have less reproductive autonomy than women?"

But I really think it's Amanda Marcotte[55] who takes the cake, agreeing that forced fatherhood is indeed unfair, and then summoning her bitchiest bitch tone to claim that for one thing, there are only about three

---

[53] http://jezebel.com/forced-fatherhood-yeah-okay-whatever-513168822

[54] http://www.salon.com/2013/06/13/there_is_no_forced_fatherhood_crisis/

men who have been forced into fatherhood, and men who don't want to become parents are "dead-beat dad" wannabes and refusing to turn your resources over to a woman you explicitly do not wish to parent with is the moral equivalent of killing your child.

It's a hat-trick of idiocy!

For fuck's sake, I can't believe the NY Times gave space to the tedious argument that because women have been graciously granted their right to reproductive autonomy (actually, it's not even remotely gracious), it's time to deal with the largely imaginary plague of "forced fatherhood", i.e. women getting pregnant and carrying pregnancies to term against the father's wishes, and then suing him for child support. This happens occasionally, though compared to men trying to force women to get pregnant against their wills, it's so rare that it's comparable to shark attacks in its frequency.

There are a number of ways that paternity can be established when it comes to women who have chosen to have children without the explicit support of the father.

Voluntary acknowledgement – the father acknowledges that he is, in fact, the father

Administrative – child support agencies contact the putative father and the case proceeds from there

Judicial – the courts contact the putative father and the case proceeds from there

Default – the courts accept the word of the woman and simply names the father

The following report[56] goes into the advantages and disadvantages of these different methods, but there is one chart in particular I would like to draw your attention to: 62% of local child support staff perceive there to be a an advantage in using any method OTHER than voluntary acknowledgement of paternity because it ensures that the correct father is identified.

Now why would that be? Why would the majority of child support workers think identifying the correct father through something other than just "she said it's true, so I guess it must be?"

Could it be because the WRONG MEN are identified as fathers rather routinely? It appears that child support workers deal with the "imaginary plague" of women having children outside of an established relationship and seeking child support from men who may or may not be the biological father ALL THE FUCKING TIME.

Imaginary plague, my ass.

Let's move on to Amanda's use of the words "paper abortion".

Focusing on "paper abortions" is a way to soften up an audience to the demands of men who want to foist all the responsibilities of child-rearing onto their exes while still getting to float in periodically to be the big hero who takes the kids to Disneyland once in awhile. If you actually go to "father's rights" forums and websites, you'll find lots of paranoia about sperm-stealing, but the men who are on the forum almost all are divorced and are bitter about writing child support checks while not getting the sexual and house-cleaning benefits of having a wife.

---

[55] http://www.rawstory.com/rs/2013/06/13/fine-would-be-deadbeat-dads-heres-a-suggestion-for-you/

[56] http://oig.hhs.gov/oei/reports/oei-06-98-00050.pdf

Yeah, that's exactly the topic we are discussing. Amanda has mixed up two very distinct group of men: fathers who are very much interested in being fathers who have been ousted from their children's lives, and men who are confronting an unintended pregnancy only to discover they have absolutely no say in how that pregnancy proceeds.

The use of the words "paper abortion" is unfortunate, and I hope it is not a common phrase uttered by those who are interested in reproductive rights for men, because it strongly implies that refusing to be a parent by disavowing social and financial responsibility is morally equivalent to killing the child outright.

It's not.

To equate refuting responsibility with death is disingenuous at the very least. Men are not asking for the right to "abort" a child. The decision to allow a child to live belongs to women, as it must. Men are asking for: LEGAL PARENTAL SURRENDER

A woman who gives birth to a child she does want to accept legal or financial responsibility for has the option to surrender that child to the state and simply walk away. The child will be given to someone who DOES want legal and financial responsibility, and the expense to the state is minimal and of finite duration.

Men should have the exact same right.

Amanda has some caveats she wants to attach to that right. Let's take them one by one.

He has to sign away all rights before the baby is born. He does not get his name on the birth certificate. The child's father will be registered as "unknown". If someone else—say his ex's new husband—wishes to adopt and coparent the child, he cannot interfere.

Agreed. No problem whatsoever.

The only exception to this is if the mother did not alert the father to the pregnancy beforehand. He should be able to provide witnesses to testify that he hadn't seen her in at least six months prior to the birth.

Uhm, no. SHE should have to provide evidence. Prove that she DID see him. Prove that a relationship DID exist. The burden of proof should be on the woman who has decided to give birth a child without knowing how she is going to support that child, and not on the man who may not even be aware of a birth control sabotage/failure.

He never contacts the child. As far as his child knows, he's a ghost. No visits, no toys, no pictures, nothing. He should also not be allowed to contact the mother. If he reaches out to the mother, she has full rights to sue him for child support, using that as evidence that he actually does want a relationship with his ex and his biological child.

How are people who may work together or live in a small community or go to the same school together supposed to avoid contact? This is an unreasonable demand.

This is for life. If you contact the child on her 18th birthday, you owe 18 years of back child support. If you contact the child when she's 30, same thing: All 18 years of child support, with interest.

Bullshit. This is for 18 years, same as in the case of legal parental surrender. At that point the child is an adult and free to pursue his or her biological origins just as any other adoptee. There is no guarantee that the father who has legally surrendered his child wishes to have a relationship, just as there is no guarantee that adopted children will have an adult relationship their biological parents.

If the court determines you were abusive to your ex, all the above is invalidated and you will pay child support with no visitation rights if the judge so determines.

Oh fuck off. Get out of jail free card, much? Allegations of abuse are routinely lobbed at men, with no basis in fact, other than her word. This caveat invalidates every previous assertion. It's straight up manipulative bullshit.

While we're at it, let's say children who don't have child support get a special stipend from the government, much like the Social Security payments they'd get if you were dead.

Let's say not. In the case of legal parental surrender, the state is on the hook for the costs of placing the child with parents who DO want to accept legal and financial responsibility, which then transfers to those parents. You don't get to make the state your husband because you have made a terrible decision.

It's interesting that a writer as virulently feminist as Marcotte would even lend her voice to this topic. That says a lot about how far reproductive rights for all has come. It needs to go a bit further, though.

It comes down to understanding that rights come with responsibilities. Women have, and must have, the sole jurisdiction over deciding whether their bodies can be used to create a new life. The right to terminate a pregnancy belongs to the person who is pregnant. But it comes with a responsibility. If you are going to create that new life, you are responsible for it. Especially if you are creating that life against the will of the father.

If you are married, you are responsible for maintaining that marriage for the long run. That applies equally to men and women. If you create a union and bring children into it, only the direst of circumstances gives you the right to dismantle that union.

If you are unwed, and have no social resources, you are STILL responsible for that child, because you exercised your right to bear him or her. You can meet those obligations by being a single mother (bad choice) or by surrendering your legal and financial responsibility. And that SHOULD apply to equally to men and women. A legally surrendered child should be offered to the biological father FIRST. He should have the right to claim sole responsibility, should he so desire.

I strongly suspect it is not babies that daddies don't want responsibility for. It's the baby-mama they're not interested in. That's just a suspicion, though. According to the PEW research council, the rate of households headed by single fathers is growing rapidly. One quarter of single family homes are headed by daddy. That strongly suggests men are more than willing to step up to the plate to care for their children.

I suspect 2-3 men will take this offer a year if it becomes law. Maybe even a dozen!

You keep telling yourself that, Amanda.

Bring the law in.

Equal rights to legal parental surrender.

Who thinks the birth rates for single mothers will collapse? Who thinks the astonishing number of children born to the rich and famous out of wedlock will collapse?

It's certainly worth taking this hypothetical out of the arsenal of "men's rights" activists.

You won't be taking anything out of the arsenal, honey.

You'll just be giving men the same weapons that women take for granted.

The right to force men into fatherhood is a right that women NEED to lose.

The sooner the better.

Lots of love,

JB

Men's desires, women's desires. Sometimes they aren't all that nice. But only men's desires are wrong. How to be a joyless feminist.

Here's Roxane Gay, writing a lovely piece of hypocrisy and cluelessness at Salon[57]. This kind of self-pitying, blatantly sexist bullshit is getting a bit tiring, but it's still instructive. Men don't have the corner on being assholes, ladies. There are plenty of asshole women, too. Roxane Gay being one of them.

What men want, America delivers

From Robin Thicke's latest songs to abortion restrictions around the country, America's all about men's desires

What women want, America delivers.

From Carrie Underwood's latest songs to reproductive restrictions on men, America's all about women's desires.

In his single "Blurred Lines," Robin Thicke sings soulfully about giving a good girl what she really wants—buckwild sex—even if she can't come out and admit it. It's a catchy enough song. Some might even call it this summer's anthem. But "Blurred Lines" is also a song that revisits the age-old belief that sometimes when a woman says no she really means yes.

In her single "Two Black Cadillacs", Carrie Underwood sings soulfully about giving a cheating boyfriend what he deserves – death – even if he doesn't come right out and ask for it. It's a catchy song. Some might even call it a you-go-girl anthem. But "Two Black Cadillacs" revisits the age-old belief that men's sexuality belongs to women and that cheating men deserve to die.

Critics have been vocal about the sexual violence undertones in the song and they're not wrong. Robin just knows you want it, girl. He just does, so shut up and let him give it to you. Scores of men and women are, apparently, on board. "Blurred Lines" is Thicke's most popular song to date. In his latest single, "Give it 2 U," Thicke doubles down on his bad boy phase with the lyrics "I got this for you / a little Thicke for you / A big kiss for you / I got a hit for you / Big dick for you / Let me give it to you." In the wake of the criticism, Thicke is fairly unapologetic, saying, "Women and their bodies are beautiful. Men are always gonna want to follow them around."

Critics have not been the slightest bit vocal about the sexual violence in "Two Black Cadillacs", and that is pretty fucked up right there. Carrie knows we want to see men die, so just shut up and let her do it. Scores of men and women are apparently on board. "Before He Cheats" is Underwood's most popular song to date. In her latest single, "Two Black Cadillacs", Underwood doubles down on her vengeful girlfriend phase with

[57] http://www.salon.com/2013/07/05/what_men_want_america_delivers/

the lyrics "Two months ago his wife called the number on his phone/Turns out he'd been lying to both of them for oh so long/They decided then he'd never get away with doing this to them/Two black Cadillacs waiting for the right time, right time."

The right time for what? Oh yeah. To kill a man.

I guess that's that. Men want what they want.

I guess that's that. Women want what they want.

In truth, I like these songs. They make me want to dance. I want to sing along. They are delightful pop confections. But. I enjoy the songs the way I have to enjoy most music—I have to forget I am a sentient being. I have to lighten up.

In truth, I like these songs. They make me want to dance. I want to sing along. They are delightful pop confections. But. I enjoy the songs the way I have to enjoy most music—I have to forget I am a sentient being. I have to lighten up.

Take Kanye West's recently released "Yeezus." It's very compelling and ambitious, with sounds that are aggressive if not hostile. I've been listening to the album on repeat. I want to love Yeezus but I can't because I hear lyrics like, "You see it's leaders and it's followers / But I'd rather be a dick than a swallower." Kanye's disdain for women overwhelms nearly every track — but then there's a song like "Blood on the Leaves," which is so outstanding you can't possibly dismiss the album.

Take Pink's recently released "The Truth About Love". It's very compelling and ambitious, with sounds that are aggressive if not hostile. I've been listening to the album on repeat. I want to love "The Truth About Love" but I can't because I hear lyrics like, "Sometimes I hate every single stupid word you say/Sometimes I wanna slap you in your whole face." Pink's disdain for men overwhelms nearly every track – but then there's a song like "Just Give Me a Reason", which is so outstanding you can't possibly dismiss the album.

This is just music, right? These artists are merely expressing themselves.

This is just music, right? These artists are merely expressing themselves.

So much of our culture caters to giving men what they want. A high school student invites model Kate Upton to attend his prom, and he's congratulated for his audacity. A male fan at a Beyoncé concert reaches up to the stage to slap her ass because her ass is there, her ass is magnificent, and he wants to feel it. The science fiction fandom community is once again having a heated discussion, across the Internet, about the ongoing problem of sexual harassment at conventions — countless women are telling all manner of stories about how, without their consent, they are groped, ogled, lured into hotel rooms under false pretenses, physically lifted off the ground, and more.

So much of our culture caters to giving women what they want. High school girls meet Harry Styles of One Direction and are lauded as adorable, not predatory. 2NE1's Dara kisses a fan boy in the audience because he is there and said, "I wanted it to be a special event for the fans who support me... I've performed the kiss four times at this point, and there are more than 10 concerts left on the tour." 10 more random boys to kiss.

The male stripper community is once again having a heated discussion about aggressive female fans who grab their asses, grope their packages and offer to pay for sex.

But men want what they want. We should all lighten up.

But women want what they want. We should all lighten up.

It's hard not to feel humorless as a woman and a feminist, to recognize misogyny in so many forms, some great and some small, and know you're not imagining things. It's hard to be told to lighten up because if you lighten up any more, you're going to float the fuck away. The problem is not that one of these things is happening, it's that they are all happening, concurrently and constantly.

It's hard not to feel humorless as a man and a humanist, to recognize misandry in so many forms, some great and some small, and know you're not imagining things. It's hard to be told to lighten up, because if you lighten up any more, you're going to float the fuck away. The problem is not that one of these things is happening, it's that they are all happening, concurrently and constantly.

These are just songs. They are just jokes. They are just movies. It's just a hug. They're just breasts. Smile, you're beautiful. Can't a man pay you a compliment? In truth, this is all a symptom of a much more virulent cultural sickness — one where women exist to satisfy the whims of men, one where a woman's worth is consistently diminished or entirely ignored.

These are just songs. They are just jokes. They are just movies. It's just a little ass groping. A little murder on the side. Flex those muscles, you're so strong, and so potentially useful! Can't a woman pay you a compliment? In truth, this is all a symptom of a much more virulent cultural sickness — one where men exist to satisfy the whims of women, one where a man's worth as a human being rather than a beast of burden is consistently diminished or entirely ignored.

Or I could put it this way. Let's say this is simply the world we live in. If there is a spectrum of misogyny with pop culture on one end and the disrespect for women's boundaries in the middle, on the other end, we have our nation's lawmakers who implicitly encourage this entire spectrum to thrive.

Or I could put it this way. Let's say this is simply the world we live in. If there is a spectrum of misandry with pop culture on one end and the disrespect for men's boundaries in the middle, on the other end, we have our nation's lawmakers who implicitly encourage this entire spectrum to thrive.

I could go on here, but really, what's the point. These twisted little mewlings are so easy to dismantle, and it isn't even fun anymore. It's always men. Men are bad. Men are evil. Men are keeping women from achieving all their greatness by getting in the way with their absurd claims that they, too, deserve to be seen as human first, and men second.

Obviously, it's men who are responsible for the fact that most women don't give two fucks about politics, especially in Canada, right? Ladies prefer fashion and celebrity gossip because men? Or because a whole lot of them are dumb twats who prefer to let the boys deal with all the icky, tricky stuff like running the state?

Take any aspect of popular or political or economic culture, and for every negative attribute ascribed to men, you can bet your ass you will find the same negativity from women. Robin sings about aggressive, crude sex? And just what do you think Rhianna's Sticks and Stones is about? Oh, I know. A woman who enjoys rough sex.

Call women gold-diggers and MISOGYNY!

Sing about your boy-toy gold-digger whom you toss out without a penny and it's all rah-rah-rah GRLZZZZ!

Star Trek has gratuitous nudity? I can't believe Abrams apologized for that.

Right, we could never understand a James Bond film without seeing Daniel Craig come sweeping out of the sea in his swim briefs. Man of Steel? Come on baby –show us your abs!

I guess I still have a hard time wrapping my head around the fact that on the one hand, feminism claims to be about EQUALITY, but on the other hand, self-identified feminist writers like Gay seem genuinely oblivious to the fact that every questionable, unpleasant, negative aspect of the culture they isolate for critique when it comes to men applies EQUALLY to women.

Body objectification? Check

Violent music? Check

Physical assaults? Check

Disrespect for physical boundaries? Check

Laws that privilege one gender over another? Check

It's completely absurd to call out asshole men who think "I got a big dick for you" constitutes a great come-on, and then give women who call their husbands "stupid" and who want to slap their "whole face" a pass. Bullshit. If Robin is an asshole, then so is Pink.

Gay keeps telling herself to lighten up. Good advice, honey. Seriously. Lighten up. Men haven't cornered the market on being shitheads by a long shot. And being a shithead isn't even all that bad. Pink's song is actually really, really awesome.

I sing it to my husband all the time. Because it's true. I guess that makes me an asshole, too. Or just a bitch. Take your pick.

> *At the same time, I wanna hug you*
> *I wanna wrap my hands around your neck*
> *You're an asshole but I love you*
> *And you make me so mad I ask myself*
> *Why I'm still here, or where could I go*
> *You're the only love I've ever known*
> *But I hate you, I really hate you,*
> *So much, I think it must be*
> *True love, true love*

I don't really hate him, but those moments when we irritate the shit out of each other? This song is just the thing! It's a free pass to call him an asshole. Kind of like when he talks about my blog, and calls me a bitch just a little too enthusiastically.

Obviously, we're perfect for another.

No one has corned the market on being obnoxious in this house. We're equals. Equally capable of being disagreeable and ornery and unpleasant.

Just like every other human.

And yes, that includes women.

Lots of love,

JB

Wanna be a Male Feminist? Okay, here's what you have to do

Our friend Hugo Schwyzer has ignited quite the little debate with his departure from internet feminism, and the mantle of Numero Uno Male Feminist is now up for grabs! Surely there are some ambitious lads here who might want to take a shot at the Crown?

Meghan Murphy at xoJane has laid out for you just how to go about it[58]. Ready?

Feminism is for everyone, but why does it seem as though those who insist they are "good guys" or self-identify as feminist grate on me?

First up, you need to understand that no matter what you do, you are going to irritate the shit out of all the ladies who call themselves feminists. You will grate. Once you understand that little chestnut, you will be much more likely to succeed as a Male Feminist.

Repeat after me: No matter what you do, you are wrong. And irritating.

It's not that I don't think men can be feminist. I know many men who clearly align themselves with the feminist movement. The problem seems to be with men who self-identify as "feminist" as a means of gaining credibility or avoiding accountability. The problem is that many men who claim to be "good men" or to respect women, don't actually... well... respect women.

You hear that? It's not enough to just claim the word. You are going to need to be credible and accountable. Those are important virtues to feminists.

Credible.

Accountable.

We'll keep that in mind.

After his video "Blurred Lines," was called misogynist and "rapey," Robin Thicke responded by arguing that OH BUT it's ok for him to objectify women because he respects them so much! "We're the perfect guys to make fun of this," Thicke said. Because HAHA you guys! Isn't misogyny hilarious?

"Blurred Lines" was called misogynist and rapey by whom, Meghan? Oh, some whiny feminists, who don't like the line "I know you want it".

Okay, let's put our credibility on the line and look at the lyrics, and not just one line.

> *And that's why I'm gon' take a good girl*
> *I know you want it*
> *I know you want it*
> *I know you want it*
> *You're a good girl*

---

[58] http://www.xojane.com/issues/unpopular-opinion-it-pisses-me-off-when-men-call-themselves-feminists

> *Can't let it get past me*
> *You're far from plastic*
> *Talk about getting blasted*
> *I hate these blurred lines*
> *I know you want it*
> *I know you want it*
> *I know you want it*
> *But you're a good girl*
> *The way you grab me*
> *Must wanna get nasty*
> *Go ahead, get at me*

Hmmm. She's not plastic. A good girl acting bad. What is Robin to do? Ooh, then SHE grabs HIM. My, my, my. She wants to get nasty, apparently. Now what does Robin do?

He invites her to make the next move. Go ahead, get at me.

Yep, pretty rapey.

Credibility score: 0

"When we made the song, we had nothing but the most respect for women," he said on The Today Show. He even went so far as to say the song is a "feminist movement in itself."

Well, as long as if by feminist you mean that women have the right to grab men on the dance floor, I guess it IS a feminist song.   I wonder what the response would be if it were Robin grabbing the women? Isn't that technically assault?

Former New York Governor Eliot Spitzer was forced to resign after it was revealed that he'd been buying sex from prostitutes. Yet he insists he's actually a feminist.

Let's see. Spitzer believes that women have the right to control their own sexuality, the right to determine how their bodies will be used, the right to attach commercial value to themselves, and he paid women fair market value for their services.

The misogynist.

Prostitution is incompatible with feminism because women CANNOT possibly understand the implications of attaching commercial value to their bodies. Unless they are soccer players. Or models. Or anything other than prostitutes. Silly women. It's only your body and your choice when it comes to killing babies.

Accountability score: 0

The deal is, apparently, that you can behave however you like so long as you plead feminism. "But you abuse women, sir..." "Impossible! I love women!" I've heard it time and time again in my own life. Men believe they love women and that that simple belief or declaration erases their sexist behaviour.

I can only assume Meghan is referring to her previous paragraphs as examples of abuse and or/sexist behavior? Not quite certain, but let's go with that. Letting sexually aggressive women decide how far they would like to take their actions and allowing women to determine how they will use their bodies is abusing women/behaving in a sexist manner.

Gotcha.

Credibility: still 0

Walter Madison, lawyer for the young men convicted in the Steubenville rape trial, painted the victim as "a party girl" and essentially accused her of being "embarrassed;" choosing to claim rape in order to avoid being labeled a "slut." Despite his victim-blamey arguments, he told Ariel Levy that he considers himself "very much a feminist."

A lawyer suggests that a young woman might try to avoid being held accountable for her behavior by casting the blame on the men. I wonder if the "victim" would have liked Robin's song? Something tells me yes.

Proposing that perhaps women are in some teeny, tiny way responsible for their own actions is clearly sexist.

Accountability: still 0

And then, of course, there's Hugo Schwyzer, who recently left the internet due to not only personal struggles but, according to an interview in New York magazine, because of vitriol from the feminist internet.

Schwyzer is clearly struggling with some very serious mental health issues and has a lot of personal work to do away from the feminist internet. But you'd think a self-described male feminist would know better than to blame "women's anger" for his troubles. "Men are afraid of women's anger," he said. Hmm mmm. Women and their scary, scary feelings and opinions. Note all the men of the world cowering in the corner because women *gasp* feel angry. Man, I wish that worked.

Pay attention here, men. Women's anger is equivalent to feelings and opinions. When you hear "I feel" or "I think", and it is coming from the mouth of a woman, you can take that to mean "I'm angry". That's a key element of how to communicate with feminists.

Assume they are all angry bitches. Meghan says they are!

And keep in mind that she would really love it if men would cower in the corner when faced with women's anger. She wishes that would happen.

You can make it happen! But be aware, that won't make her any happier. She will still be angry.

Now, no fistfights over who gets to take on this job.

The interviewer said: "One reason you became a punching bag is that there just are not many men writing feminist columns online," prompting Schwyzer to complain: "If you look at the men who are writing about feminism, they toe the line very carefully. It's almost like they take their cues from the women around them."

Toe the line.

Carefully!

Take your cues from women. And only women.

Well yes. That's the idea. While feminism is a movement that can include and benefit men and women alike, at the end of the day it's also a movement to end patriarchy and has always been led by women. To say that "It's very hard for men to stand up to women's anger" is to imply that, somehow, white men in feminist spaces are being persecuted or silenced.

Your persecution complex will have to go, gents. It's true that feminists want you to cower in the corner, toe that line carefully and prepare to be led by and take your cues from angry women, but there is NO PERSECUTION INVOLVED IN THAT.

Just shut up already.

Credibility? Crap. Still 0.

Women have long been silenced by being told they are hysterical or aggressive or out of control or "too angry" when they stand up for themselves or speak out. To call in such a sexist stereotype in order to gain sympathy displays the same kind of entitlement expressed by all these baffled men who say "But, but... I RESPECT WOMEN" when called out on their anti-feminist behaviour.

Wait. I'm confused. Meghan just SAID that when feminists think or feel, it's the same as anger. But no calling them angry! And no being baffled!

"I'm a feminist," when coming from a man, always feels to me like demanding a pat on the head. "I love my mother," they say, puffing out their chests, as though it excuses their visit to the strip club the previous night.

What the hell does loving your mother have to do with making sure strippers can put food on the table? I'm not sure, but I think you either have to hate your mother or let those bitches dancing in clubs starve.

Accountability? Hovering right at 0.

An evil man I was in a relationship with once told me I was being "cunty." I looked at him with shock and disgust. "You realize it's not ok to call women 'cunts' or 'bitches' or 'sluts' or any of those other gendered words used to degrade women, right?" I responded. "Oh, well some women I know say it and they think it's fine," he mansplained. "It isn't. Especially when it's coming from a man. Especially when you're saying it as an insult," I said. (As though being called "cunty" could be anything but insulting). CONTEXT PLEASE. This man insisted he was both progressive and feminist. He, therefore, was free to use sexist language against women. It wasn't sexist when he said it!

It's perfectly acceptable to call men evil, and you should probably prepare to have that accusation lobbed at you, kind sir applying as Male Feminist, but do NOT refer to any woman as "cunt", "bitch" or "slut".

Even if the woman really IS "cunty". Which Meghan definitely IS.

"Oh do I seem mad? Too bad. You still can't call me 'cunty'"

The point here is that women, and only women will define what terms are and are NOT acceptable and you will toe the fucking line, you evil creep!

Similarly, Thicke tries to pin his creepshow video on women. Supposedly he preferred the clothed version of the video, but then said: "I showed it to my wife and all of her friends and everyone's immediate response seemed to be 'This is amazing. You have to put this out.'"

That's like saying: "But that feminist just called herself a slut! Therefore, it's ok for me to call my girlfriend a slut." Or, like: "But all those women are posting porny photos on Instagram! So it's ok for me to creep their accounts." Nope! Or, I suppose you can but don't do it while simultaneously pretending to be feminist. Pro tip: We can all see when you "like" those #sxy #babe #hot #girls #asss shots on Instagram and we are all judging you.

Women: yes, you CAN post porny ass shots on Instagram. You may NOT sell that ass for actual cash (see above) and you may not shake that ass on a stage (see above). You may call yourself a "slut" or any other word you prefer.

Men: you will not look at Instagram or use the same language as women.

Didn't we just cover this?

WOMEN DEFINE THE TERMS OF DEBATE, TOE THE LINE, FUCKER!

"I don't want to be sleazy, I'm a gentleman," Robin Thicke insisted on BBC's Radio 1. Well, too bad bud. If you don't want to be "sleazy" then don't make a video that's essentially a celebration of male power and rape culture.

Oh, oops. My bad. I thought feminists just defined the actual language as acceptable or not. Turns out they will also be in charge of policing music and videos, too.

This is looking like a lot of fun!

Men who insist they are the "good guys" without actually changing their behavior or interrogating their beliefs about women and what gender equality really means do more harm than good. It's manipulative more than supportive. It's silencing. And if you're silencing feminists or objectifying women while claiming to respect us, you're doing it wrong.

I think it will take duct tape and possibly several tubes of crazy glue and probably some well-placed sutures to silence Meghan, but that doesn't mean you can't at least TRY, guys. You will NOT be considered a "good guy" until you have ceded all language and music to feminist determination, until you pick up that line and toe it, subject yourself to interrogation about gender and equality, and while you're at it, would you mind cowering in the corner?

Thanks ever so much.

Credibility: I think we're gonna have go with negative integers at this point. -1

Men need to do much more than call themselves "feminist" in order to be allies, which is why, generally, when men claim the label "feminist" I feel more irritated than elated.

Yes, honey, we know. You're angry and irritated all the time.

I want men in this movement and there are men in this movement. But the men who I see doing the work and changing their own behavior both in their personal and public lives to support women aren't going around advertising their feminist status and demanding we all recognize. They're just doing it.

So, addendum to toe the line: TOE THE LINE SILENTLY

And don't silence anyone else with your silency silence.

Credibility just took a severe nosedive. -20

So you want to be one of the good guys. You want to join team feminism. You want to respect women and be an ally. Awesome. Now stop telling everybody how much of a feminist you are and start acting like one

I'll recap what that requires just in case you got lost:

> You are grating
>
> You are irritating
>
> You must be credible
>
> You must be accountable
>
> Women are allowed to grab you
>
> You are a rapey rapist under all conditions
>
> Women are not accountable for their behavior and you will not expect them to be
>
> When feminists think or feel, it means they are angry. Deal with it.
>
> You will cower in the corner
>
> You will toe the line
>
> Carefully!
>
> You will be led by women
>
> You will take your cues from women
>
> You will accept persecution without any stupid complex
>
> You will not call women angry
>
> You will not be baffled
>
> No baffling!
>
> If you love your mother, you can't help strippers feed their kids
>
> If you hate your mother, go ahead
>
> You are evil and creepy
>
> You will not use language that has not been approved by feminists
>
> You will not look at asses on Instagram. Twitter might be okay. I'll have to get back to you.
>
> You will be interrogated
>
> You will shut up

All righty then! Taking applications for Male Feminist in three – two – one ……..

Guys? Hey guys? Where did you go?

Oh right. You're cowering in the corner, holding fast to your line, and being silent. Awwww. Good dog! Here's a cookie.

See? Sometimes, feminists LOVE cookies (see below)!

And obviously, they love men.

Me too!

Lots of love,

JB

DO NOT give feminists cookies. Feminists hate cookies. NO COOKIES!

OK, so North Carolina is considering some pretty draconian measures against abortion, which will effectively restrict women's reproductive freedoms, bringing them more in line with the reproductive choices men have: have a baby or don't have sex.

Obviously, there are a whole bunch of women who think having the same rights and freedoms as men is utterly and completely unacceptable, and they gathered outside the Governor's mansion, decked out in 1950s costumes, to protest the new legislation.

As is their right.

Governor McRory went out to greet the protesters, and then he slapped them in the face with symbolic viciousness so breathtakingly cruel and malicious it makes wearing a Nazi uniform to a Bar Mitzvah seem positively uplifting.

He offered them cookies.

I'll give you a moment to recover from the shock. How could anyone be so heartless?

Cookies, people! They may even have been home-baked! They appear to be chocolate chip!

Governor McRory lends new meaning to the word "diabolical". It defies imagination that anyone could be so hateful and spiteful and detestable. Giving protesters cookies. It's beyond the pale.

Cookies, you see, are a universally acknowledged symbol of oppression, and handing them out is pretty much the same thing as saying "Welcome to the gulag, ladies. Surrender your souls". How do we know this is true?

Because Amanda Marcotte says so[59]! And it's not just cookies she has a hate on for, it's sandwiches, too. I suppose we could consider the fact that the Governor ONLY offered cookies, and not the devastating cookie-sandwich combination a redeeming quality?

Next to sandwiches, cookies are probably the most potent edible symbol of the belief that women's role is to shut up, give up their ambitions, and return to the kitchen.

Cookies: they will shut you up (as long as you abide by the "don't talk with your mouth full of cookies" rule), destroy your ambitions (it was an abortion protest, so I suppose the ambition we are talking about here is to kill unborn children?) and send you to the kitchen (where the ingredients and tools to actually make cookies are conveniently located).

Governor McRory, you bastard. I hope you burn in hell. Roast alive at 350F for 10-12 minutes (longer if you prefer a crispier cookie).

I was gonna write "it's almost funny", but it's not "almost funny". It IS funny. Holy fuck, Amanda, are you for real? In addition to the multitude of other oppressions that keep you in a state of perpetual victimhood, you are now adding cookies to the list?

Wow.

Here's another bit of crazy to add to Amanda's: Madeline Alpert, writing at xoJane, who would also, no doubt, be horribly offended if offered a cookie. Hahahahahahahah! I Googled Madeline, and look what I found!

She's making cookies! Too precious. Don't give one to Amanda, Madeline. She will probably punch you in the face if you even think of making such an insulting gesture. And trust me, Madeline is no stranger to insults, her latest post at xoJane being a perfect example.

The best part about all of this anti-misandry nonsense is that misandry isn't real! There is no such thing as an inveterate systematic hatred of men and there never has been. Misandry exists only as an exaggerated Internet joke and as a way in which women who have been directly or indirectly hurt by men to express their frustration and anger.

The whole article is quite the astonishing read, amounting to an argument that, okay, sure, misandry is REAL, but only because men DESERVE to be hated. A charming story all around. Let's just look at this one paragraph.

Inveterate, systematic hatred of men. Inveterate means "long established and unlikely to change". Systematic means "following a plan". Hatred means "intense dislike or hostility". A long established and unlikely to change plan demonstrating intense hostility to men.

Madeline, are you familiar with something called the criminal justice system?

---

[59] http://www.slate.com/blogs/xx_factor/2013/07/30/pat_mccrory_signs_a_bill_dismantling_abortion_access_but_that_s_okay_because.html?wpisrc=flyouts

Of all offenders convicted in U.S. district courts in 2003, 82.8 percent of the males were sentenced to prison but only 57.5 percent of the females. Among offenders convicted of violent crimes, 95.0 percent of the males and 76.4 percent of the females were incarcerated. For these offenses, the average sentence was 90.7 months for men and 42.5months for women

(Sourcebook of Criminal Justice Statistics Online 2003 N.d., tables 5.20.2003 and 5.21.2000)

Forty-two percent of the male offenders sentenced by state court judges in 2004 were sentenced to prison, compared with 27 percent of the female offenders. The average maximum prison sentence was 61 months for males and 42 months for females.

(U.S. Department of Justice, Bureau of Justice Statistics 2007g, tables 2.4 and 2.6)

There were 3,228 prisoners under sentence of death on December 31, 2006; of these, only 51 were women.

(U.S. Department of Justice, Bureau of Justice Statistics 2007a, tables 4 and 12).

Among offenders convicted of felonies in 1994 in Cook County (Chicago), Illinois, 28.3 percent of the females and 63.9 percent of the males were sentenced to prison. The corresponding proportions of offenders who were incarcerated in Jackson County (Kansas City), Missouri, were 16 percent (females) and 45 percent (males). The figures for Dade County (Miami), Florida, were 60.2 percent (females) and 69.2 percent (males).

This isn't some shit I just made up, Madeline. Look at the death sentences data[60]. Over three thousand men sentenced to death, and only 51 women. Between 1976 and 1997, approximately 60 000 murders were committed by women, and almost 400 000 murders were committed by men.

1% of male murderers face the death penalty. 0.08% of women get the same penalty. Is there anything that expresses hate more fully than actually killing someone?

If misandry is a way that women who have been directly or indirectly hurt by men express their anger and frustration, can we not also call misogyny a way that men who have been directly or indirectly hurt by women express their anger and frustration?

If it's okay for women to lash out with hateful, spiteful rhetoric against men, then why is it not okay for men to lash out with the same hateful, spiteful rhetoric? David Futrelle delights in cherry-picking expressions of anger and frustration from men, all the while giving women a free pass to rage away.

> *The male is completely egocentric, trapped inside himself, incapable of empathizing or identifying with others, or love, friendship, affection or tenderness. He is a completely isolated unit, incapable of rapport with anyone. His responses are entirely visceral, not cerebral; his intelligence is a mere tool in the services of his drives and needs; he is incapable of mental passion, mental interaction; he can't relate to anything other than his own physical sensations. He is a half-dead, unresponsive lump, incapable of giving or receiving pleasure or happiness; consequently, he is at best an utter bore, an inoffensive blob, since only those capable of absorption in others can be charming.*

Unfair to quote a wingnut like Valerie Solanas? The woman who shot Andy Warhol? But Madeline ~~references Valerie right in her headline!~~

[60] http://www.bjs.gov/content/pub/pdf/wo.pdf

WHERE'S VALERIE SOLANAS WHEN YOU NEED HER? WHAT IT REALLY MEANS TO MAN-HATE IN 2013

If you're going to accept misandry as a thing, but only because those fucking men deserve it, then let's be fair and accept misogyny on the same terms: those fucking women deserve it.

Or, we could look at actual instances of inveterate, systemic discrimination and decide to address them. You won't find much systemic discrimination against women anymore. Most of those issues were redressed over 70 years ago, although the feminist industry continues to insist there are still "issues" that require copious amounts of funding, from which they draw their salaries. No conflict of interest there, at all.

Systemic, inveterate discrimination against men? Here are just a few topics you might want to look into, Maddy.

Child custody

Criminal justice

Suicide

Health care funding

Selective Service

Pediatric psychotropic medications

Domestic violence

False accusations of rape

Legal parental surrender

Look at those issues carefully, Madeline, and then tell me they amount to an internet joke. If you actually open your mind and let your preconceived notions of victimhood and perpetual oppression go, you might find a whole new world opens in front of your eyes. One in which there really IS inveterate, systemic hatred for one gender in particular.

It's not women.

And Madeline, please don't give Amanda Marcotte any of your yummy looking cookies. She's a fucking bitch and doesn't deserve any cookies, ever.

Fuck you, Amanda Marcotte. Is it possible to say that enough?

I don't think so.

Lots of love,

JB

Richard Dawkins hands feminists a fabulous argument and not one of them touches it. I wonder why not?

I am an atheist.

I do not believe in God.

I do not believe in the "afterworld".

I do not believe any sort of imaginary force, being or energy controls or created the universe.

I don't KNOW how the universe was created and neither does anybody else. That information will be discovered soon enough, and until then, I am not compelled to make up a story to fill in the knowledge gap.

Richard Dawkins, perhaps the most famous atheist in the world, found himself in the midst of a Twitter tsunami when he tweeted "All the world's Muslims have fewer Nobel Prizes than Trinity College, Cambridge. They did great things in the Middle Ages, though."

Oh dear. Cue the shitstorm. Dawkins takes down his critics beautifully in a post on his own blog[61], and the relevant passages are:

1. "There are 1.6 billion Muslims, nearly a quarter of the world's population, and we are growing fast." There is even, sometimes, a hint of menace added. In the words of Houari Boumediene, President of Algeria, "Le ventre de nos femmes nous donnera la victoire" (the belly of our women will give us the victory).

2. "Islamic science deserves enormous respect." There are two versions of this second claim, ranging from the pathetic desperation of "the Qu'ran anticipated modern science" (the embryo develops from a blob, mountains have roots that hold the earth in place, salt and fresh water don't mix) to what is arguably quite a good historical point: "Muslim scholars kept the flame of Greek learning alight while Christendom wallowed in the Dark Ages."

Putting these two claims together, you almost can't help wondering something like this: "If you are so numerous, and if your science is so great, shouldn't you be able to point to some pretty spectacular achievements emanating from among those vast numbers? If you can't today but once could, what has gone wrong for the past 500 years? Whatever it is, is there something to be done about it?"

Dawkins targets early childhood education as a principal defect in Muslim culture: they are not educating their children for scientific achievement, and appear to be incredibly successful at achieving nothing scientifically.

I don't think skin colour has the slightest bearing on ability to win Nobel Prizes, whereas it is highly probable that childhood education in a particular religion does. Educational systems that teach boys only memorisation of one particular book, and teach girls nothing at all, are not calculated to breed success in science.

Has something gone wrong with education in the Islamic world, and is it a problem that Muslims themselves might wish to consider? Just to throw in a separate piece of information, colleagues lecturing to aspiring doctors in British universities inform me that Muslim students boycott lectures on evolution. And I have myself interviewed, for television, pupils and teachers at one of Britain's leading Islamic secondary schools – one with impeccable Ofsted ratings – where I was informed by a teacher that literally all the pupils reject evolution.

Just as an aside, do you know that Noah's Café in the Creation Museum offers gluten-free meals?
[61] http://www.richarddawkins.net/foundation_articles/2013/8/9/calm-reflections-after-a-storm-in-a-teacup

Hahahahahahahahahahahahahah! Oh, I'm sorry. Do you lack the genetic variation necessary to digest wheat? Has an over reliance on wheat based foods for the past ten thousand years created a sensitivity? Is your digestive tract still adapting to this novel food item?

ARE YOU EVOLVING*?????????

Professor David Sanders, Consultant Gastroenterologist at the Royal Hallamshire Hospital and University of Sheffield, says, "Only for the past ten thousand years have we had wheat-based foods in our diets, which in evolutionary terms makes wheat almost a novel food. If you put that in context to the 2.5 millions years that mankind has been on earth, it makes sense that our bodies are still adapting to this food, and more specifically, the gluten that it contains."

http://www.science20.com/news_articles/being_glutenfree_determined_evolution_says_gastroenterologist-91578

Who wants to bet they caution people to use the handsanitizer, too? Use anti-bacterial soap in the kitchens and bathrooms? Gotta watch out for those superbugs! Pretty nasty flu virus going around this season. Can't be too careful.

Can't be too stupid either, by the looks of it.

*Yes, I understand that evolution happens over countless generations and not just one person. It's still an example of extreme cognitive dissonance to believe you can't digest a plant because you lack the necessary genes and deny evolution at the same time. Is there genetic variation across human populations that responds to environmental stimuli or is there not? Pick one, for fuck's sake.

Okay, so Dawkins is wondering if the lack of scientific achievement in the modern Muslim world can be linked to faulty education. Perfectly valid question, and he's probably right that YEP! The scientific method, which is the basis of all discovery CAN be discovered by accident, but it's better to teach it systematically, especially to children.

But Muslims are not the ONLY group who are A) numerous, and B) boastful about their supposed abilities, and C) devoid of any actual achievements.

Women have fewer Nobel Prizes in scientific achievement than Trinity College, too.

Women have been awarded 44 prizes (Marie Curie was honored twice, so only 43 women have won), but when you ditch Literature, Peace and Economics, the number collapses to 16. Trinity College claims 32 prizes. 31 prizes in scientific achievement. One college beats Muslims, and women hands down.

Now why might that be?

Can we blame the educational system? Are women being socialized as young children to ignore science, to discredit irrefutable theories like evolution and gravity while boys are not? Is the school system rigged to make sure boys direct their attention and energy towards all the really hard thinky subjects like math and engineering and biomechanics, leaving the girls to study literature and home economics?

Hmmm. Doesn't look like it. In California, women now outnumber men in high school math and science courses.

At the high school level, female enrollment exceeds male enrollment in every core subject area except computer science, where females lag males substantially[62] (p7).

But it makes no difference. Girls get all the same training as boys, but do NOT translate that into even low level achievement.

The results of the analysis indicate that high school boys lag girls in English, foreign language, and social science but that girls are 10 percent less likely than boys to take physics and 43 percent less likely to take college-preparatory computer science classes. These last two areas of study prepare students for some of the highest-paying jobs in today's labor market. Girls also lag boys in Advanced Placement (AP) course enrollment in calculus, chemistry, physics, and computer science.

Girls take all the core subjects, but not at high levels and not to prepare to do advanced work in those subject areas.

There is no flaw in the education system.

But you won't hear that reported anywhere in the media. Girls outperform boys in math and science around the world, except in Canada, the United States and Britain. But they do not translate that outperformance into achievement.

Because patriarchy, obviously.

The US Department of Education has found that girls "who have a strong self-concept regarding their abilities in math or science are more likely to choose and perform well in elective math and science courses and to select math and science-related college majors and careers".

The department emphasizes that: "improving girls' beliefs about their abilities could alter their choices and performance ... particularly as they move out of elementary school and into middle and high school."

Oh wait. You mean girls who are actually interested in math and science tend to pursue math and science? Wow! What an incredible insight. People do things that interest them. Genius! I'm glad we cleared that up.

Most girls aren't interested in math or science.

But don't you dare suggest that the girls are making a conscious choice that reflects those interests, or lack thereof! Larry Summer's did, and he was crucified! How hilarious that he was run out of Harvard for speaking truth. Harvard's motto, of course, is **VERITAS**.

Which is Latin for "shove your truth up your ass, you sexist prick".

Unlike Muslims, who did in fact have some glory days back in the Middle Ages, women have NEVER contributed very much to the world scientifically. Well, except in one way.

They gave birth to great scientists.

Lots of love,

JB

---

[62] http://www.ppic.org/content/pubs/cacounts/CC_201ADCC.pdf

Dating, Sex and Relationships

Of all the requests I get for advice, dating and relationships stands at the top. And of all the hate mail, I receive, my admonition that men never date single mothers garners the lion's share. The fact that men have no reproductive rights, and women are not penalized for their bad choices, colors all possible relationships between men and women, leaving everyone worse off. The ones who suffer the most, of course, are the children. We can have a robust conversation on how to address the poor life outcomes for the overwhelming majority of children raised by single mothers, but it is impossible to deny that the most effective way to blight a child's chances of success is to raise him or her without a father.

Understandably, men are reluctant to enter into relationships with women, given that women have all the power, and children suffer when that power is wielded to make selfish choices. But all is not lost. There are many, many women who understand that having power is not the same as using it, and finding those women is possible. It's not easy, but it's possible.

Begin by rejecting single mothers. There goes 50% of your dating troubles right off the bat. Let's look at why.

Dating single mothers? Just say NO! A note for all the single dudes.

First up, let's clarify our terms. A widow is NOT a single mother. Her husband died! Lumping her in with single mothers is an insult to his memory, to her and to her children. So don't even think of doing it. Especially war widows. If you ever find yourself referring to a woman whose husband died on a battlefield as a single mother, you should immediately pour Tabasco sauce into your eyes, because you deserve to weep all the tears I'm certain she has.

Divorced mothers are also NOT single mothers, although a huge flashing PROCEED WITH CAUTION sign is definitely in order. We'll get to these charming ladies later.

A single mother is a woman who had a child outside of any established relationship, or a relationship so fragile the thickest retard in the world ought to have been able to see bringing a child on board was a FUCKING TERRIBLE IDEA. Single mothers are bona fide idiots and here is why you should never even consider dating one:

First, this is a woman who clearly doesn't give a shit about her child's well-being and future prospects. Children of single mothers do poorly on every imaginable scale[63]: they have more emotional problems, experience more stress, are more likely to grow up poor, they have lower educational achievements and experience way more behavioral problems than children who grow up with married parents. Depression, suicide, drug abuse, jail and psychiatric medications are all more common in populations of children raised by single mothers.

Ladies, this is why abortion exists! If you screw up and get pregnant, don't screw up even more and bring an innocent child along with you! The rest of us who have to LIVE with your fucked up, emotionally scarred children will PAY you to have a fucking abortion. Be sensible, for the love of god.

63

http://futureofchildren.org/publications/journals/article/index.xml?journalid=37&articleid=107&sectionid=692

Second, single mothers are clearly really, really shitty at making life decisions. Having a child out of wedlock is pretty much the number one thing you can do to fuck up your life. You can pick up a heroin addiction, drop out of high school, rob a bank or decide to write the great American novel financing yourself on your credit cards. All of those things can be fixed. You can go to rehab, get your GED, get parole, and pay off those cards. But once you have a child, you cannot take it back. It's done.

Third, single mothers profoundly misunderstand men. There are few men who are overjoyed to spend their blood, sweat and tears on some other guy's genetic offspring. Remember the Cinderella Effect? It's real. A modern man doesn't turn up his nose at a woman with some sexual experience who might have learned a trick or two from previous lovers about what men REALLY like, or more likely, she learned how to FIND OUT, but the majority of men would like to see a NEW sign on her uterus. No previous occupants. When a man picks a wife, he wants to know he won't be competing with some random babydaddy who was there before him.

A woman who cares so little about her children, her own prospects, and her future husband is NOT going to make a great wife. Sorry. It's just not going to happen. A great wife and mother places the needs and happiness of her husband and children ABOVE her own needs, and in doing so, finds her greatest happiness. So politically incorrect to say so, I know. But a woman who makes YOU the center of her life is going to be a great wife. Oh, and in return, you have to make HER the center of your life.

See how that works? Yeah. Not really a huge mystery. You live for one another. You both put each other's happiness above your own. Exactly what single mothers do NOT do.

Now divorced mothers, who are a breed of single mothers, MIGHT be a little different, but whenever you approach one, sing this little song in your head: it takes two to tango.

Never, ever assume a divorced woman is some innocent blushing maid cruelly abused by some terrible man. Oh, that's the story she'll spin for you, because really, what women is going to sit there and say "I'm an unbearably controlling and irrational cunt who made my husband's life such hell he decided he would rather be a weekend Dad than spend one more second with me".

When you meet a divorced single mother, immediately start looking for the flaw. It's something big. Something that drove another man to pledge his undying love to her, to have and to hold, from this day forth, and then sometime later decide "fuck this shit. I'm outta here". Stand firmly on guard. Scan the horizon, dude. Something wicked this way comes. Or it soon will.

Divorced moms who escaped abusive marriages with drug/sex/gambling/whatever addicts should not get a free pass from you, either. Even if it's TRUE that the husband was a colossal fuck-up, you need to ask yourself what kind of imperceptive moron couldn't spot that? What kind of insecurities plague a woman who thinks getting married to a drug addict is good idea? What kind of delusional self-image does a woman have, if she can fall for a con artist with a gambling habit that would shame Charlie Sheen? Be very cautious around a woman who takes none of the blame for her failed marriage. You might not be the FIRST man she blames all her problems on, but you sure as hell can be NEXT.

Don't be.

On the whole, give single and divorced mothers a pass. And for the love of god, if you decide to give one a spin, STAY AWAY FROM THE CHILD. That child is aching for a man to call his or her own. Every child of a single mother lies awake at night in bed, longing for the Daddy he sees on TV, in books, in the lives of the other kids at school. He wants you so badly. Don't let him fall in love. You'll break his heart. Or hers. Little girls long for daddies as much as little boys.

That's the real danger. The children of single mothers have already been wounded so deeply by the lack of a father. To give them some hope that it might be YOU, and then leave them is unspeakably cruel. It's the worst thing you can do. You can't save those little innocents, but you can save them from hurting even more.

Don't date single mothers. It's just not worth it.

Lots of love,

JB

Sluts lower the value of all women. Here's how to compete with them.

Margaret Wente, a columnist with Canada's Globe and Mail newspaper knocks it out of the park with her article on the sexual economics of today's young men and women[64]. And her assessment for young women is harsh, but so fucking true:

"A lot of women are in no hurry to get married, either. But it might not work out so well for them. They've watched too much Sex in the City. They think they'll still have the same choices at 35 and 40 that they had at 25. They have no idea that men's choices will get better with age (especially if they're successful), but theirs will get worse. Believe me, this sucks. But it's the truth."

Basically, women are so quick to give up sex, there's no incentive for men to work for it, and men working for sex is what BUILT THIS CITY. Sluts offer up their vaginas (but not for cash, so don't get excited, whores!) for very little effort and in effect, make it hard for ALL women to create lasting and meaningful relationships with men. Left to their own devices, men CAN and WILL sample as much of the herd as they can, and that's hella fun! For both men and women, but eventually a woman will start looking around for a provider (unless she voted Obama, in which case she can depend on ALL men to support her through the wonders of taxation). Babies are time sucking assholes who need their mamas fulltime for YEARS, and in order for a woman to do a good job raising her offspring (and no, hiring an illegal immigrant to raise your child is NOT doing a good job), she needs a man.

Dependable, reliable, loyal, strong. A man. The kind of man women's studies majors HATE. #sorryfeminists.

What is a sensible, reasonable woman to do in the face of sluts throwing their vaginas around like confetti at a wedding? In truth, it's not that hard to compete with sluts. What you'll need are some domestic skills and a sense of loyalty to match your man's.

True story: when we were in grad school and just dating, I asked Mr.JB for the keys to his room and he gave them to me. He told me later that he expected to come home to his room and find me splayed in some kind of exotic lingerie and he was a bit worried about living up to whatever romance novel induced fantasy I had concocted for the two of us. Although that DOES sound kind of fun, I had a different fantasy in mind.

I went to Mr. JB's room and collected all his laundry. I washed it and then, using a piece of cardboard, folded it into beautiful Gap store origami and arranged it on his shelves perfectly. He came home to a room

---

[64] http://www.theglobeandmail.com/commentary/why-wont-guys-grow-up-sexual-economics/article5172942/

that smelled of Tide and Bounce, with his shirts ironed and hung and his t-shirts lined up on a shelf with military precision.

Yeah. I did his laundry.

He fucking died. He told me later that THAT was the moment he knew he would marry me. We have a long standing joke about choosing me randomly, because Mr. JB, handsome and tall, was quite a catch on campus. He had been to a hot tub party at the Faculty of Law and acquired the number of a hot young law student who happened to share the same first name as me. So he had two "JBs" on his cork board and he picked one to call one lonely Friday night, and it was me!

He swears he knew it was me. Yeah. Right. No harm, no foul! Who cares? It was me!

During our 18 months at grad school, I continued to do his laundry. I learned what he liked for breakfast and had a tray ready for him every morning. I fetched him hot food when he was tied up in long meetings, got him coffee when he looked tired and rubbed his back after eight hours of lectures in a chair designed for someone six inches shorter. I folded his laundry, made his bed and listened to his frustrations.

What did he do for me? It doesn't matter. The answer is: LOTS! But we're not talking about quid pro quo here. If your first instinct was to set up a mental balance sheet and make sure all of YOUR thoughtful actions are being returned in EXACT PROPORTION to your outlay, you might as well give up now. You don't know shit about men, or relationships of any kind.

As our relationship progressed, I made sure that Mr. JB knew I had a deep care taking instinct. At the beginning of our relationship, we lived in student housing and went to a cafeteria every day. In actual fact, I CAN cook. I'm a terrific cook, but he didn't know that until we had been married for over a year (we lived in China for our first year and ate out pretty much every meal). What he DID know was that I cared about what he ate. I cared if he was hungry. I would not hesitate to trudge across campus in rainy, shitty weather to bring him a hot dinner.

And he loved me for it. Sucks, doesn't it? Food, clean clothes, tidy room, sex and a shoulder to lean on. Yep, it's really that simple.

That's how you compete with sluts. Be a wife. Be a woman. Look at the man, and care about him deeply. Don't create a scorecard. Don't keep tally about who brought coffee to whom. Let the balance swing in his favour dramatically.

What will you get in return? Oh, just a husband. A man who loves you completely. Loyalty, protection, honesty, reliability, dependability. A rock who will weather any storm for you. Who lives for you. As long as you live for him.

That's how you defeat sluts. Because at the end of the day, sluts are in it for themselves. They don't give a shit about any particular man, and will toss whatever man they DO manage to snare under the fucking bus the second they think something better has come along. To hell with the man, to hell with their children, to hell with everything but their own insatiable desires. For something they will never have.

Love. True love. It's a verb, ladies. Show it. Do the fucking laundry.

Lots of love,

JB

Slutty feminist WOMEN with fucked up personal lives are heroes. Slutty feminist MEN with fucked up personal lives are mentally ill traitors.

It's interesting to me to see the compassionate response the complete meltdown of male feminist Hugo Schwyzer has elicited from the very men he has repeatedly attacked for their supposed "misogyny" and hatred of women.

Paul Elam at A Voice for Men[65] expresses his sorrow at the mess Hugo has found himself in, and places enormous truth value on Hugo's claims that he suffers from a fairly serious mental health problem.

To be completely honest, for the first time I actually feel sympathy for this troubled soul. His unchecked sociopathy and childlike lack of governance over his base impulses have led him to a place few gender ideologues will ever go: To simultaneous personal and professional destruction.

William Pierce at The Spearhead[66] has similar thoughts: Hugo has some crazy in his pants, and while Pierce doesn't demonstrate quite the compassion that Paul does, he takes the prospect of Schwyzer being suicidal quite seriously, although he is quick to place the responsibility right where it belongs. Fair enough. Men do commit suicide at alarmingly high rates that amount to a national healthcare crisis.

Finally, I'd like to point out how topsy-turvy things are when we have male feminists fooling around with porn stars and flying to Ukraine (Lord knows what Hugo was up to there) while manosphere writers cause scandals by settling down in monogamous relationships. It's a crazy world out there...

Hugo, when you behave in this manner, it isn't your critics who are causing your problems: it's you.

I'm not criticizing any man who lines up behind Hugo, or demonstrates empathy or concern. In fact, it's a pretty terrific example of exactly how NOT cold-hearted and quasi-violent men who question feminist ideology are towards those who routinely attempt to shame them into silence.

When a man is hurting, other men at least pause to consider that someone here is hurting.

That's a pretty beautiful sentiment.

When it comes to Hugo, I don't share it. Not for one second. I think Hugo is being a total pussy and missing out on a fantastic opportunity to point out the fucking hypocrisy of the ideology he has thrown himself behind professionally and personally.

What Hugo should be saying is "Step off, bitches. You do the same shit and spin it as liberation and freedom. My personal life is none of your goddamn business".

Let's start with the Grande Dame of feminism herself: Simone de Beauvoir[67]. She supposedly had an "open relationship" with Jean Paul Sartre, and she pursued him for her entire life.

Yet in this lifelong relationship of supposed equals, he, it turned out, was far more equal than she was. It was he who engaged in countless affairs, to which she responded on only a few occasions with longer-lasting passions of her own. Between the lines of her fiction and what are in effect six volumes of

---

[65] http://www.avoiceformen.com/misandry/sycophants/schwyzer-bows-out/

[66] http://www.the-spearhead.com/2013/08/01/hugo-schwyzer-caught-with-pants-down/

[67] http://www.theguardian.com/world/2005/jun/10/gender.politicsphilosophyandsociety

autobiography, it is also evident that De Beauvoir suffered deeply from jealousy. She wanted to keep the image of a model life intact. There were no children. They never shared a house and their sexual relations were more or less over by the end of the war, though for much of their life and certainly at the last, they saw each other daily.

Is de Beauvoir a pathetic simpleton who can't get it through her head that her cheating genius will never, ever ruck up with a ring and a dress? Is she mentally ill to allow her life to be dictated by a man who openly sleeps with other women while she seethes at home alone with jealousy? Does anyone question her feminism because she plays the role of the dupe? All her passions governed by one man, whom she cannot have?

Nope. She's a goddamn hero.

Erica Jong launched sluttiness as a virtue in 1971 with her book Fear of Flying. Married four times, she reveled in the fuck and run mentality.

"The zipless fuck is absolutely pure. It is free of ulterior motives. There is no power game . The man is not "taking" and the woman is not "giving." No one is attempting to cuckold a husband or humiliate a wife. No one is trying to prove anything or get anything out of anyone. The zipless fuck is the purest thing there is. And it is rarer than the unicorn. And I have never had one."

The book is one long erotic fantasy of just grabbing and banging whatever guy gets your motor running, and women embraced the challenge rather thoroughly, all the while lauding Jong for her audacity and the liberating effects of zipless, no strings attached fucking.

Eat, Love, Pray? Hell yeah, ladies, ditch your husband and kids and go on a sex and food tour. It's good for you!

Sex and the City? Ladies, if you are not cultivating greed, avarice, tons of stupidly expensive shoes and bedposts notched to toothpicks, you are doing feminism WRONG[68]!

...to dismiss the programme entirely on the basis of its shortcomings as a feminist text would also be to lose out on what it does deliver. Just to take the most headline-grabbing example, that includes some pretty frank discussion of sex, in which female sexual pleasure and agency is obviously considered a fundamental right, rather than a privilege.

Ladies, you have a fundamental right to be a slut! Okay, I'll buy it.

Why don't men have the same fundamental right? Why doesn't Hugo?

Granted, Hugo has been a bad, bad boy.

Sex with undergrads.

A botched attempt to murder a girlfriend while high on who the hell knows what.

Cheating on his wife with a 27 year old sex worker.

All the while railing against older men lusting after younger women.

---

[68] http://www.theguardian.com/lifeandstyle/2008/apr/16/women.film

And cheering for monogamy.

Yeah, so Hugo is a giant fucking hypocrite. This is news? The real question is why, Hugo, do your lady friends get a pass for all their shitty behavior without anyone questioning their ideological commitment or veracity, while you are driven to the brink of suicide by doing the exact same shit?

Riddle me that.

Sex with students? When the teacher is a woman, that's just all good fun[69]!

"There is still a double standard out there, and it's almost a joke — 'Hey, he got hit on by some pretty teacher, what's he complaining about?' " said Ramsland, who has worked with the FBI's Behavioral Science Unit. "Many don't see it as much of a crime, and one of the factors that women are getting off easier is some don't see them as a big of a threat as a man.

Getting a pass for attempted murder? There are too many to even cite, but I love this woman who hired a HITMAN (who was really a police officer) to kill her husband and she got the full out pussy pass. No penalty of any kind.

Women's justice groups are urging the Supreme Court to stand by a decision that acquitted a Nova Scotia woman for trying to hire a hit man to kill her estranged husband due to years of abuse.

The abuse was so severe the husband was awarded custody of their daughter. Must have been really bad, right? Or complete and utter bullshit.

Older women lusting after younger men? Why, that's just natural[70]! All that young, virile sperm. And the muscle tone of a young man! Ooh, baby. Bring it on.

As women decline in fertility, their sex drive gets a supercharge in order to maximize their remaining baby-making chances, new research from the University of Texas at Austin reveals. Women in the low-fertility group (ages 27-45) were much more likely to report having more sex, wanting more sex, and having more (and more intense) sexual fantasies. "If you're trying to maximize your remaining fertility, it makes sense to seek out a younger partner because his sperm is healthier," says lead researcher Judith Easton.

And monogamy? What's that? Why should women embrace that dreary old shit? I particularly love this story, plastered everywhere, about how Simon Cowell knocked up his best friend's wife! She is apparently delighted to have snagged the BabyMama Crown from the grasping hands of the other members of the Aching Ovaries Brigade.

None of these issues, or women, are being called out on feminist media sites. Nothing to see here. La la la la. The top stories on Jezebel?

What to do with your slobbery drunk friends? Fuck 'em, is basically the advice. Gosh. Lovely to see women lining up in each other's corners, no?

What to do when your period is so heavy you can't go to work! Jesus. How heavy does it have to be? What is your job? Shark tamer?

---

[69] http://www.denverpost.com/news/ci_18726100

[70] http://www.psychologytoday.com/articles/201101/field-guide-the-cougar

Lindy West, who gets bigger with every new post, had a breastmilk lollipop. Ewww. Do you have suck everything that comes near your mouth, Lindy? Really? No limits at all?

The rest of the stories are just as compelling. Jezebel has lots to say, but very little of it focuses on the issues that Hugo is being excoriated for all over the feminist media.

Hugo, ask yourself why. Why is it that WOMEN get a pass for doing all the same shit you do, or at the very least are met with some pretty deafening silence, while YOU are basically being deprived of your ability to make a living or contribute to society in a way that you want to contribute.

Notice something else, too.

Look carefully at who came to your defence. It wasn't the pack of fucking bitches who are willing to toss you under the bus for committing the exact same infractions they extol when women are the protagonists.

It was men. And a few men in particular.

You're a fool, Hugo, if you cave into the demands that you present yourself as mentally damaged, in need of medications and self-flagellation. Your lady friends might forgive you this time, but you will always walk that tightrope of being barely acceptable and you will always be the first one they sacrifice.

You went to the Dark Side in search of cookies, Hugo, not seeming to realize that feminists HATE cookies.

Come into the light. We have cookies, and everything else too!

And please, whatever you do, do not give them the satisfaction of destroying you utterly. They won't mourn you. Not for one second. Don't become another tragic statistic. Your crimes were not crimes at all. Being human is not a crime.

Even if you happen to be male and human at the same time.

Lots of love,

JB

Hook-up Culture is a thing white kids do? Why are more than 70% of black children born out of wedlock then?

Let's start with a definition: according to Urban Dictionary, hook-up culture is "The era that began in the early 1990s and has since prevailed on college campuses and elsewhere when hooking up has replaced traditional dating as the preferred method of heterosexual liaison".

There have been a few high profile articles[71] about this so-called hook-up culture circulating around the internet lately, mostly focused on the women who participate in it, and then predictably, complain afterwards that they hate being treated like interchangeable blow-up dolls by men who don't find them particularly appealing as people. Women interviewed (anonymously, which is telling in itself) at Penn State recognized that they were not going to succeed in their desires for a boyfriend, and decided to just join the blowjob party in exchange for what they COULD get:

---

[71] http://www.nytimes.com/2013/07/14/fashion/sex-on-campus-she-can-play-that-game-too.html?pagewanted=all&_r=0

"It's kind of like a spiral," she said. "The girls adapt a little bit, because they stop expecting that they're going to get a boyfriend — because if that's all you're trying to do, you're going to be miserable. But at the same time, they want to, like, have contact with guys." So they hook up and "try not to get attached."

Now, she said, she and her best friend had changed their romantic goals, from finding boyfriends to finding "hookup buddies," which she described as "a guy that we don't actually really like his personality, but we think is really attractive and hot and good in bed."

Haley describes how the hook-up culture works in practice:

"You go in, and they take you down to a dark basement," Haley, a blond, pink-cheeked senior, recalled of her first frat parties in freshman year. "There's girls dancing in the middle, and there's guys lurking on the sides and then coming and basically pressing their genitals up against you and trying to dance."

Dancing like that felt good but dirty, and like a number of girls, Haley said she had to be drunk in order to enjoy it. Women said universally that hookups could not exist without alcohol, because they were for the most part too uncomfortable to pair off with men they did not know well without being drunk. One girl, explaining why her encounters freshman and sophomore year often ended with fellatio, said that usually by the time she got back to a guy's room, she was starting to sober up and didn't want to be there anymore, and giving the guy oral sex was an easy way to wrap things up and leave.

Not all women embrace the hook-up mentality, but those who don't feel insecure about their choices.

"Am I allowed to find the person that I want to spend the rest of my life with when I'm 19?" she said. "I don't really know. It feels like I'm not."

Susan Patton, that "Princeton Mom" thinks women at colleges have heard the message loud and clear, even though it goes against what most of them actually want:

At one point, she asked the young women if any of them wanted to marry and have children. They at first appeared shocked by the question, then looked at one another for reassurance before, she said, "sheepishly" raising their hands.

"I thought, 'My gosh, what have we come to that these brilliant young women are afraid to say that marriage and children are significant parts of what they view as their lifelong happiness?' " Ms. Patton said.

"They have gotten such strong, vitriolic messages from the extreme feminists saying, 'Go it alone — you don't need a man,' " she added.

So basically, young women are given a message that men, children, marriage and families are unimportant, they are entitled to sex, and they should happily engage in random acts of swallowing (or spitting, I suppose, depending on your preference) with men they barely know and don't even necessarily LIKE.

"We don't really like each other in person, sober," she said, adding that "we literally can't sit down and have coffee."

And gosh, they need ALCOHOL to get through this disaster of a dating scene?

There's a shock.

Much of the response to the hook-up piece in the NYT has been to moan about "where the men are". Why aren't men being interviewed about all this? How do the men feel? How are we supposed to blame the men if we aren't even engaging them in the conversation?

Oh, now, don't you worry your pretty little head about that. Actual men are not required to blame all men. Amanda Marcotte can blame men for everything, at all times, with no evidence of any kind because EQUALITY FAIRNESS PATRIARCHY FEMINISM VICTIM SNOWFLAKE!

Responding to Tina Brown, who thinks young women are making a big mistake to play along, Marcotte has this to say:

Brown's understanding of this situation is that the boys these young women are encountering are selfish in bed, treat women like they exist to serve them, and are crass and rude. But the young women are nonetheless supposed to make these young men their boyfriends or else they're "editing out tenderness, intimacy, excitement, somebody respecting them". I don't mean to be an asshole here, but how? If a guy treats you like a blow job machine whose pleasure is irrelevant, then he's not going to be a source of tenderness, intimacy, etc. He's just a dick, and trying to make him your boyfriend is a waste of your time— and these women are clear they have better things to do.

Selfish dicks.

Selfish dicks.

Selfish dicks.

Did we get that?

Men are selfish dicks who treat women like blowjob machines. Apparently, it has not occurred to Amanda that perhaps the reason men treat women like blowjob machines is because the women are ACTING LIKE BLOWJOB MACHINES!?!?

I wonder why Amanda can't see that?

Girls who buy the line that there's something wrong with them if they don't have or want a boyfriend at that age end up spending a lot of time sitting around a messy college apartment, being ignored by their "boyfriend" while he plays video games with his bros. I saw it. Hell, I did it. It sucks.

You did it? I'll bet you did, sweetie.

The reality is that many of the young men who are all caught up in masculine posturing in college mellow out afterwards and become completely eligible bachelors who are totally capable of offering love and support in return for getting it. Part of what helps a lot of them on their journey is realizing that you can't actually keep a girlfriend if you don't treat her well. They are not even remotely helped, therefore, by encouraging women to cling to them like life rafts, lest said women get accused of being cold-hearted bitches. By having some fucking standards and not trying to turn "texts you for a beej and boots you out the door" guy into your boyfriend, these young women are probably speeding up the process that turns a belligerent young man who is afraid that intimacy will make him grow vaginas to a young man who puts all that behind him to enjoy the pleasures of actually hanging out with and enjoying the company of women you have sex with.

Hahahahahahah!

That's just too funny. Yeah, hand out blowjobs like party favors at a McDonald's restaurant opening, because that will make men eventually grow up and love you!

Good plan.

I sincerely feel sorry for any woman who takes Marcotte and her ilk seriously. Embrace your slut! Accept those booty call texts! Go down on as many randoms as you can! You're actually helping them understand the value of women! Make sure you're good and trashed when you do it, too. And if it doesn't work out quite the way you hoped, you can always accuse him of raping you.

Ah, romance!

Competing with sluts is actually really, really easy, and Marcotte's advice makes it even easier! Any young lady that takes my advice will have her pick of men, who will be devoted to her, as long as she is devoted to him. And if it requires alcohol to carry out my advice, he's the wrong guy. Or you're an alcoholic. Either way, it's wrong.

The conversation took an interesting turn today at Jezebel, where the ladies proclaim that hook-up culture is a rich, white girl thing. All the other ladies have the whole relationship thing worked out, and know how to encourage intimacy and attachment and establish meaningful connections with their sexual partners.

...many young black kids have a desire to disprove the historical assumption that black people are "hypersexual" and therefore are more careful about their sexual activities.

I'm reading a very fascinating book by a man named Tom Burrell called "Brainwashed: Challenging the Myth of Black Inferiority". Tom is not some liberal arts trained PhD student desperately trying to wade through the stickiness of post-modernist/feminist/heteronormative/cis-gendered/bullshit theory, like so many other people who write on issues of race and class and gender.

No, Tom is one of the founding partners of Burrell Communications, an incredibly successful and profitable advertising agency that specializes in targeting black consumers, so his words are written through the lens of what works in practice, not in theory.

I'll take an adman over an academic, any day.

Burrell's chapter on black sexuality and family formation is disturbing, to say the least. He charts out how the legacy of slavery and early emancipation was deliberately designed to fracture black families and make it incredibly difficult for black men and women to see each other as fully realized humans.

A common, modern critique of black culture is that plenty of other groups have had a rough go in terms of being dehumanized, vilified, and outright murdered throughout our long, sad history, and have still managed to maintain their basic orientation towards family and community. Most notably, Jewish people, subjected to the Holocaust, mass murder and plenty of anti-Semitism across the globe have still managed to be productive, functional members of civilized society.

The Holocaust lasted 12 years.

Slavery lasted 250 years.

That's a whole lot more time to destroy the foundations of a culture. And the reverberations have carried across a wider gulf of time.

The effect of slavery on families is pretty much a no-brainer. Children could be, and were sold away from their families. Marriages were either outright forbidden, or destroyed at the will of the slavemaster. Once it became illegal to import new slaves, existing slaves were used as breeding stock, and the bonds of family were completely and utterly irrelevant.

What I found very interesting was how early welfare laws STILL acted to destroy black families. In order for a woman to be eligible for benefits, she could not have a man in the house. She had to choose between her children and her husband.

Here is how Burrell lays out the historically rooted dysfunction in black families:

Disrespect: words of mutual contempt, ridicule, wide mistrust of mates

Roots: Black family life, not conducive to a slave based economy, was disrupted, disrespected, and destroyed. Black men and women were stripped of their roles as parents and protectors. Soceity, through the welfare system, dismissed black fathers

The beat-down: disproportionate rates of physical, verbal, spiritual, and psychological abuse in black families

Roots: Slaves and descendants were conditioned to accept physical and psychological abuse. Emulation of slave-era dominant males norms continues today with a misplaced sense of "manhood" and reaction to powerlessness

Can't be true to my Boo: the acceptance and expectation of infidelity

Roots: Result of male slave emasculation and bearing witness to misogynistic, humiliating crimes against black women. Black men portrayed as unreliable and unable to protect. Black women portrayed as the property of white males. Unquestioned belief in black male and female unworthiness.

Icing: Emotional shutdown and distance that fosters unhealthy relationships

Roots: Slaves learned to endure conditions outside their control. Protective mechanisms to provide family safety fractured during slavery. Generational acceptance of trauma and instability of black life.

What I find most compelling about Tom's book is that he is not offering EXCUSES for how black culture operates, nor is he asking for ACCEPTANCE. He is offering an EXPLANATION, and using his analysis of how and why certain aspects of the culture came to be as a means of charting a way out of the mess that exists now.

And he very clearly points out that white, especially liberal, thinkers are a key part of the strategy to CONTINUE to represent black people as inherently inferior all the while pretending to be sympathetic and understanding.

The Jezebel article about hook-up culture is a perfect example. By claiming hook-up is a white thing, the writers can pat themselves on the back for NOT engaging those nasty racial stereotypes about "hypersexual" black folks just wanting sex and popping out babies willy-nilly. Of course, they still have to make sure the stereotype gets engaged by mentioning how they are NOT engaging the stereotype, but they conveniently put the words into the mouths of black students themselves.

It would be racist for Jezebel to say such a thing directly.

It's even more racist to ignore it.

By only focusing on the elite, the successful black college kids who keep it in their pants, Jezebel ignores and therefore allows all the young black men and women struggling through a massively dysfunctional culture to seem normal, natural and ultimately responsible for their own predicaments.

And ultimately, they are. But that doesn't mean there are not a whole lot of structural and psychological factors that come into play. Again, those factors are NOT excuses, they are explanations and they offer a road map for how to tackle the issues facing the black community.

Seven out of every ten black children are born out of wedlock, into families that have no fathers present on a permanent basis.

How does that sneak by the "hook-up" culture radar? The real headline on the Jezebel piece should have been "White girls better at birth control and abortion", which leads to a whole different set of critiques. Or maybe it should have been "White girls better at blowjobs", since it's pretty hard to get pregnant from a blowjob.

I have often pointed out that feminism, upon closer examination, appears to actively hate women. Marcotte's advice to engage in casual, meaningless oral sex as a means to teach men to value women falls right into that camp. Women need to be drunk to override their basic impulses NOT to do that, but feminism still goes all rah-rah-blowjobs-for-everyone! Rather than treat women's basic instincts as right and proper and valuable and worthy, feminism seeks to get women to deny their most simple needs.

Articles like "hook-up culture is a white thing", while superficially appearing to be race-progressive (tee hee – only white girls are sluts!) is an active part of the dialogue to ensure that black families continue to be subject to the pressures that make their formation so damn difficult. Black women are right to be very suspicious of feminism.

Feminism isn't just about female superiority: it's about WHITE female superiority. The vast majority of white, college-educated women will go on to marry and produce children within the legal bonds of matrimony, because white women aren't stupid[72]. There are enormous advantages to being married, and it remains one of the very best ways to create wealth and transfer it to the next generation. Marriage is what allows the divorce industry to flourish, so even when those smart, white ladies decide it's time to trade in for Husband 2.0, they still keep most of the families accumulated wealth.

And there is a competitive advantage to keeping the number of married, stable families limited to white ones. It's pretty easy to compete against the single mamas and fathers paying child support to six different women when you're a rich white lady married to an equally rich white dude.

Pointing out that hook-up culture is NOT a white thing, and that it is having a devastating effect on black families is not racist.

Ignoring it, all the while congratulating oneself on being so liberal and progressive, most definitely IS.

The problem is not what a bunch of drunk white sorority girls do during their downtime at college. It's how that culture takes an already problematic idea and makes it so much worse for everyone who is NOT a drunk white sorority girl. The empowered slut trope makes it virtually impossible to discuss subjects like

[72] http://www.livescience.com/8049-college-educated-women-stay-married.html

fidelity and kindness and intimacy and connection and attachment and commitment and marriage without coming off sounding like some Bible-thumping Puritan intent on shutting down all fun forever.

By and large, white folks don't NEED to discuss fidelity and kindness and intimacy and connection and attachment and commitment and marriage, because we haven't been subject to centuries of social engineering to make sure those things are almost impossible to achieve.

There are, however, some people who DO need to openly, actively, proactively and strategically discuss those topics. By shutting down that conversation, we ensure black culture continues to flail around in darkness. Feminism doesn't want black men and women to have that discussion.

Why not, ladies? Are you afraid to compete? Afraid that a culture coming out of such turmoil and devastation might discover what younger white women, having lived through the nuclear devastation of their mother's feminism are coming to understand in ever increasing numbers?

We are meant to live in harmony with one another. We are meant to have children and raise them in loving, stable families. Men and women are meant to complement, and not compete with one another. Humans are social creatures. We are meant to live in families. And the more of those families that are black, the better off we will all be. Keeping black culture in turmoil by engaging white liberal guilt is a key part of denying that families matter. That children matter. That men matter.

"Go it alone — you don't need a man"

That's a message far more black women receive, and act on, than white women. It's not racist to point that out.

It's racist NOT to.

Lots of love,

JB

Attention high school girls: please don't fall in love with a boy because that is an excellent way to get abused. Just give blowjobs instead.

Hook-up culture is STILL getting all the proper lady writers in a tizzy, and it seems like the blame for this sad state of affairs has not been laid squarely enough. It really looks an awful lot like a whole bunch of ladies are just sluts, but then again maybe the whole thing is a figment of everyone's imagination?

Hanna Roisin[73] at least takes a stab at trying to understand what it all means, and remarkably, she suggests that "people" have a fraught relationship with sex in general.

Maybe it means that people don't take sex as seriously as they used to. Maybe it means women are less afraid of it than they used to be. Maybe it means that young people have learned to incorporate sex into their definition of friendship. Maybe it means sex isn't so loaded, and doesn't put you on a path to marriage or a real relationship anymore.

73
http://www.slate.com/blogs/xx_factor/2013/08/15/hookup_culture_doesn_t_exist_new_study_shows.html?wpisrc=flyouts

Well, Hannah clearly needs to be spending more time with her fellow Double XX bloggers, because hook-up culture is far more than just "sex", my pretty. Hook-up culture is actually a very clever strategy designed to allow vulnerable young women the opportunity to escape the inevitable abuse that comes with having a relationship with an icky, violent, cootie-ridden BOY.

Yuck.

Boys.

First they infect you with their childish crudeness, then they beat the hell out of you because once you admit you like a boy, everyone knows it's punching bag city from there on out.

Right?

According to Amanda Hess, that's exactly the risk young women run when they think in terms of anything OTHER than fly-by blowjobs after gym class.

Women in their teens and 20s still face an elevated risk of abuse and assault. But confining their relationships to casual sexts instead of jumping into intense relationships could actually help girls avoid violence from their partners now and later in life.

Hess, who apparently has a sliver of conscience left when it comes to perpetuating deeply hateful stereotypes against boys in particular, admits that rape and domestic violence in the population at large are declining at precipitous rates.

...when it comes to real crimes, modern American relationships have actually become a lot less "extreme" in recent decades. Incidents of rape have declined by as much as 85 percent since the 1970s (and when they do happen, victims are more likely to report the crime). Domestic violence incidents have also dropped precipitously since the '90s.

But those menacing boys tipping from adolescence into fully realized adult manhood still scare the bejeebus out of her. Even though women can and will chuck a few head shots themselves, and plenty won't hesitate to settle their disagreements with a little bloodshed, Amanda is still deeply concerned the poor duckies might find themselves trapped in an abusive relationship with an intimate partner[74].

During the past two-and-a-half decades, official statistics suggest that female delinquency has undergone substantial changes compared with male delinquency. Between 1980 and 2005, arrests of girls increased nationwide, while arrests of boys decreased (Federal Bureau of Investigation, 2006)

Facts don't bother Amanda, though.

[Boys] are seen as predators, and girls, their prey.

Boys trapped in abusive relationships with their highschool sweethearts are shit out of luck. Man up, you pussies! Who lets a girl hit them?

What's a girl to do? Well, concentrate on school, of course. Give yourself alternatives to endless beatings at the hands of your teenage Romeo! What Juliet needs to do is shift the balance of power into HER corner.

---

[74] https://www.ncjrs.gov/pdffiles1/ojjdp/218905.pdf

...intimate partner violence also drops "as women's alternatives outside their relationships improve," they found. As women secure higher educations and increase their earning potential, they're "able to achieve self-sufficiency in the long-run." When "battered women can support themselves, they are both more likely to leave and have more power within their relationships if they stay."

And see how brilliantly hook-up culture fits into that?

Sexting is not "something that creates a very secure relationship," child development specialist Dr. Robyn Silverman tells Lauer. Kids tell her that "hook up culture makes it so they can get a competitive edge in college and high school. They're not worried about the relationship. They're focused on school and the things that matter to them."

And what things matter to kids, anyways? According to her own article, it's not the pleasures of random sex with people you barely know.

...boys "often expressed a desire for a deeper connection with girls, but felt confused about how to make it happen."

...when the boy sent her another message telling her that "he liked her," she became "intrigued" by the possibility of a real relationship with him.

Let's keep in mind that these are HIGH SCHOOL boys and girls we are talking about. Despite their own stated interests in actually exploring intimate, connected, meaningful, emotional relationships with one another – something BOTH boys and girls aspire to - Hess and her ilk continue to insist that boys really ARE predators, and girls really ARE prey. No matter how ardently, or clumsily the aspiration for a deeper connection is expressed, girls need to always keep in mind that BOYS ARE DANGEROUS.

A disgusting text from a boy is bad, but a serious commitment with the sender could be a lot more dangerous.

Some young ladies, of course, are simply not going to buy into the myth that a relationship with a boy is pretty much asking to be regularly back-handed, and the name we have for those girls is STUPID. No matter. We'll do our best to help them choose the least rotten apple!

First up, try and avoid the 50% of young men who volunteer and give back to their communities. I mean, sure, philanthropy is nice and all that, but when boys volunteer they still have to be all BOY about it, taking on physically demanding and challenging activities, and helping people younger than themselves learn about fair play and rules and winning and losing and all that sort of nonsense.

Boys were more likely to undertake physical activities such as environmental cleanup or working with younger children in sports, while girls were more likely to help the homeless and other needy people or to work with arts groups.

Boys are just practicing for the inevitable moment they will get to overpower and abuse the girls silly enough to think they are, oh, lovely, caring human beings. Don't buy the lie, ladies!

Stay away from all those boys involved in extracurricular activities, especially sports and student governance, which lead to high self-esteem and the development of leadership qualities! High self-esteem in boys can only mean they feel free to beat the crap out of their girlfriends. Predator/prey, remember[75]?

75

A considerable difference was observed between males and females in athletics and sports team participation in both school- and community-based activities. School-based extracurricular activities were appraised as most beneficial to the development of self-esteem and leadership role development.

And for heaven's sake, steer way clear of those young entrepreneurial men who are increasingly one of the driving forces of innovation and development, not just in the modern economies, but around the world! Ladies have good reasons not to dirty their pretty mitts with tough and scrabble, live or die BUSINESS.

In other words, in contrast to young men, young women are less likely to see opportunities, have a higher fear of failure and therefore, less likely to engage in entrepreneurship.

Those boys are just trying to get money and power so they can abuse their girlfriends.

Teenage boys: more likely to get involved with their communities and schools, volunteer with children, create meaningful business ventures and do the dirty work we need as a culture to survive.

Data from the U.S. Bureau of Labor statistics for all workers suggests that male workers are much more at risk than female. In 2009, 93 percent of the workers in America who died in the job were men.

- Also in July, 17-year-old plumber Benjamin Graham died in Albany, Georgia after being electrocuted while working under a home on a water pipe.

- In August, 16-year-old Damon Springer of Osgood, Ohio was struck by a bobcat frontend loader while working with his father in a family tree service company. Springer's father did not see the boy and accidentally backed into him, crushing him.

- In September, 17-year-old Stephen N. Tiller was killed when crushed by a garbage truck while working for a family-owned sanitation company. Tiller was riding in the front of a front-loading garbage truck when the truck hit some bumps and sent the boy and another worker flying in front of the truck, which then ran him over.

- In October, 16-year-old Armando Ramirez died in Lamont, California after inhaling hydrogen sulfide in a drainage tunnel at Community Recycling and Resource recycling company

Amanda Hess is rather audacious to draw an analogy between prey and predator in her writing. Does she honestly think that some of us, especially the mothers of sons, won't see the truth? These grown women who sit in air-conditioned offices with their high heels and manicures, chastising their younger counterparts not to trust or love young men are the predators.

And both young men and women are the prey.

When a grown women who presumably has a modicum of sense and humanity and understanding tells young women that random blowjobs are a good idea because hey, at least you will avoid being abused by that evil boy, it's time to question who is speaking in our culture, and what damage is being done.

The TODAY show panel talks about that like it's a bad thing, but "real relationships" don't erase the potential for abuse; in some cases, they leave girls more vulnerable to repeat offenders.

---

http://lin.ca/Uploads/cclr10/CCLR10-112.pdf

The repeat offender here isn't the hapless boy sending poorly worded texts to a girl he likes. The repeat offender is Amanda herself. The need to spin stories ever more crassly, to point blank treat young women as if they are stupid and young men as if they are monsters is telling in itself.

The cracks are beginning to show. The rhetoric of hate is becoming so amplified, it can only lead to one outcome: revolution.

The sadness of the women's movement is that they don't allow the necessity of love. See, I don't personally trust any revolution where love is not allowed.

Maya Angelou

Me either, Maya. And one revolution always follows the next.

Sooner or later.

I'm betting on sooner.

Lots of love,

JB

I went to college and there aren't enough men! Wah! I stayed home and there are too many men! Wah! Jesus, bitches, could you pick one?

So, the always lovely, always articulate Amanda Marcotte has a new post up at Slate's XX blog about how much it sucks to live in a town with men[76].

Apparently, there is an oil patch in North Dakota (who knew?!) and since working in an oil patch is scrubby, dirty, physically demanding work, there are a whole bunch of men about! Interesting that Amanda doesn't touch that little nugget, isn't it? Let's see, shitty, dirty, strenuous , back-breaking labor – of course men are doing it! For six figure incomes.

Nope, Amanda just lets that slide. What she wants to talk about is NOT the fact that the world's most difficult, demanding work is done by men, but rather the fact that these men SUCK. They move to small towns, where the work happens to be, in small Northern States (with "conservative" cultures) and suddenly whammo, blammo! They're ENTITLED to treat women as garbage. And by garbage she means "notice" and "try to talk to", which, as we all know, is what no woman wants ever. Especially not Amanda. (Hey, maybe she's a lesbian? I don't know. In which case, of course she doesn't want men to talk to her and oops, my bad. I really have no idea, though.)

[Men sucking is] a result of the heavily transitory population that comes with oil fields and the highly conservative culture of rural North Dakota, where men feel entitled to treat women like garbage in a way they don't feel—or can't express, at least—in places where "feminism" is actually thought to be a good thing.

Why, you fuckers!

---

[76] http://www.slate.com/blogs/xx_factor/2013/01/16/sex_in_the_non_city_the_dangers_of_a_small_town_where_single_men_outnumber.html

If the abundance of (crappy) men in small towns comes as a surprise to women dwelling in cities or on college campuses, well, that's because you ladies have the RIGHT SORT of men, there's just not enough of them.

And the sisterhood of sluttiness means that the RIGHT SORT of men don't have to settle down with any one woman when all the vaginas are theirs for the taking!

Oh my. Well this is a right mess, isn't it? Go to the cities, and there are not enough men. Stick to the countryside, and all the men suck. What is a lady to do?

Amanda's article is a perfect example of HYPERGAMY, (colloquially referred to as "marrying up") - the act or practice of seeking a spouse of higher looks, socioeconomic, caste or status than oneself.

These oil patch lads, well, they have money, and the work keeps them in fairly good physical shape, but they just don't have the STATUS a proper feminist wants. Most of them probably haven't even BEEN to college. Sure, they know to weld and fit a rigging and understand how couplings work, but I'll bet they have never even heard of Monique Wittig and they have no idea how completely irrelevant they are!

What these men are is, well, MEN. These do not look like the sort of essay-writing, feminist-leaning, soft-bodied boys you find on college campuses. They do not appear to be the sort of men willing to put up with a lot of shit. You spend a day on an oil rig, and I highly doubt you have plans to come home and negotiate who will be microwaving Lean Cuisine for dinner. Men who do men's work (and oil rig workers ARE men) expect to be treated like men, and to act like men, and that right there is what gets Amanda all in a tizzy.

There is one group of women who really, really love oil patch workers: prostitutes. Now there is a group of women who understand what men want and they are willing to provide it. For cash. And good for them.

Amanda doesn't like competing on those terms. And she doesn't want other women competing on those terms, either.

Hmm. I wonder why? If men can simply buy sex, then women who are interested in something more will have to offer something more!

Ladies, don't let Amanda scare you! Methinks the lady has a bad case of "I WISH men would hit on me". There is nothing wrong with small towns, nothing wrong with men who work dirty jobs (for lots of money!), and the idea that men who live in small towns feel entitled to treat women like garbage is just straight up slander.

Here's my advice: leave Amanda to her cat. They look happy together.

If you have something more to offer men than just your pussy and a bucket of sneering contempt, load up your car and head for North Dakota. And forget about wearing white for a while. Crude oil is hell to get out.

Lots of love,

JB

Katie Rolphe thinks online relationships are more real than real ones, explaining once again, why she is single.

I have a love hate relationship with Katie Roiphe, ever since she published her first book, *The Morning After: Sex, Fear and Feminism*, in which she argues, among other things, that expanding the definition of sexual assault to include any kind of sex a woman is later unhappy with ultimately results in a culture that fails to take rape seriously. Whiny, boo-hoo bitches who wake up ashamed have made it nigh unto impossible for victims of violent sexual assault to secure justice, or even just have anyone believe they didn't consent to be dragged in a back alley and raped.

One of the triumphs of feminism: when every sexual encounter can potentially be defined as rape, every man becomes a potential rapist. Schrödinger's rapist is a popular meme, playing off of Schrödinger's cat, a thought experiment in physics in which cat in a box is either dead or alive, depending upon a random interaction between subatomic particles which may or may not have triggered the release of lethal radioactivity.

The general idea captured by Schrödinger's Rapist is that every man should be treated as a rapist, no matter what the circumstances. Check out this little piece and allow me to draw attention to one passage in particular, addressed to MEN, the potential rapists:

"...you must be aware of what signals you are sending by your appearance and the environment."

Wait a minute!? Are you saying that the clothing you are wearing and your general appearance and attitude can convey signals to people that they may or may not interpret correctly?? It's neat how that applies to men, ALL MEN ALL THE TIME, but never to women.

Let's get back to Katie. In this piece at Slate[77], she argues that online flirtations and relationships conducted across a computer screen are MORE real than relationships in real life.

It's interesting that in all three examples she cites, it's the man who is the cheating, dirty, scumbag and the woman who is the innocent, unsuspecting, put-upon victim. Actually scratch that. It's not interesting at all. It's getting downright wearisome to listen to the message over and over again. Yeah, yeah, we get it Katie. Men suck.

Just what is it about cheating online that seems so much more real to Katie?

Received wisdom tells us online communications are unreal, fake, and distant, but they can, in fact, be the opposite; they can represent very intense fantasies, distilled versions of romantic yearning, including its darker, more narcissistic sides, honest articulations, for better or for worse, of the inner life.

So relationships that are REAL, according to Katie, involve intense fantasies, romantic yearning, narcissism and the inner life. Hers, one presumes.

Oh, Katie. You're operating on a set of assumptions that virtually guarantees you will never have a relationship of any length or meaning with anyone in your life.

Real relationships don't involve fantasies. They are all about facing the nitty gritty details of life with humor and cheer and compromise and most of all, an infallible sense of being together in the storm. You can't imagine away your partner's flaws, nor your own. You have to face them, and try to keep your head and stay rational and sane even when you feel like you will lose your mind if he fails once again to break down the empty cereal box before piling it up on all the other recycling.

---

[77] http://www.slate.com/articles/life/roiphe/2013/02/online_dating_is_it_more_real.html

You hear that, Mr. JB? BREAK DOWN THE BOXES. That's how you prevent an unwieldy pile of cardboard from sliding down the back stairs!

Real relationships may start with romantic yearning, but what are you yearning for? For love? Acceptance? Affection? Physical pleasure? Those things develop over time and grow more intense the longer you are together. They require the physical presence of another person and can never be replicated by a name on a screen or words on a page. Words can portray the intensity of feelings, but they cannot substitute for feelings themselves.

Narcissism and the inner life. There's the nail in the coffin, darling. The key to happy relationships that last forever is that you always, always put the other person's happiness first. And that applies to both people in a relationship. My happiness comes before his, his happiness comes before mine.

It's the opposite of narcissism. Selflessness.

For the past seventy years, feminists have been shrieking at women to reject this definition of relationships. Selflessness is just another word for oppressed. No one's happiness or well-being should come before a woman's own. The only acceptable priority for any woman is HERSELF.

How'd that work out for ya?

Poor, Katie. Sitting in her apartment, typing on her computer with her sperm donor kids out with the nanny, wondering why she doesn't have a relationship. She has all the qualifications: fantasy, yearning, narcissism and a pre-occupation with her inner life.

Like the proverbial cat in a box, wondering if she will live or die based on seemingly random events.

Here's my advice: close the computer and get out into the real world. Go and meet some real, live flesh and blood men, and when you find one you can love, make a choice: put his happiness above your own. Choose selflessness.

That's how the cat gets out alive.

Every time.

Lots of love,

JB

Sluts tend to be fat and ugly, so stick to the pretty girls, lads. Unless you want to get laid, that is.

Well, file this one under "No Shit Sherlock", but in a study published in *Biodemography and Social Biology*, Elizabeth McClintock at Notre Dame has discovered that "very physically attractive women are more likely to form exclusive relationships than to form purely sexual relationships; they are also less likely to have sexual intercourse within the first week of meeting a partner." In addition, "for women, the number of sexual partners decreases with increasing physical attractiveness, whereas for men, the number of sexual partners increases with increasing physical attractiveness." And finally, "for women, the number of reported sexual partners is tied to weight: Thinner women report fewer partners. Thinness is a dimension of attractiveness for women, so is consistent with the finding that more attractive women report fewer sexual partners[78]."

[78] http://chronicle.com/article/The-Emotional-Costs-of-Hooking/65960/

Hmmm. Pretty, thin woman seem to have some upper hand in the dating market, and they use that to secure meaningful relationships that are based on something other than just sex. Why, it's almost as if women value emotional and intellectual connections, and dislike the social pressure to have a huge number of sexual partners.

Gorgeous ladies, why aren't more of you sluts?!? Don't you know that being a slut is empowering and a sign of your personal liberation from an oppressive patriarchy that values you only in terms of your looks? You must fight this, oppression, ladies, and get out there and fuck a stable full of guys!

Because that will make you happy!

Except that it won't.

Check out this article celebrating sluts in XOJane[79].

To me there's nothing negative about being a slut. Sluts are FUN! Sluts do whatever they want, whenever they want, and they don't regret anything. Sluts dive as voraciously into sex as they do their other many passions. Sluts like their own bodies, and other people's too. Sluts are enthusiastic! Sluts will do a lot for a good story.

Sluts are confident and have great shoes. Sluts are pretty. Sluts find something to love about all different kinds of people. Sluts are brave. Sluts laugh a lot. Sluts challenge gender roles. Sluts are fearless. Sluts love adventure! Sluts will try new things without worrying about looking stupid. Sluts high-five after sex.

This is an article aimed at pre-teen girls! XOJane claims to be a magazine for 18-24 year olds (which is hardly any better), but the truth is that the website is a huge favorite amongst pre-teen and teenage girls and continues to be.

Why would a website try to dissuade an entire age group from visiting a site that caters directly to them? Why would an editor shun all teenagers after her co-worker had expressed that the site was geared towards those 18-49? (By the way, 18 is a still a teenager.) It does this for the same reason that liquor and tobacco companies claim to be targeting older age groups. Simply, the site posted irresponsible content for young women and instead of admitting that, they've decided to swear off teenagers for good. Oh, they'll continue to write content that teenagers will find interesting, but it won't be "for" teenagers.

Now add on a culture that tells young women it's perfectly fine to be fat and slovenly and that men should "like them for who they are and not what they look like", and there you have a recipe for perfect disaster.

Why do older women (and you can bet your ass that all the editors of these magazines are older women) try to convince younger women to be fat and slutty? What's in it for them?

Could it be that fat sluts increase the value of the older women dramatically? Instead of having to compete with young, thin women who prefer relationships over hook-ups, older women can corner the dating market by making sure men have no options in the younger pool. And younger men go for it in droves, because hey, fat sluts!

Men who are interested in casual sex only have a lot of options out there, but men who want something more, some deeper, more connected relationship with a woman, the landscape looks at little different. Finding a woman he can love and respect and admire and cherish is a lot harder when the market is

---

[79] http://www.xojane.com/sex/reclaiming-the-word-slut

flooded with overweight, ballbusting tramps who have no idea how lonely and bitter they are going to feel when they end up in an apartment with a cat at age 40, with no hope of a husband or children or family.

My advice for men who want more: start by looking for pretty, thin women. Those ladies know their own value, and in knowing their own, they understand yours. Attractive women are not attractive by accident. They understand and respect male desire, and that is the beginning of any meaningful relationship. Knowing that what men and women value is different, and understanding that different is not just better, it's awesome.

Fat sluts? Give them a pass if you're looking for more than a blowjob. And if sex is all you want, Christ -wear a condom! Those girls get around!

Lots of love,

JB

Valentine's Day is bullshit. Except for chocolates. I'll take those.

So the mathematical wizards over at Jezebel[80] have worked out a formula that determines how much money one has to spend on Valentine's Day to ensure sex with a paramour happens. The ladies are not just handy with numbers, people, they are wordsmiths, too. Sex is described as "going to Poundtown". How romantic.

$218

This comes in the form of dinner and presents and presumably one should bring either a calculator or the receipts in order to determine if the correct amount of cash has been outlaid to secure sex.

And needless to say, this is the MAN buying sex from a WOMAN. Split the bill on VDay?!? Surely you jest. That's not the kind of equality women are interested in. No, sir. On VDay, dudes spend their money and ladies spread their legs.

We should just start calling it Vagina Day and be done with it.

I've never been one to get overly excited about Valentine's Day and not because I'm a cynical bitch who is too clever to fall for a commercial holiday crafted by chocolate makers, florists and greeting card companies. I think that's a pretty stupid objection, actually. St, Patrick's Day, Halloween, Mother's Day, Father's Day, hell even Christmas and Easter are pretty much just straight up commercial holidays, and who cares?

They're fun!

No, my principal lack of interest in Valentine's Day stems from the fact that to me, it feels like a children's holiday. Cinnamon hearts and pink cupcakes and exchanging Valentine's at school and making hearts out of doilies and red and pink construction paper. It's lovely and fun and sweet and poignant, but it just seems like something CHILDREN do.

In our house, I'm not the one who gets in to Valentine's Day.

---

[80] http://jezebel.com/5983174/your-vagina-is-worth-about-218-on-valentines-day-youre-welcome

I've already told you the story of how I came to be in possession of a diamond engagement ring, but I also happen to be the owner of several other pieces of jewellery, all gifts from Mr. JB.

True story: When Mr. JB was a young man, working in Japan, he went on a tour of the famous Miki Moto Pearl Diving Facility and watched the divers harvest pearls and ate oysters and had romantic thoughts about the wife he had yet to meet. He wanted her to have pearl earrings to wear on her wedding day, so he purchased two matching, glossy pearls and set them aside for his one-day bride.

We met in August, and by February, we both knew that we had found our life partners. So for our first Valentine's Day, he had those pearls set and I found them under my pillow in the morning. Under his pillow, actually. We spent the night in his room. On a single bed. Christ, we must have been in love!

I did not wear them until our wedding day. I'm not good at keeping track of my things, so I gave the pearls back to him for safe-keeping, and I've only worn them a handful of times since. The thought of losing them makes me feel ill, so they live in my jewellery box, safe and sound.

At one point, Mr. JB ended up with Dr.K in Thailand, and he purchased a beautiful blue sapphire for this bride he had yet to meet, so she could wear "something old, something new, something borrowed, something blue". I found the sapphire under my pillow on our second Valentine's Day together.

So much for the idea that men don't spend any time thinking about their wedding day. The amount of minutes I have dedicated in my entire life to pondering my nuptials: ZERO. Never gave it a thought. I thought about being married, but the wedding didn't capture my imagination at all.

Valentine's Day just seems to bring out the poet in Mr. JB, and not the one that writes limericks.

And I suppose that's how I feel about Valentine's Day, in general. If it's a day you genuinely enjoy, that feels romantic, feels like a celebration of love, then by all means, carry on and have fun. Caveat: the person who cares about the day should foot the bill for it.

But if it's just a cynical, opportunistic and narcissistic way to cast yourself as the Princess in your own fairytale, then I'm not so much into it. If you're going to be a sulky cow and insist that your boyfriend/husband ruck up that $218 dollars, you're not celebrating love, you're celebrating prostitution.

And hey, why not? Go for it.

Nothing wrong with a little VDay prostitution, but don't pretend it's about love, unless by love, you mean "$218".

As always, I will find a thoughtful, lovely present under my pillow on February 14th and a romantic card with a handwritten sentiment. And in exchange, I will give Mr. JB his favorite present. The one money can't buy.

Oh wait. Scratch that. Money can buy it. From this gorgeous lady, for one[81].

But Mr.JB prefers to get his at home.

Happy Valentine's Day!

Lots of love,

---

[81] http://gracebellavue.com/

JB

Zerlina Maxwell says we need to teach men not to be sexually aggressive. All the other women say "fuck that".

Oh my! Well this was quite the little dust-up. Zerlina Maxwell, a political commentator and social media analyst, went on Hannity and put forth the suggestion that the way to solve the "rape crisis" is to teach men NOT to rape.

What a brilliant idea! We could solve a lot of problems with this advice. An epidemic of car theft? Let's line up all the men and teach them NOT to steal cars. A record number of home invasions and robbery? Line up, lads, and we'll teach you NOT to break into houses and steal other people's stuff. Skyrocketing rates of arson? Bring your lighters and cans of gasoline over here, gentlemen. We're gonna teach you how to NOT burn shit down.

Now, now. I realize that only a small percentage of men steal cars, break and enter and start fires, but that really isn't a relevant fact. SOME men do, so that means we need to treat ALL men as if they do. Some women are up to that kind of craziness, too, but shush now. We're not talking about them.

Here is Zerlina's strategy for teaching men not to be rapists:

Teach young men what the word consent means. You know, your average fifth grader knows what that word means, but let's start with the assumption that men are just straight up stupid. And never mind the fact that the vast majority of men are not sexually violent. Ah, yes. An excellent start.

Teach young men to see women's humanity, instead of seeing them as sexual objects there for male pleasure. Make sure your humanity is visible under your push-up bra and don't step on it with those 4 inch stilettos!

Teach young men how to express healthy masculinity. Which will be defined by women, of course.

Teach young men to believe women who come forward and not to blame the victim. And always buy that time-share condo in Florida. Those people never lie!

Teach young men about bystander intervention. Dudes, you MUST notice each and every lady that appears to be in distress and immediately leap from your white steed and charge to her rescue. Because equality.

Hey about we spin that around and make a list for WOMEN on how not to get raped?

Teach young women what the words implied consent mean. If you leave the keys in the ignition of your car, the law takes that as your implied consent to have people steal your car. We're working on teaching people NOT to steal cars, but so far, no luck.

If you get really trashed, start making out with a man, go to his room, remove your clothes, then change your mind AND DON'T SAY ANYTHING, you have implied consent. Claiming you were "paralyzed with fear" is bullshit. If you have changed your mind, you have to SAY that. Otherwise your actions have implied consent. You can't wake up the next day and decide you were raped.

Teach young women to see men's humanity, instead of seeing them as sexual objects there to flatter female vanity. Women don't wear low-cut tops and miniskirts and high heels or tousle their hair and put on make-up and expect men to ignore them. Not a fucking chance. Women do those things to signal their sexual status to OTHER women, and to try and attract the highest quality man.

Instead of ranking men according to what they can provide, how about you just start treating them like people, with a wide range of interests and talents and personalities? Stop chasing after those star football players and you might find they stop treating you like a status whore.

Teach young women how to express healthy femininity. It begins by accepting responsibility for the choices you make, good and bad. You need to understand that the circumstances of your birth or your socialization are EXPLANATIONS for why you find some things difficult, and not EXCUSES that allow you to blame others for your own decisions. I really don't give a fuck if your Mama socialized you to defer to every man at all times. You are a grown-up and you figure out how to work around what your Mama gave you. That's what being a grown-up MEANS. If you're that much of an emotional cripple that you can't speak your own mind, you shouldn't be interacting with anyone other than your cat and your therapist.

Teach young women not to lie about being raped. And no, not because false accusers make it difficult for other women to be believed. It's actually really easy to convict someone of a crime: have some evidence. Voila!

You don't lie about being raped because you are RUINING another person's life. False accusations carry a social stigma far greater than any stigma a rape victim will face in her life. It's one of the shittiest things you can do to a man. So don't. End of story.

Teach young women they do not have an automatic right to male protection. While it's awfully nice to have the protection of men who will intervene on your behalf, there is no way in hell any woman should go through life thinking she is entitled to that protection. There are things you can do to protect yourself from distressing situations, and you have some responsibility to do so. You can take reasonable precautions to prevent assault, robbery, car theft … any number of crimes. And yes, you can take steps to prevent rape.

Ultimately, Zerlina wants us, as a culture, to teach men to be "less sexually aggressive". You want that Zerlina, and pretty much NO ONE ELSE,

Guess who is still required to make the first move? Guess who is waiting to be approached? Guess who has to take the emotional risk of rejection[82]? Guess who is passive? And who is aggressive?

A great majority of women, 93%, preferred to be asked out -- only 6% preferred to do the asking. The majority of men preferred to do the asking, 83%, while 16% preferred to be asked out on a date. It is interesting that more men preferred to be asked out (16%) than there were women who preferred to do the asking (6%). That difference suggests that 10% of men may be waiting quite a while for a woman to ask them out on a first date.

The truth is that both men and women like and expect men to be sexually aggressive. While no one (one seriously hopes) wants to see that aggression taken to the extreme of rape, the suggestion that we can fix "rape culture" by making men less aggressive runs exactly contrary to what we actually WANT and DO.

The death and rape threats Zerlina received after making her statements are disgusting, and no matter how stupid or ill-conceived her ideas are, she doesn't deserve to be gang-raped for them! Let's point out that her

---

[82] http://www.psychologytoday.com/blog/the-how-and-why-sex-differences/201104/why-dont-women-ask-men-out-first-dates

ideas are based on some completely hateful stereotypes about men, and that her suggestions run exactly counter to what we want, but we'll draw the line at rape threats.

And that's an equal opportunity line. Most of my rape threats come from women, so let's join hands together and teach both men and women NOT to make rape threats on the internet.

Isn't that so much better?

Lots of love,

JB

Sex contracts? Sounds like so much fun. How do you enforce defaults?

Tracey Cox, who writes a sex advice column at the Daily Mail has some advice for couples who aren't having the amount of sex they would like[83]: what you need to do is think about all the things your partner considers romantic or seductive and then set the stage so that you can deliver those things, whatever they are. If flowers and candlelight are the things that make your partner's heart beat faster, then pick some up on your way home and turn the lights off when you get there.

If your partner finds it hot that you sit beside him on the couch watching footie, wearing nothing but his favorite team jersey, well, put the kids to bed and find a game to watch.

The key thing is to put your partner's pleasure above your own, and use his or her preferences to encourage a little more time spent pursuing one of life's great pleasures.

No, silly, that's not how you have more sex with your partner. What you NEED to do is think about what YOU want, and then write a detailed contract specifying all the particulars and then you both need to SIGN THAT CONTRACT (blood is optional, apparently) because nothing says "I love you darling and want to have sex with you" quite like the concept of CONTRACTUAL OBLIGATION.

Sigh.

So romantic.

Usually, contracts come with some penalty for defaulting. That opens up a lot of possibilities, doesn't it?

You know, I can't quite figure out where the caricature of the modern career lady as a dour shrew sucking the joy out of everything comes from?

And it seems that you can use this technique of contractual obligations for more than one aspect of life and love, too. Look! Jezebel has instructions for *How to Make a Dude Sweep the Kitchen Floor (Correctly), Without You Even Having to Tell Him*[84].

Make him!

[83] http://www.dailymail.co.uk/femail/article-2292519/Would-sex-contract-work-FEMAIL-sexpert-Tracey-Cox-thinks-so.html

[84] http://jezebel.com/5989991/from-the-dept-of-finally-how-to-make-a-dude-sweep-the-kitchen-floor-correctly-without-you-even-having-to-tell-him

Correctly!

Mindlessly!

Wow. Life with these ladies sounds like so much fun.

Here is just SOME of Jezebel's list of considerations:

Do I do half of the laundry and half of the dishes every day?

Do I buy half of the clothes and toys?

Do I take on half of the management of my care providers?

Do I write half of the lists and notes?

Do I wake up in the middle of the night to calm the baby half of the time?

Do I change half of the diapers?

Do I plan half of the travel?

Do I track half of the household budget?

Do I put the kids to bed half of the time?

Do I make half of the grocery, sports, and afterschool lesson runs?

Do I write half of the e-mails to my kids' teachers?

Do I watch the kids for half of the weekend and for half of every weeknight?

Seems like they forgot something, no?

DO I EARN HALF THE MONEY THAT COMES INTO THE HOUSE?

DO I WORK HALF THE HOURS IT TAKES TO EARN THAT MONEY?

This just leaves me with my head shaking. In what world does this make sense?

Women work fewer hours

At idiotic jobs (Hello, File Clerk! – Good job knowing your alphabet! Yay!)

That require little to no physical effort

Make less money

And still demand the right to define what gets done in a house and by whom.

Here's an easy way to add more sex to your marriage: stop being such an irrational witch and do the damn housework yourself!

You know what really confuses me? Why do men marry these women? How is it even possible that they HAVE husbands? What do men get out of relationships with these women? Contractual sex, a shit ton of housework, and the thankless task of bringing home more money and working more hours at more physically demanding jobs.

I think I'd rather be single.

Short post today – my kids are off school for the week and they are trashing the joint. I won't be setting up any Excel spreadsheets to make sure I have correctly bitched out Mr. JB for not doing exactly half of all this additional work.

Oh, and I'll probably get laid tonight, too.

Lots of love,

JB

Hey, Ivy League ladies: If you want to marry up, you need to marry young, so get out there and nail down a freshman!

A bunch of Princeton ladies went to a careers advice lunch with some older Princeton Lady Alum, hoping for some direction and inspiration and they ended up talking about …. men, marriage and children.

Of course they did. This inspired Susan Patton to write an article for the *Daily Princetonian*, urging young women at Princeton to get married while at college, because they would never again have such a pool of worthy men to choose from. And Susan quite rightly points out that earlier is better. As a freshman, you have the classes above you to choose from, but each year, the senior class graduates, removing them from the fish barrel, and you yourself will advance a year, meaning the new incoming class is now out of reach.

If a lady waits until her senior year to snag that solitaire, she has only the senior class of males to choose from, while those males still have ALL the classes and those hot little bitches entering their freshman year are some kind of competition!

I'm being a bit snarky here, but I actually think Susan's advice is spot on. If you WANT to marry and have children, it's best to do that while you are young. You can launch your career later, after your children are safely off to school. Very sensible.

What gets my hackles up is the idea that it is only behind the walls of an ivied tower that you are going to find men worthy of a lady from Princeton. That the only men worth considering are those above you in the social order. It may be true that ONLY a man from Princeton could possibly endure the snotty, snobby, so fucking full of yourself personality disorders that seem to plague the ladies from Ivy League schools, but that just means Ivy League ladies are snobby, snotty cunts.

Here's my favorite comment from the Jezebel spin on Susan's article, from a commenter who calls herself SingleLeaguer (she'll probably be able to keep that handle permanently):

I've literally had the following interaction with men on multiple occasions:

(After a sustained period of flirting)

Him: So, where did you go to school?

Me: I went to Yale. You?

Him: Oh wow. Well, it's been nice talking to you. (Walks away)

That's what my friends and I like to call the Y-Bomb.

And this may sound snobby, but often times it's a lot easier for me to relate to men who were also Ivy Leaguers. It may stem from our similar academic background, or because I know that we're not going to have that above interaction. And where is it easiest to find a large pool of eligible, heterosexual Ivy League men? At your Ivy League school.

Oh wow. You dropped the Y-Bomb, did you? I wonder if she knows the Y stands for yappy: as in an annoying little yutz that jabbers stupidly and shrilly.

It's incredible that she can't see how her "I went to Yale, see how much better I am than you" conversational style might send the lads running, but so be it. I guess when you major in nuclear physics, you get to think yourself a bit better than average, no?

Oh now wait a second. Nuclear physics? Hahahahahahah!

Nope. Women at Yale are primarily enrolled in Arts and Humanities programs. 58% of all Humanities degrees in 2010 were conferred on women.

67% of the English degrees

87% of the Art History degrees

84% of the Religious Studies degrees

70% of the Anthropology degrees

You know what you say to someone who graduated with an Art History degree from Yale?

Venti 1 pump caramel, 1 pump white mocha, 2 scoops vanilla bean powder, extra ice frappuchino with 2 shots poured over the top (apagotto style) with caramel drizzle under and on top of the whipped cream, double cupped.

Hope she's smart enough to get that on the first run. Also, I fucking hate wankers who order shit like this at Starbucks. Yeah, yeah, we get it. You're sooooooooooooooooo unique and special.

Okay, that's not fair. There are SOME clever gals at Yale.

29% of Economics degrees were conferred on women

40% of Political Science degrees

33% of Biomedical Engineering degrees

17% of Geology and Geophysics degrees

0% of Chemical Engineering degrees (oops!)

0% of Mechanical Engineering degrees (double oops!)

But wait!!

87.5% of Women's Studies degrees were conferred on women.

Clearly, the ladies at Yale rock! So much smarter than the boys! So much more accomplished. Why it's obvious that any man at Yale wants a Yale lady for his own!

Let's look at the value conferred by those degrees. The average humanities graduate earns $35 000. The average engineering graduate earns $59 000. If you're looking to marry up, you'll have to bypass all those boys with humanities and head straight for the engineers. Too bad there are so few of them.

Only 8% of Yale undergrads are male engineers. Boo!

What is a lady to do?

Oh my! Look at this. The average salary for a man with a trade is $55 000! Why that's almost the same as an engineer.

What, you mean those grubby, dirty, tool-belt wearing Neanderthals who probably don't know a malbec from a syrah and couldn't quote Blake if their lives depended upon it?

When my mother died I was very young,

And my father sold me while yet my tongue

Could scarcely cry " 'weep! 'weep! 'weep! 'weep!"

So your chimneys I sweep & in soot I sleep.

William Blake, Songs of Innocence, 1789

I wouldn't count on those men not knowing any poetry. One of the most manly guys I know can recite Robert Frost for you at the drop of a hat. While hanging drywall. Wearing a toolbelt.

The institutionalized cultural snobbery against men who work at physically demanding jobs has a lot to do with an institutionalized hatred of all things masculine. In the End of Men, Hanna Roisin writes:

What if the modern, postindustrial economy is simply more congenial to women than to men? For a long time, evolutionary psychologists have claimed that we are all imprinted with adaptive imperatives from a distant past: men are faster and stronger and hardwired to fight for scarce resources, and that shows up now as a drive to win on Wall Street; women are programmed to find good providers and to care for their offspring, and that is manifested in more- nurturing and more-flexible behavior, ordaining them to domesticity. This kind of thinking frames our sense of the natural order. But what if men and women were fulfilling not biological imperatives but social roles, based on what was more efficient throughout a long era of human history? What if that era has now come to an end? More to the point, what if the economics of the new era are better suited to women?

It's a seductive siren call for women who really, truly, deep down believe that women are better than men, and that if only women were in charge of everything, the world would be a better place. Women who desperately want to believe that men are irrelevant and useless and will be trampled into dirt by the ides of March sweeping across the landscape.

The same women who walk into their dark houses, built by men out of materials invented, acquired and crafted by men, who flip a switch on the wall and expect electricity to magically be there while they congratulate themselves on their economic superiority.

Let's just consider the power grid and nothing else. The US is facing a crisis with nearly 45% of power grid engineers heading for retirement within the next few years.

Who works to maintain the power grids?

Yep. That would be men. And that isn't going to change any time soon. Go back and look at the Yale data again. 0% of the 2010 graduates in Mechanical Engineering were women. Not one. Not one single one.

Across all production and craft industries, 91% of the workforce is male.

And that isn't going to change, either. What IS changing is that younger men have abandoned a lot of the traditional male occupations for the kinds of cushy jobs that women like and admire and do not find threatening, which has resulted in a severe labor shortage for skilled trades and craftsmen.

That is driving the price of skills and trades through the roof, which is an excellent thing. Those higher wages will bring more men back to the trades.

So chicky who dropped the Y bomb on that guy in the bar? I hope he wasn't a power grid worker, because you just lost your shot at a man who brings home the bank. It's probably lucky for him, though. I'm pretty sure that after he spends a day climbing up utilities poles in shitty weather, he isn't going to listen to you piss and moan about whose turn it is to do the laundry after you've spent the day filing shit alphabetically for some man with your art history degree.

Even if it is from Yale.

Men who work hard want one reward for that: a woman who appreciates him, sees that he works hard, and makes dinner.

Yep. It's pretty much that simple. You want to really drop a bomb on that guy? Finish the night with a back rub and sex.

I'll bet they don't teach that at Yale though.

Lots of love,

JB

Yoo hoo! Hey all you career ladies with no time for a husband! And all you single mamas! And all you older ladies hitting the wall! I have the solution to all your man-hunting woes!

If you're on the market for some serious scientific data to support your hypotheses about various types of human behavior (or anything else, for that matter), you need only look as far as Yahoo! They do surveys! With people! They met on the Internet! Why don't we just let Yahoo take charge of ALL the science!?!

Take this "study[85]", for example: more than 40 per cent of single men and women simply don't have time to search out their soul-mates.

Hey, n = 1000. Good enough!

Okay, I'm just poking fun at my source material, but there is quite a bit of conversation surrounding the fact that high-powered careers leave little time for the pursuit of happiness, and this is a cause of consternation amongst the ladies in particular. Why, some of them even feel guilty for thinking that a relationship with a man might be nice!

God forbid you should suggest that women use their time at college to look for a husband though! That's just straight up oppression and misogyny!

Never mind that fact that college educated men aren't the only ones worth pursuing! Sssssh. We're not talking about that. NO MEN EVER are worth pursuing. If life isn't about YOU and ONLY YOU, you're doing it wrong.

And it doesn't get any easier for single moms, either. In some shocking news, ladies who come with more baggage than Heathrow's Terminal One have a hard time snagging (the next) Mr. Right. Nothing says "Pick me! Pick me!" like a long string of really poor decisions and a complete lack of self-reflection.

And once you reach that "certain age" and are hitting the wall in terms of looks and fertility, well, oof! The search for Prince Charming just took a turn to GoodFuckingLucksVille.

The key to dating after 35 is to treat the entire process as a kind of mergers and acquisitions deal.

Greenwald is the hottest thing to hit America's dating scene since Sex and the City. She is a slick graduate of the elite Harvard Business School who believes the ruthless rules of commerce can be applied to the hunt for a mate. Out go roses, chocolates and eyes meeting across a crowded room. In come 'branding' and 'marketing'. Romance may not be dead inside this room, but it certainly seems to have gone corporate.

Oh my god, that is so romantic! I can see the men lining up for a shot at one of these lasses. The queue must go right around the block, assuming we're talking about a lego block.

But never fear ladies! JudgyBitch is here to share her incomparable brilliance relating to bag of rocks stupid women who have no clue what men want or what will make them happy.

The solution to all your man-hunting woes is....

POLYGAMY!

Bear with me now.

Let's start with the busy busy busy worker bees. Life is long, but the days are short, dammit, and there is just no realistic way to work 60 hour weeks as the senior editor of a fashion magazine (or whatever pointless fucking thing you're doing, because it sure as hell isn't likely to be curing cancer), fit in trips to the salon and the masseuse, get to yoga class, have drinks with the girls three nights a week, do some shopping, attend mandatory therapy sessions, update your Pinterest board and your status on Facebook AND have time for a man, too.

It's just too much. Overwhelming! And obviously, you need priorities. But the solution is so simple! Let's say you, and two or three of your best girls, get together with your laptops and compile your perfect man.

---

[85] http://www.dailymail.co.uk/femail/article-184511/Workaholics-busy-love.html

Locate the qualities that overlap in your mutual lists (Venn diagrams are helpful), and then find yourselves a man that meets at least one criteria for each of you and SHARE THAT MAN LIKE A LEMON MERINGUE PIE.

It's a win-win situation. You all have money and can take care of your own bills. Maybe you could chuck a cardboard box in the bottom of one of the closets for him to keep some stuff in on the days he's YOUR husband, although a sturdy backpack might be a better option. He doesn't need to leave ANY shit at your place at all.

Men like variety, and have been known to get really sick of putting up with women's shit on a day to day basis, and since you're all special and unique individuals, it's unlikely you'll all be pulling the exact SAME shit, so he gets a welcome break (not from shit, just from YOUR shit).

Shouldn't be too much work to write an algorithm that allows each of you to have one weekday and one weekend day with your husband, and for the rest of the time, you are as free as a little jaybird!

Win-win, and you're welcome!

Now, for the single mothers. Well, you have all gone and fucked yourselves quite nicely. But hope is not lost! Polygamy can work for you, too! You're probably going to be in need of a little cash to go with your shared sausage, so you'll be hunting for a different sort of man. He'll need to be rich, or at least capable of supporting you partially, in addition to his first wife and family.

If you're living in a trailer park in Arkansas, we're not talking Donald Trump. A good solid middle class salary ought to suffice. Sadly, you won't have the same kind of equality of status that the career ladies have. You'll have to settle for being the lesser wife. Hierarchies suck, especially when you're at the bottom, but you probably should have considered that BEFORE you decided to become a single mama.

You'll have to focus on the BENEFITS. First, your children will have some sort of male role model, and you should never, ever discount the importance of that. Children need their fathers, and if they can't have their OWN fathers, then someone else's will have to do. It's better than nothing. Second, you'll have some help with the bills. Becoming a single mother goes hand in hand with poverty, but apparently the meaning of the word poverty has been lost somewhere in translation, because millions of women continue to opt for that life, for both themselves and their children.

And third, you will have a real, honest to god, flesh and blood husband! You won't have him full time obviously, and your scheduled times will be at the whim of the primary wife, but again, it's better than nothing. Think of how nice it will be for your husband, who doesn't have to worry about all the bullshit intricacies and the tangled webs of infidelity and stepping out. He can step out whenever he likes! With his OTHER wife!

And if you're smart, you'll be sure to suck up hard to the Primary Wife, because she just might decide to babysit while you have your time with your shared husband. How perfect is that? Father figure for your child, a little extra cash, a man of your (sort of) own and a built in babysitter.

I'm a goddamn genius, I tell you.

And now for the older ladies. The lonely cougars with aching ovaries who just left the whole husband and kids thing a little too late. Polygamy is your blessing, too. Like the single mamas, you will have to accept a slightly downgraded status in terms of where you rank on the wife scale, but that's not such a big price to pay, is it? The alternative is life as a cat lady, so I think not.

The older ladies, provided they have minded the shape of their ass and have cultivated at least SOME sexual skills can bring the pleasures of variety to a man minus all the difficulties of infidelity, and they have an outside shot at confirming his virility by producing that last heir. And it's not like you'd be a single mother, for goodness sakes! Being a second (or third, or fourth) wife is still being a wife.

Polygamy: just one giant win! The ladies get a man, and all the benefits that come with that, and the men get a variety of booties to hit without all the drama that comes with cheating. Obviously, there won't be any drama of any kind in these sorts of arrangements, right? What could the source of conflict be? Maybe some scheduling squabbles? Well, Christ, a good iPhone app can deal with that. If McDonald's can get that Happy Meal on the tray in under three minutes, you can figure out how to divide your time between a couple of families.

Divorced folks do it all the time, just without the benefits of continued sex. Easy peasy. And if you think this whole post has just been one giant joke, you need to read this:

Polygamy is the new face of Britain. Can the rest of the Western world be far behind?

What can possibly go wrong? Riddle me that.

Lots of love,

JB

Ladies, stop being so mean to sluts. Sluts make excellent friends! Said no woman ever, including other sluts.

Poor, sad, lonely little sluts of the world – what are we going to do with them? All their hard work, banging random men they meet in bars, and what does it get them? Well, other than outstanding blowjob techniques, I mean. The rewards of vagina slinging are denied to the slutty ladies who have racked up 20 partners (or more!), and this is clearly a problem.

Zhana Vrangalova, a graduate student in the field of human development in the College of Human Ecology at Cornell University (hope she's looking forward to a long career at Starbucks) asked a bunch of women if they thought they might like to be friends with a real, bona fide, the password to my pussy is PASSWORD, sluts.

Eh, no. Even other sluts don't like sluts.

Gosh! I wonder why?

"Sexually permissive women are ostracized for being 'easy,' whereas men with a high number of sexual partners are viewed with a sense of accomplishment," Vrangalova said. "What surprised us in this study is how unaccepting promiscuous women were of other promiscuous women when it came to friendships – these are the very people one would think they could turn to for support."

She added that prior research shows that men often view promiscuous women as unsuitable for long-term romantic relationships, leaving these women outside of many social circles. "The effect is that these women are really isolated," Vrangalova said[86].

---

[86] http://medicalxpress.com/news/2013-05-women-promiscuous-female-peers-friends.html

Oh dear. Well this is terrible news. Nobody likes a slut. Not even other sluts. Of course, Jezebel has to jump on the bandwagon, defending sluts from all the big meanies who think sluts are disgusting, disease ridden scourges on the sexual landscape.

And true to form, they get the details of the actual study dead wrong.

Nine out of ten women surveyed listed promiscuity as a negative trait in another woman, while men were more lax about this attribute in the female profile.

Nope. Men didn't read the women's profiles. Only same-sex friendships were explored. #sorrysluts

Men with a higher number of sex partners favored men who had less experience, but specified that it was due to evolutionary mate-guarding.

Nope. Men with a high number of sexual partners did NOT prefer less experienced men in eight out of ten tested attributes. Men preferred less experienced men as friends on TWO attributes: mate guarding and dislike of sexuality.

Possibly because less sexually experienced friends are less likely to make a play for your girlfriend? "Mate-guarding". Such a confusing term. So difficult to make out what that might mean. Science is hard!

Jezebel doesn't even get the sample size correct. 751, not 721. Come on now, Barbie. You just had to READ the number. It's not like you had to count to 751 all by yourself.

Why do I read this shit?

Here is what I find interesting about the research: it refers to prior research that indicates men do not consider sexually promiscuous women suitable long term romantic partners. And again, this is what irritates the crap out of me about writers like the Jezebel ladies or Amanda Marcotte, who will cheer loud and hard for slutty sluts slutting it up, and ignore the fact that there are consequences for women's behaviour.

Consequences most women will not like.

I honestly have no problem with sluts. If fucking a boatload of random men is your idea of fun, have at it. It's your life, you do as you please. What I HATE is when women who really are not the least bit slutty listen to all the lies (coming from other women) about how empowering and liberating treating your sexuality like a commodity can be.

And it's mostly young women who believe it. They listen to their older sisters and older women in the media and then act contrary to their instincts because they do not understand THEY ARE BEING LIED TO. And none of the big-mouthed ladies will mention that, oh, yeah, along with feeling like a total piece of garbage after sex with a man whose name you barely remember, you will be socially ostracized and considered an inappropriate romantic partner.

Go ahead and wear your slutty school uniforms, little ladies. You should do whatever the hell you want, at all times, and damn the consequences!

It's funny that Amanda uses the words "self-respect" because that is exactly what encouraging slutty behaviour in young women does NOT do. In order to respect yourself, you have to know yourself, and then go ahead and behave in a way that respects what you know. If you honestly, genuinely are capable of completely separating sex and emotion, and it's just straight up physical pleasure for you and nothing more, then go ahead and hump away.

Biologically, that is simply not true for most women. The simple act of hugging a man causes a spike in oxytocin levels, the hormones that promote bonding. Guess what else? Oxytocin has the EXACT SAME EFFECT ON MEN. Indeed, men produce greater amounts of the love hormone than women in response to sexual activities.

It has been assumed that women have higher levels of oxytocin than men do. While the hormone estrogen does indeed make women more susceptible to increased oxytocin, studies show that men produce greater amounts of the hormone during intimate activities such as hugging, kissing and intercourse.

So Slut Culture doesn't just lie to and about women; it lies to and about men, as well.

Sex connects humans to one another emotionally. That is a simple biological reality. Sluts violate reality by denying the emotional connection between sexual partners. This hurts women deeply, and most of them will come to regret their sluttiness.

Sluts also hurt men by acting as if men have no emotional investment in sex. Men learn to shut down their emotional connection with promiscuous women, and the effect lasts a long, long time, something sluts don't seem to understand.

In the words of Dr. Dre, you can't make a ho a housewife.

Now this this is one of them occasions

where the homies not doin it right

I mean he found him a hoe that he like

But you can't make a hoe a housewife

And when it all boils down you gonna find in the end

a bitch is a bitch, but a Dogg is a man's best friend

So what you found you a hoe that you like

But you can't make a hoe a housewife (wife)

So why should sluts in particular dislike other sluts? Because it's like looking in a mirror. A promiscuous woman knows that she is untrustworthy, and she knows that she is not respecting herself. When she sees another promiscuous women, she understands that such a woman will make a terrible friend.

It's not about competition. It's about self-reflection. Sluts don't like what they see in the mirror.

And neither does anybody else.

Sluts: ashamed of themselves. As they should be.

Lots of love,

JB

All teenage girls need advanced training to understand they are NOT sexually entitled to their male classmates.

Lately, the scandals just keep on coming about teenage girl's sexual harassment of their male classmates. The headlines bring up a number of questions (in addition to a rising feeling of nausea) about female sexual predation: Are young women biologically, unstoppably, wired for sexual aggression? Or are they only sexually volatile if the culture where they grew up or where they do their work supports ideas about the sexual domination and objectification of men?

OK, we already know a lot about the answer to this question. Yes, there is some biological underpinning for female sexual aggression but also young women will have different sexual beliefs and behaviors based on their early models (both family and friends): whether or not they had close relationships with brothers or male friends, and whether they have been exposed to a culture of respect or disdain for men.

Young women are not helpless slaves to their DNA or their hormones. Your average Mom or girlfriend is not surreptitiously videotaping men in a school shower. On the other hand, a female teacher at an area highschool has been accused of doing just that, and taken with the variety of sexual offenses that seem to be epidemic in highschools, one might reasonably assume that there is a vulnerability in a certain kind of woman, in a certain kind of environment, for foul sexual behavior. (Can men be guilty of similar sexual trespass, yes, but it is rare, and not systemic in any institution.)

This proclivity for ignoring men's right to choose who sees them naked or who has sex with them is a manifestation of an unhealthy gender culture in highschools, but it isn't unique to that institution. Many women still believe that their sexual appetite is irresistible, and that sexual access to men, by any means necessary, is a natural, even inalienable, right of women. Tempt women by putting men in a girl's club, and what do you expect?

I am not too sympathetic with this line of reasoning. If we follow its logic to its natural conclusion, we'll need to cover up young men everywhere, institute American purdah and get teenage boys out of the public eye so that young women can harness their sexuality and focus on their educations. But that isn't going to happen.

Then what will it take to end this seemingly endless parade of scantily clad young women who harass and undermine their male classmates? I think we need a serious re-education program for all teenage women. Most young women will not have reviewed their sexual values or thought about why they feel or act the way they do in sexual situations before they enter highschool.

But particularly as more women enter traditionally male subject areas (STEM), young women need to learn more about their own sexual psyche and why they may have feelings of aggression, entitlement or expect sexual privileges. I am not so naive that I believe a program or series of programs will change all women into ladies, but it will change many of them into safer colleagues and partners. Those women who can't be respectful need to be expelled from school.

This isn't an immediate fix. These kinds of programs would have to be instituted for every woman at every grade level throughout each year of highschool. Why? Because let's face it: You can only have so many cases of foxes guarding the hen house until you know that contempt for men's sexual rights is threaded through the leadership as well as the rank and file.

Tell me how several women, who were in charge of sexual harassment policy, were implicated in sex harassment? What kind of careful selection process for those jobs would have produced the result of the enforcer becoming the offender?

Ultimately the debate over women's true sexual nature is of minimal importance. I don't care if we can prove that women are horny by nature; civic and social life is by definition unnatural. We all have to learn how to work with our desires and operate in ways that respect everyone's integrity and safety. If we change the gender culture in highschools by changing women's hearts and minds, their sexual "nature" won't be a problem.

Now take out every reference to "highschool" and replace it with "the military". Take every reference to "women" and replace it with "men", and you have word for word, Pepper Schwartz's attack on all military men published on CNN[87]. These are the same men, by the way, whose blood and strength and sacrifice have made it possible for Pepper to sit in her cushy office with her perfect manicure complaining that men are shitty and they suck and they all need to be rounded up in a big group and subjected to massive brainwashing so they can grasp just HOW shitty they really are, and how much they really DO suck.

On behalf of the 285 000 men buried at Arlington Cemetery, I have this to say: fuck you, Pepper Schwartz.

Fuck you so hard.

Lots of love,

JB

Is there no subject feminist writers can't turn into a bitchfest? Now there are gender rules for where you have to sit on a date.

I don't know why I clicked on this story at Slate today. The image came to my mind of a call girl, sitting against a bar, looking for a man who might be in need of some company.

I personally have never sat at the bar on a date with someone, but it's been a long time since I went on a date, so what the hell do I know?

True Story: my first "date" with Mr. JB (as in he called me up and asked me if I wanted to have dinner with him) took place in the men's washroom of our student residence.

We lived in a four story dormitory and the Graduate Students (who tended to be older than the undergrads) were all housed on the top floor. The whippersnappers who lived beneath us dubbed the fourth floor "The Geriatric Ward" and were constantly putting up signs admonishing others to be quiet because Elderly People Sleeping.

When you're eighteen, twenty-five seems like a lifetime away! The little jerks.

Mr. JB has a hidden talent for hair cutting, and he was running a barbershop in the men's room, taking his payment in the form of liquid assets, AKA beer. It was a price a lot of our fellow students were prepared to pay. He had intended for us to go to the campus bar and have natchos or cheeseburgers or something else equally elegant, but his customers kept showing up and when he had to choose between taking me to a proper sit-down eatery and forgoing beer, well, that was a no-brainer.

Beer, obviously.

---

[87] http://www.cnn.com/2013/05/24/opinion/schwartz-military-sex/index.html?hpt=hp_bn7

Someone was doing a McDonald's run and popped their head in to see if we wanted anything, and that ended up being our dinner. I sat on the counter in the men's washroom with my feet in the sink, eating a Quarter Pounder and watching Mr. JB cut hair and collect beer.

I'm not sure the last guy got the best haircut of his life, but it sure was cheap!

Okay, let's jump into this Slate slime[88]! It's a short article, but packed with so much vacuous cuntiness that I can't resist. The lovely Katy Waldman in italics.

Last week, an Atlantic Wire piece explained all about the beauty of eating at the bar when you're alone. Not having to stare at the empty seat across from you reduces existential angst, it said. You enjoy better access to drinks and conversation via the bartender. You don't feel rushed, or guilty for taking up an entire table. All true, all pretty obvious. The more difficult claim—one the writer breezed right by—is that there is an equivalent beauty to eating at the bar when you're on a date.

"It's less depressing eating alone at the bar. When you're eating alone at a table with only an empty chair to look at, you have visual proof of how lonely and cold this world is. The bar gives you a brief distraction from this depressing reality,"

How cold and lonely this world is. Or how unlikeable and friendless you are? I could see if you just moved to town, you might experience a bit of loneliness, but if you begin with the assumption that you are not entitled to companionship in this world, and that in order to be appealing to other people, you need to consider their needs and likes and wants, that whole "no one to share a meal with" problem should disappear.

We'll keep that sense of entitlement firmly in mind.

The greatness of this seating arrangement cannot be overstated: The two of you are looking at something besides each other, which can provide conversational fodder. ("That bartender sure has moves." "Did you ever see the movie Cocktail?" "Ugh, what happened to Tom Cruise? He had so much promise!" And so on.)

So, you are on a date with another actual human, but you prefer not to actually have to look at this human. Hmmm. Interesting strategy to encourage connection and intimacy.

You wish to have a conversation, but not based on your observations about how the other person is responding or how much enthusiasm they show for a particular subject. Something superficial and trite fits the order of the day. Ooooooooookay.

You are more likely to get away with having something stuck in your teeth, or quietly spilling water on yourself, or dropping your silverware, in the forgiving ambit of his peripheral vision.

God forbid you should stop thinking about yourself for ten seconds all at once. My teeth! How are my teeth? Check your reflection in the bar mirror. How's your hair? Is your lipstick smudged? Is that push-up bra delivering the promised boobage? Maybe a little discreet lift and tuck is in order?

Me me me me me me me me me me me ….meeeeeeeee!

God, it must be exhausting to think about yourself so much.

---

[88] http://www.theatlanticwire.com/entertainment/2013/07/beauty-eating-bar/67135/

The side-by-side posture is both equalizing and intimate—and if he's a dud, you might be able to catch a glimpse of the game while pretending to "get to know him." (Or he might do the same to you, in which case, eating at the bar is bullshit.) But the best part of perching with your date at the bar is that it allows you to circumvent the gender seating wars.

I'm sorry, but why are even on a date if your intention is to watch the game while pretending to "get to know him"? The outright declaration that you don't really have any interest in this person as a human being is a little creepy, to be frank. He better be valuing YOU as a human though - that game only plays one way.

The fact that Katy can see where she sits as a "gender war" really says pretty much everything we need to know about her, doesn't it? You're on a date with someone you don't really want to look at, you don't want to have any deep conversation with, you don't particularly want to "get to know", you can't stop thinking about yourself and how you appear and where you sit is a declaration of war!

How does this woman ever get a date in the first place?

An unspoken Hammurabi's Code seeks to dictate where men and women park themselves while dining together. (Same sex couples, I'd imagine, are spared some of this aggravations, or maybe the ambiguity just compounds the problem.) As I understand it, the lady sits with her back to the wall, facing the room, while the gentleman gallantly takes the seat with the more limited view. This is supposedly chivalrous, because the room-facing seat is perceived as more desirable, based on an ancestral antipathy to being caught unawares in the savannah, with your back to the lion.

Uhm, no. That is not why the man sits with his back to the room.

"Think of the woman as the guest of honor," says Post, "and the guest of honor always gets the best seat, which is with her back to the wall, looking out over the room." When applicable, the man should also offer her the seat with less "aisle traffic" passing from behind. If it's a table positioned in the middle of the room, then let her choose where she wants to sit, says Kirsch.

It's actually a compliment to the lady, and the man is seated, presumably, between the lady and any danger that might arise, no matter how improbable. Ultimately, you'll note that a gracious man allows a woman to choose.

But leave it to Katy to twist a compliment into an insult.

It is not (necessarily) chivalrous. Certainly the men (sometimes) mean well, but I would much rather feel free to get up and leave at any point, rather than being boxed in by a seating arrangement that has me wedged between the table and the wall.

Is it just me, or does that whole thing sound kinda rapey? Boxed in. Wedged. Vulnerable. Freedom to just get up and leave curtailed. First date, and Katy already has her gentlemen companion wedged into the "all men are potential rapists" box.

How charming.

Other women will disagree, and that's part of life, and dating—learning about another individual's preferences, deciding whether or not you can accommodate them. But the rigidity of the Code makes it highly awkward, because I often want my date to sit where he'd prefer to sit anyway, and it's weird to be constantly issuing disclaimers about how you truly don't mind having your back to the room, especially if the guy is already pulling out your chair with a look of pained martyrdom on his face.

Other women most certainly disagree. I have a question though: how are you supposed to learn about another person's preferences when you don't want to look at him or talk to him and prefer to watch the game while pretending to "get to know him"? Really. How is that supposed to work?

It's weird to be constantly issuing disclaimers? You would prefer that your date sit where he wants? I have a suggestion for you Katy. Stop issuing disclaimers. Shut the fuck up. And stop thinking about what you would prefer. Give his preferences top priority, and let him be gracious if he so chooses (although hell if I know why anyone would be gracious to you). Try, just try, for the course of one evening, not to be an irritating, mouthy cunt.

Can you do that?

Probably not.

That's why he's wearing that pained expression of martyrdom, sweetheart. He can't wait to get the fuck away from you!

Enter the bar. The bar means parity, escape from the gender seating wars, an end to the passive-aggressive dance of "no, no, you pick." Plus there are nuts.

Oh, there are nuts alright. Beginning with the guy who agreed to date you.

So there you are, at the bar. No need to look at him. No need to have any meaningful conversation. No need to miss the game. You can just pretend to "get to know him" while checking your teeth in the bar mirror. No feelings of vulnerability, being wedged into an escape proof seating arrangement, in case your date gets all rapey on you. It's all tickety-boo.

Why are you out with him in the first place? Katy, you sound like a terrible date. Like you're entitled to male attention but with no obligation to return it or even make a passing gesture of acknowledgement like LOOKING at your companion.

So what's the motivation? Why put yourself, and him, through this exercise of bitchiness and dismissiveness?

Bartender? Check, please!

Oh, my. Well, there we have it, don't we? I guess that image of the call girl waiting for a customer wasn't too far off the mark, was it?

Yeah, Katy, you sit at the bar. Smart men will see you instantly for what you are.

The rest of us will be seated with our backs to the wall, enjoying the company of men we are interested in looking at and speaking to, and with hardly any requirement at all to "get up and leave at any point".

Well, pee breaks, obviously. And when your first date is actually in a washroom, that's not a problem at all!

Lots of love,

JB

How to be attractive to other people? Be really self-absorbed and don't make any efforts to please anyone else.

Ah, Lindy West. One of my favorites. Here is Lindy[89] with some advice for people who are chronically alone and incapable of attracting other people, particularly people of the opposite sex. It's worth wading through, because it's an impressive articulation of what is wrong with our concept of what a relationship, particularly a long term relationship, between two people is supposed to look like.

1. The opposite of confidence isn't shyness—it's fake confidence.

It seems like a good plan—to just mimic the confidence you see in others and hope it passes for genuine—but it's not. It is a bad plan. There's a big uncanny valley when it comes to confidence, where you think you're swaggering around like James Bond but really you're just frenetically fumbling through magic tricks and insulting everyone at the bar like a fucking freak. It's disconcerting for those of us on the receiving end. And by the way, if you take a look at how James Bond actually picked up women—mostly he was just like, "Hey."

A way better plan is to stop trying to carve yourself into this socially prescribed shape that you think deserves confidence, and start finding actual confidence in the things that make you you. If you're unhappy with your body or your mind or your social life, that's one thing—but change yourself for you, not for some faceless ringwraith you plan to bone some day in the future as soon as you get good enough at kettlebell squats. That's bad for you and dumb.

Lindy is correct in stating that having confidence is a big factor in whether someone finds you attractive, but what she gets wrong is CONFIDENCE IN WHAT? Lindy says you need to be confident in the things that make you you. It's a trite, hackneyed sentiment that is repeated endlessly, and it also happens to be dead wrong.

What you need to be confident in is are the things that make you GREAT MATE MATERIAL. And that requires you to think about the other person first and foremost. What do you bring to the table? For most men and women, those are different things entirely, although not always.

Most women are looking for men who are physically bigger than they are. Men of imposing physical stature are attractive, relative to your own stature, because they are perceived by both men and women as dominant and strong.

Applying an evolutionary psychology perspective, we predicted that taller individuals are seen as more leader-like because they are perceived as more dominant, healthy, and intelligent. Being fit and physically imposing were arguably important leadership qualities in ancestral human environments—perhaps especially for males—where being a leader entailed considerable physical risks. In line with our expectations, our results demonstrate that by manipulating an individual's stature height positively influences leadership perception for both men and women, though the effect is stronger for men[90].

For men, especially shorter men, what you need to signal is your confidence in your ability to lead DESPITE not having the advantage of height. HOW you do that will be as individual as each person, but the key is that you are signalling your ability to lead OTHERS, especially her.

It's already pretty obvious why feminists don't like that: the reality that most women want a leader for a mate is an uncomfortable truth that doesn't sit well with the ideology of perfect equality. First Officers who answer to a Captain who has the ultimate authority are not beloved when the First Officer is a woman.

---

[89] http://jezebel.com/i-appreciate-this-but-i-am-also-frustrated-by-it-your-627815071

[90] http://gpi.sagepub.com/content/16/1/17.abstract

Naturally, men as First Officers are okie-dokie, in theory. In reality, not so much. Men who relinquish authority are well on their way to a cheating wife[91].

The flip side of this is that women need confidence in their ability to be led, which really comes down to confidence in their ability to ADVISE, because that is the main role of the First Officer. Women need to demonstrate that they are intelligent and loyal and honest and that they are willing to use those qualities to make a TEAM work. Again, how you display that confidence will be different for each woman, but the focus needs to be on the TEAM, not on the individual.

Something as simple as getting drinks or fixing plates for both of you, and not just yourself signals that the other person has top priority in your mind, without requiring martyrdom or self-effacement, neither of which are attractive.

Show that you care. Not that hard. That's the confidence you need. Women need to be able to confidently demonstrate that they can put someone else's needs above their own, and men need to have confidence that they can accept responsibility for someone other than themselves. Granted, there are some dangers in accepting responsibility for people who are not worthy, but isn't that what dating is? Sorting out the worthy?

It's funny that feminism won't hesitate to hold men responsible for women's decisions when those decisions are bad (hello rape culture) but when it comes to personal, happy, functioning relationships, they rebel against the idea that women like strong, confident leaders.

Leader/Advisor is not the only thing that factors into our perceptions of attractiveness, and all those other qualities also require a show of confidence, but they come down to one thing: be confident that you are worthy by actually having the qualities the other person is seeking. That means you have to spend some time thinking about what the other person is seeking!

Some women really ARE Captains, and they are fully prepared to take on the leadership of their team. Some men are very natural First Officers. That's perfectly fine. Know what you bring to the relationship, and figure out how to signal that. Stop thinking about what makes you YOU, and start thinking about what makes you great for the other person.

2. If you trick someone into liking you by being full of shit, you end up dating someone who wants to date a bag of shit.

Honesty is so great! Here's what happens if you're completely honest about yourself with people you might want to date: You end up maybe dating people who actually like you instead of people who like that weird character you made up. (Plus, cuts down on continuity errors.) Here's what happens if you're not honest: You end up hanging out with dicks you don't like. Worse than being alone! Hooray!

Really? If someone doesn't like you, that makes him a dick? Wow. This whole paragraph reeks with aggression and dislike of men. And Lindy's missing the same point as above. Instead of being completely honest about the sort of person you want to date, how about being completely honest about what sort of person might want to date YOU?

Begin with the other person. What qualities do you have that someone else might value and admire? Work on those things first, and then worry about whether the other person has qualities YOU like and admire. Begin with yourself. What do you have to offer?

---

[91] http://www.dailymail.co.uk/femail/article-1211104/Think-men-unfaithful-sex-A-study-shows-WOMEN-biggest-cheats--theyre-just-better-lying-it.html

3. People are attracted to love, not hate.

About six months into dating, my current boyfriend and I discovered that, coincidentally, both of us had spent a few (dark-ish) years obsessively listening to the Ricky Gervais podcast every night as we fell asleep like weirdos—like a kind of fucked up, screeching security blanket. It's not something we do anymore, or ever did together, but it's one of the many threads that make up our big tangly connection. He doesn't love me because of how much I hated being alone. He loves me because he sees how much I love the things I love.

If you want people to love you, you should love stuff. Bitterness is like Citronella for vaginas. Are you interested in anything? Do that thing. You never know who you might meet in Thing Class—and even if you don't, hey! You got to spend a bunch of time doing your thing!

No, no, no. This is really bad advice. Do NOT do "your thing" in the expectation that you will meet someone who shares your interests and a romance will blossom thanks to mutual love of whatever that "thing" happens to be.

If I had taken this advice, I would have spent all my free time at advanced crochet seminars (yes, I'm a hooker), bread-making classes and riding my granny bike around the duck pond. Not a whole lot of men share those interests, and the ones that do are probably First Officers like myself and not what I am looking for. Had Mr. JB taken the exact same advice, he would have spent all his free time watching Benny Hill marathons and inspecting massive construction projects for fun, and we would never have run into one another.

My "thing" is period costume drama.

His "thing" is diggers. And bulldozers. And really big cranes. And trucks with giant wheels.

We agree to have different "things", and while we do love how much the other person loves their "thing", there is no requirement that we share in our passions.

Your mate does not have to be your friend, any more than the Captain of your softball team has to be your friend. He/she needs to be someone you trust, love, and to whom you can give every ounce of your ability and skill and intelligence and every other great quality you possess in service to the TEAM.

Have some qualities the other person values. Again, you need to spend some time thinking about what other people might value, and cultivate those things in yourself. Your "thing" is just that. Yours. And their "thing" will also be just that: theirs. Never mind the "things".

They are not important.

4. A great way to endear yourself to women is to fight against the societal structure that oppresses them and made you lonely in the first place.

All this shit—your "type," the "criteria" you think you need in a mate—is arbitrary. It's social conditioning. I used to think I wanted to date someone tall (I'm tall), until I started asking myself why I felt like that and couldn't come up with a single coherent answer. Then I dated some dudes who were way shorter than me, literally never even noticed after the first 2 minutes, and then literally never thought about it again. Because THEY'RE PEOPLE. That arbitrary people-criteria you think you really, really want but can't get? Just try to imagine not wanting it. Voila! Now go out and bang whomever, Criss Angel. You can do this. Now please stop making eye contact with me.

Nope. Having a "type" is not social conditioning and it's not arbitrary, and the sooner you accept that, the closer you will be to finding your mate. That's not to say you can't overcome instinctive preferences and desires, but I would never advise anyone to try that: it doesn't work very often.

It's not about having the Aussie supermodel or the 4% body fat cross fit champion. It's about understanding what you personally find appealing and understanding that it will be very, very hard to overcome an instinctive revulsion. In some cases, the qualities you dislike will become amplified over time and things will get so much worse.

And naturally, you have to understand that other people will find certain things about YOU revolting and repulsive. Some of those things you can change. If you are seriously interested in seeking out a mate, then you will make some effort to understand what things have a tendency to repulse others, and deal with that.

You CAN manage your weight. You CAN manage grooming. You CAN control what you wear and how you present yourself, and if you care about another person, you will do those things. For THEM. And they will do things in return to appeal to you.

How interesting that Lindy broadened her dating pool to include short men. The one thing you CANNOT control. Height. And implicit in that generosity is that men should be broadening their pools by including …. short women? tall women? How about…. fat women? Nice way to sneak in a little man-shaming there, Lindy. Men cannot control baldness or height. Everyone can control their weight and grooming habits, and they should do so in deference to what others find attractive.

Take shaving and hair removal, for example. Some women do NOT like beards or scruff or moustaches or chest hair. I'm not one of them, but whatever. If you want to be attractive to a woman who dislikes facial or body hair on men, then you will shave. For her pleasure. Her pleasure takes priority over the annoyance of having to shave every day.

And it goes both ways. It baffles me that women don't seem to understand the point of Brazilian waxing. It's not an expression of paedophilic tendencies when men prefer a smooth genital area. Porn culture may have introduced the concept, but the reason for that sort of personal grooming has nothing to do with men imagining you are a little girl and everything to do with the fact that hair in your mouth is squicky!

You do those things for HIS pleasure, and that leads to ….. YOURS!

And that is how relationships work: you make his pleasure and preferences YOUR priority and he makes your pleasure and preferences HIS and you both end up pleasing and being pleased. The whole relationship should work that way: there is very little room in any functional relationship for selfishness. If it's all about you, and you are waiting for someone to agree that it really IS all about you, you had best hit up the local Humane Society for a kitty or two.

Why is there such resistance to the idea that the way we appeal to one another as human beings is to consider what our potential mates might find appealing, and try to be those things? Why is there such a fierce push-back against the idea that others people's likes and desires not only matter, but ultimately matter more than your own?

I think it's the fault line in feminism showing up again. Feminism is supposed to be about social, political and economic equality between men and women, but it's not. It's a philosophy and an ideology that women should never make anyone else's needs matter more than their own, but men should continue to exist in service to others.

Nineteen of them died this weekend[92], fighting a wildfire in Arizona. Nineteen men, whose whole lives were dedicated to serving others. Nineteen men, who made other people's safety more important than their own.

When is the last time you heard of nineteen women dying in service to others? In accidents, in crimes, in lethal weather and other acts of God? Yes. But in service to others? Show me. Show me the nineteen women who suited up and strode across the blackened landscape to battle flames leaping 80 feet into the air, for the sole purpose of protecting others.

83 firefighters died on duty in 2011. 82 were men. 1 was a woman[93].

Give me an all-woman fire crew, and then I will believe feminism is about equality. When 83 firefighters die and HALF of them are women, I will believe feminism is about women competing head to head with men, and not just enjoying the protections of men while disavowing any need for reciprocity or even gratitude.

You want to appeal to the opposite sex, ladies? Imagine that every man you see is a firefighter. He will give his life to save you.

Think about what you will give him in exchange for that.

Think hard.

Now be those things. Be what he wants. What he needs. What he desires. And know that every moment you put into considering what someone else wants and needs, will be a moment spent in making yourself appealing.

It's not what makes you you that matters. It's what makes you worthy of him. And what makes him worthy of you.

There are four questions of value in life... What is sacred? Of what is the spirit made? What is worth living for, and what is worth dying for? The answer to each is the same. Only love.

Johnny Depp

To the firefighters in Arizona:

Thank you.

May you rest in peace.

Lots of love,

JB

Ladies, are you short a little cash? Here's a quick and easy way to beef up your bank account and it's filled with LOL, too. Fun for everyone!

---

[92] http://www.cnn.com/2013/07/01/us/arizona-firefighter-deaths/index.html

[93] http://www.usfa.fema.gov/downloads/pdf/publications/ff_fat11.pdf

So, you're a responsible girl, right? A totally modern woman, down with premarital sex and physical pleasure and you know all the right moves when it comes to preventing pregnancy. You've been on birth control for most of your adult life and you have Plan B in your medicine chest just in case some catastrophic failure happens and the fruits of your loom decide to weave you up a darling little bundle of joy.

You have the abortion clinic on speed-dial.

Good for you! Yay! Abortion is dirty, nasty business that it's best to avoid if possible.

But all the responsibility in the world won't prevent those moments when the Visa bill comes and you find yourself financially screwed once again. Damn those credit card companies, giving you so much free money!

Courage, my love! There is a solution.

There are two ways to go about this little money-making scheme – one for amateurs and one for the more experienced ladies. Both require that you have a boyfriend with some assets (or the ability to acquire them), and the first step will be to accurately evaluate what resources your sweetie can come up with.

Is he a shiftless musician playing in dirty dives most weekends and delivering some pizza on the side?

Well, he can sell his guitar and his car, right?

Is he a staff accountant at a prestigious firm? Not rolling in the dough quite yet, but chances are he can qualify for a nice tidy line of credit at the corner bank.

Is he a stockbroker lining up for a wicked Christmas bonus? Oooh. Jackpot!

Let's get the moral quandary out of the way right off the bat, shall we? Men rule the world. They have all the money, all the power, all the opportunities and all the privilege.

So fuck them.

My plan for profiteering is not only perfectly moral, it's pretty much REQUIRED just as means to get the balance a little more right. Men have had it too easy for too long and it's time for a little comeuppance.

People only feel guilty for doing the WRONG thing, right? So don't feel guilty, because none of this is wrong. It's fairness. Justice. Follow my advice and know you are acting with integrity and walking the path of righteousness, redressing centuries of wrong with one cool trick.

Let's go the amateur route first. What you are going to do is get a positive pregnancy test and then inform your astonished boyfriend that you will need money for the abortion. Based on your calculations of his available resources, select a clinic with a fee set as close to that number as possible. Screen cap the payment info and have it close at hand for the conversation.

Practice looking wretched. Rub a tiny bit of Vicks or Tiger Balm on your eyes for the full flood effect. Weep your little heart out. Let him know you never, ever wanted this to happen and you can't bear the thought of ruining his life. Cast him as the hero who alone can save you from the terrible fate of bearing his child.

Make sure you get cash.

And set a calendar alert for the day you are having the "abortion" so that you don't accidentally forget and get caught out shopping with your new moola! Spend two days on the sofa clutching your tummy and a teddy bear, and ask him to order in all your favorite foods, which you can freeze for lunches for the next week!

See?

How clever.

You're very welcome.

Now, let's move on to the more professional ladies. You're not in it for a couple hundred bucks. Fuck that. All of this rests on the assumption that your boyfriend has some serious resources, which you are entitled to because he only has those assets in the first place because he's a man and the world happens to consider his Masters in Finance oh so much more important than your Barista of Arts degree. Obviously bullshit.

You will not need any Vick's or wretched looks. Oh no. You need to be excited! Cautiously excited, but excited nonetheless. Your boyfriend, you see, will not just be paying for the abortion, he will be paying you TO CHOOSE abortion.

Wonder out loud, as you giggle about how surprised your mother will be, just how much child support you will be able to count on. Throw out a wicked number for the nursery and preschool fees. What you want to do is get him to think about just how expensive this little bundle is going to be, and then the negotiations begin.

Maybe the baby isn't a good idea. Maybe you want to pursue your dreams of creating a felt installation that will get you into the MOMA. Give him an opening. Let him talk you into a settlement. If the money he is offering isn't quite what you want, switch back to enthusiasm until he gets it up near what you deserve.

Again, cash only please.

See how easy this is?

All you need is positive pregnancy test without actually being pregnant.

Well, fuck me. Guess I didn't think this one through very well. How are you going to get a positive pregnancy test? I guess you could follow a pregnant woman home and search her garbage, but by the time you can SEE she's pregnant, the testing period has long passed by.

If only you could BUY positive pregnancy tests from women who really are pregnant. If only it were possible to purchase a stick covered in some other woman's pee containing those knocked-up hormones. If only there were women brave and dedicated enough to offer such an item for sale to help redress all those many wrongs that have accumulated over the centuries.

Oh, look![94]

Pregnant Women Selling Positive Tests Online

And only $25.

---

[94] http://www.nydailynews.com/news/national/pregnant-women-selling-positive-pregnancy-tests-online-article-1.1443432

Sweet!

All right, ladies. Get to it! Bundles all around!

Of cash, of course.

Not babies.

Ewww. Ick.

Who wants those?

Lots of love,

JB

Marriage

My husband and I married in 2016, after dating for a full year. We became engaged and lived together while we finished our MBAs in Manchester. The episode of living together was a test for how we would share our space and our lives, with an end date set in stone. We married in August of 2000, in a park, with only a dozen close family and friends with us. We went for pizza and beer afterwards. We spent less on our wedding than many women spend on just the dress, and I have not a single regret! We actually had a rather considerable sum of money that Mr. JB was willing to spend on a wedding, but we decided together that the money was much better spent on a doctoral degree for him. Our approach to getting married is not the approach every couple needs to take, obviously, but culturally, we place way too much significance on the wedding, and not nearly enough on the marriage.

It's often said that being married is hard work, and I personally disagree with that sentiment entirely. Being married is a choice, and sometimes that choice requires some frustrating compromises. That's not "hard work", that's life. The reality of modern marriage is all the risk falls on men, and all the rewards to women. Marriage is a dangerous prospect for men, but not without its rewards, either. Provided you pick the right wife. Let's kick off this section by looking at how to pick a wife.

It's not as simple as falling in love.

How to pick a wife. Advice for single men.

I love it when this happens: some single guy friend of Mr.JB, hungry for some family time, ends up sitting at our dining room table, a plate of something warm and delicious in front of him, children cavorting silly and funny all around, a cat curled up under his feet and a glass of something fortifying at hand. He looks around, sighs, and says, "JudgyBitch, why aren't there more of you?"

The truth is there ARE lots of women like me: women who value home and family more than cash and credit in their own names. Women who like being First Officer and are happy to have a Captain who takes the main responsibility for the crew. Women who make other people's happiness their own, and who don't have to TRY to do that, it's just how they are.

The trick is to be able to recognize those women when you meet them, and to see the red flags that tell you when you're going down the wrong track. Here is my advice for single men on how to find a wife.

How much does she weigh?

People come in all different shapes and sizes, and there is no wrong or right shape. There's only what you prefer, and you are entitled to your preference. Start with that. Do NOT marry someone you do NOT find physically attractive. It will not get better. It will get worse, and that's a terrible position to be in - married to someone you don't fancy. Having said that, you need to ask IS HER WEIGHT STABLE? Whether you prefer the softly rounded or the slender, the athletic or the sturdy, a stable weight goes hand in hand with a stable mind. Look at pictures of her over time. Wildly fluctuating weight is a sign of mental disturbance, and that is just what you do NOT want.

How much does she care about her clothes?

Again, it doesn't matter what your preference, fashion-wise is. A pretty country dress, blue jeans and t-shirt, yoga pants or metropolitan chic. WHAT she wears doesn't matter, but how much she CARES certainly does. First of all, it can cost a shitload of money to keep a fashion conscious girl in circulation. That is NOT what you want to spend your family's money on. Second, someone who invests a lot of time thinking about herself and what she looks like is not likely to be spending a lot of time thinking about YOU. And fuck that right there. Check out her closets. Are they stuffed to the seams with clothes and shoes and boots and accessories? Yes? Pass on her. Not what you want.

Does she care if you are hungry?

Young women today have very few domestic skills, a sad result of growing up with mothers who preferred cubicles and frozen pizza to a kitchen and fresh bread. Those skills can be learned, however, and all it takes is practice and desire. Don't panic if your lady friend cannot boil water or make the proverbial sandwich. She can learn how to do those things. What she CAN'T do is learn how to care. She does or she doesn't. A woman who will bring you take-out, or heat soup from a can or pick up some bread and cheese from the bakery because YOU are hungry is on the right path. It's all about attitude. Wanting to go out for dinner because SHE wants to is very different from wanting to go get dinner because YOU have had a long shitty day and she's knows your favourite Mexican restaurant is just what you need. Caring about you starts with caring about what and when you eat. It's really that simple.

Does she have a loving family and close friends?

Women who DON'T have these things should not be off the table automatically, because no one chooses their family, but a woman without a family or friends should be dealt with very cautiously. There might be a good reason she has no friends. Beware of women who say things like "I don't like hanging out with women. They're so bitchy/catty/dramatic/blah blah. I prefer the company of men." That's a huge red flag right there. There are plenty of women I hate and would not voluntarily spend one second with, but I also have a group of like-minded ladies who walk through life with me and I LOVE them to pieces. A woman who prefers the company of men over all women has a problem with lack of male attention. She probably grew up in a single parent household, and it's unlikely she is going to be satisfied with just YOUR attention. Give her a miss.

Does she have an inner life?

A woman with an inner life does things that allow her to contemplate the world from someone else's perspective. Whether that involves reading or analyzing baseball games or volunteering at the animal shelter, it means she has some capacity to consider the needs of others. There's a clue there, dudes. If you're actively looking for women who read/analyze/volunteer, you should spend some time at the bookstore/arena/shelter. Become a familiar face and you might find a willing conversational partner and then take it from there.

Does she like children?

That's a deal breaker. A woman who doesn't like children is a woman who doesn't like vulnerability, chaos, responsibility, obligation, patience or cheer. Lots of women will say "oh, I would love my OWN children, I just can't stand other people's children." That is a woman who considers children personal property and you are in for a hot mess of hurt and a lifetime of child support if you fall for one of those ladies. The slightest hint of not liking children should send you running for the hills. The failure to see children everywhere as little people deserving of love and guidance and patience and tolerance is fatal flaw. Run, lads!

Does she want a big wedding?

In certain cultures, big weddings are an expectation and par for the course. My youngest brother, UPSGuy, married into a huge Italian family, and the wedding was insane, but necessary. Mrs.UPSGuy would have been happy to elope, but her 285 cousins would have killed her. So a big wedding it was, but in general, the desire for a big wedding is a hint that you have found a Princess, and not in a good way. A Princess is an entitled narcissist who thinks everything and everyone should be about HER and her Big Day! You are an accessory and not much more. That's not a good thing. Princesses expect life to treat them royally simply by virtue of being born and they have little concept of what their duties and responsibilities are in relation to the kingdom. Ditch the Princess and look for a Queen. A Queen is different. She understands that she has obligations and that her privilege comes with a price, which she is more than willing to pay. A Princess will see you as a Daddy, who ought to take care of her and indulge her every whim. A Queen knows you are the King, and commands alongside you.

A word about the dress, though. The Dress lives in every woman's imagination and it will cost a lot for something that only gets worn once (although I wear mine every anniversary). But there is a LOT and then A WHOLE FUCKING LOT. A big creamy taffeta and silk confection can be had for a couple hundred dollars and that is a lot of money, but if you can afford it, it will melt her heart and make her feel like she is living in a dream. With you.

Does she wear sensible shoes?

Ok, this one is a personal peeve. I just think a girl in sensible shoes has her head on straight and knows that sometimes life will throw you a curveball and you need have your feet on the ground, solidly and be ready to catch or get the hell out of the way. Sensible shoes doesn't mean ugly shoes. It means practical, comfortable and affordable. Just what your wife should be.

So there you have it. What to look for in a wife. Where to find her? Hell if I know. But she's out there. Don't settle for anything less.

Lots of love,

JB

How to Pick a Wife – 2.0

When I first wrote my post *How To Pick a Wife*, I failed to take into consideration the very real, and potentially devastating legal environment that marriage occurs within. Devastating for men, that is. Marriage is, and remains, the sweetest gig a woman can possibly get, which is the primary driver, I think, behind the Men Going Their Own Way (MGTOW) wars. MGTOW men hate marriage, because it is just so damned unfair to men, given the current environment. Changing that environment is one of the principle aims of the MHRM, and one that will happen, although it will take time.

In the meanwhile, for humans who are deeply drawn to pair-bonding (and that's most of us), here is an updated list of how to pick a wife, aka mitigating risk factors. Many men will never marry, until reproductive, marriage and divorce laws become fair, and that's a rational response to an irrational bias towards women and against men. I intend no shame towards those men who reject marriage and women outright, although that is obviously not a strategy that is going to work in the long-term. It's nihilism.

There are ways to make marriage safer. And even bringing these topics up for discussion will let you know very quickly just what your beloved has on her mind. A day for a Princess or a life for a Queen?

Ask her about circumcision

Prepare for a great deal of ignorance, because many women (and men) have given this zero thought at all. A woman who is instinctively repulsed by the thought of harming a child in this way gets one gold star. A woman who declares that a mutilated penis pleases her sense of aesthetics should immediately be shown the door. A woman who mistakenly believes genital mutilation is about sanitation and health is merely ignorant. She should be given an opportunity to learn and demonstrate her compassion for infant boys. Not caring about hurting babies is a deal-breaker, IMO.

Find out her thoughts on abortion.

This is obviously deeply personal and complicated. I'm not even sure what I think about abortion, but I have never faced needing one. My chain of thought at the moment is that at some point that little clump of cells divides to the point that a person exists.

A tiny little brain becomes active, even at a primitive level, and an "I" exists. I would like to see us be able to detect that using prenatal technology, at which point I am very comfortable banning all abortion for any reason. That is no longer your body, and no longer your choice.

Whatever your personal feelings about abortion, you will be able to deduce a lot from a woman based on her opinions. You can't legally prevent a woman from aborting your child, so if that's a deal-breaker for you, you need to find out sooner than later.

Never trust her with birth control

Sorry, just don't. You are legally fucked if you do. There is no way around that except to take control of birth control yourself.

An exception might be if she has an implantable birth control device because you can physically feel that under her skin. You buy (or acquire) the condoms yourself, and you never let her touch one.

When I was writing a post about birth control sabotage, I poked well over 40 holes in a condom, right through the package. Neither me nor my husband could detect a single one, not even in bright light. Try it yourself.

She never touches the condom. Never leave a used one anywhere she can get it. You will be held legally responsible if she is able to impregnate herself with a used condom. Calculate the value of child support based on your income over the course of 18 years. Think of your used condom as a little pile of cash for that exact amount. Would you leave that cash out where she can get it?

Have emergency birth control on hand. If a condom breaks and she refuses to take it: pray. That is your only option. No matter what happens, never legally marry a woman who refuses to involve you in her reproductive decisions.

How do you want to raise children, if you want them?

My husband I both wanted our children raised at home and we were explicit about that pretty much from day one. We met in MBA school and I agreed to shelve my career ambitions (which I honestly had few of to begin with) to make that possible. It's a personal decision, but if you are both not on the same page, you need to know that up front. Ultimately, you will have to use your judgement, since she can renege on her side of the bargain, any damn time she likes.

Sign a prenuptial

A woman who balks at a fair prenuptial is, to quote Taylor Swift, a nightmare dressed as a daydream. Prenuptials should include:

A financial settlement that reflects what you have both put in to the marriage

Child custody arrangements

Division of assets based on your mutual earnings

You should only consider getting married in a state where your prenuptial will be enforceable.

I can imagine most women reacting to these conditions: with a loud scream!

When you find one willing to consider why these are of vital importance to men, a woman who understands she has a loaded gun and is willing to give you the bullets, that is a woman worth considering.

Many of you will read this list and say oh hell no, and that's a valid response. For those men who do long for a mutually beneficial marriage that lasts for the long term, or in the alternative, isn't completely life-destroying, these are vital considerations.

How to choose a wife? With your eyes open and your armor on. It doesn't guarantee you victory, but it helps prevent the most grievous injuries.

Sad, when war has become an appropriate metaphor for marriage. Victory is the child of preparation and determination. Determination won't matter much. But preparation will.

Most of all, be prepared for a lot of women calling you a misogynist for caring about fairness and equality.

Par for the course, I'm afraid.

Lots of love,

JB

Katniss Everdeen is an awesome role model for girls because her life is all about children and family. And she will kill you if you try to fuck with her.

Katniss Everdeen is a girl with a useless twat of a mother who goes into crippling depression when her husband dies and is fully prepared to let her children starve to death. So Katniss has to take responsibility and become a mother and in doing so, she models for young women what a mother should be. Her own mother is self-absorbed to the point of catatonia, and when she DOES finally get her shit together, she pays more attention to her "job" than her children. Nice.

Katniss can't do it alone, of course. This is no "strong single mother" narrative. She has not just one, but two men who help her. Peeta goes first, tossing her some bread and then Gale, who helps her hunt and teaches her different techniques, like snaring. She is never alone. She lives in the woods with Gale. Peeta lives quietly in her heart, until the Reaping. When Katniss' daughter/sister Primrose is selected to fight to the death, Katniss does what any good mother would do – she offers her life in exchange for her child's. Exactly what Katniss' mother did not do for her two children.

When Peeta gets chosen as the boy tribute, it sets in motion a story that is all about protecting a husband and children and family and being prepared to kill anyone who threatens that family. Katniss' own desires are secondary to protecting and caring for others. Her love for Prim puts her in the arena and she kills only to protect her other child, Rue. When Katniss is unable to save Rue, she spirals into grief, but it does not cripple her. When the gamemakers announce that two tributes can be crowned victors if they both originate from the same district, Katniss is determined to save Peeta. Peeta becomes her husband at that moment, whether she sees it or not. She ACTS like a wife, and shows young girls what it means to be loyal and strong and brave and to put family above all else.

Katniss nearly loses her life when she goes to get medicine for Peeta. Clove, a mentally deranged psychopath with a penchant for throwing knives battles with Katniss and very nearly kills her. It is not an accident that Clove is a young woman. Woman are always the cruelest to other women. And once again, Katniss is saved by a man. Thresh kills Clove and lets Katniss live as a reward for her kindness and care towards little Rue. The message is clear. Care for children and love them properly and men will love you. Spend your time perfecting your skills (like throwing knives for fun and murder), attack women who are willing to sacrifice everything for their husbands and families and you will have your neck snapped like a dry twig.

When the gamemakers rescind their rule and try to get Katniss to kill Peeta, she reacts with a great big FUCK YOU. She would rather die with him than triumph with her own life. And she wins. By putting Peeta above her own desire to live, she wins the game and goes on to take down the whole system that would punish her for loving a man and children more than her own life.

Katniss Everdeen is truly a hero for young women. Young women are growing up in a culture that tells them they should always put their own needs and desires first. That it is a moral triumph to live only for yourself. Your needs, your desires, your goals, your ambitions, your own personal fulfillment should trump everything and everyone else. Even your husband. Even your children. I hope young women who read the Hunger Games get the message and respond to the wider culture with a great big FUCK YOU. Choose Peeta, girls. Chose Primrose. Choose Rue. Choose love. Choose their lives over yours. You just might find it the most fulfilling thing of all.

Lots of love,

JB

A decade of dishes will turn a girl into a woman, and a sensible one, at that.

According to Business Insider[95], the highest unemployment rates for people who graduated from college are for architecture majors (13.9 % unemployment), arts majors (11.1%) and humanities and liberal arts majors (9.4%).

Hmm. Just the disciplines women tend to cluster in. How perfect. Spend $50 000 plus dollars on a degree that doesn't even get you a job. Too bad the Gawker site has been affected by Hurricane Sandy, because they run a regular feature about unemployment, and you should hear the moany liberal arts graduates blaming everyone but themselves for their unemployment.

Yeah, because normally there are tons of jobs for cultural anthropology/women's studies majors.

---

[95] http://www.businessinsider.com/unemployment-by-major-2012-1?op=1

It's called being a barista at Starbucks.

So what is a young lady to do when she's ready for college but has no real idea of what she wants to do or be or how to support herself once she's done? Easy.

Don't go.

Find a husband, have some children, stay home and raise them yourself and give yourself time to turn into a mature and responsible woman. Raising your own children and taking care of your own home will help that process. And believe me, after a decade of folding underpants and doing dishes, you won't be talked into chucking fifty grand of your family's money into fine arts or children's literature or any other of the useless liberal arts majors you can declare.

Nope. You will be interested in acquiring some skills that will get you a job and earn you and your family some money. Accounting will become mighty attractive. Hell, you'll probably do the sensible thing and go to trade school and grab some actual job market skills.

Young women are narcissists. They want what they want, and they are surrounded by a culture that tells them HELL YEAH YOU SHOULD DO WHAT YOU WANT. Except that what they want is fucking stupid. Spending a shit ton of money (that you probably had to borrow and it will take you twenty years to repay) on a useless piece of paper that qualifies you to work at McDonald's is just plain old dumb.

Grow up before you make that decision. Do a real job with real responsibilities before you decide how you plan on making money. Be a wife. Be a mother. Do a good job at both.

Only then will you be wise enough to pick a college major.

Lots of love,

JB

No, my husband doesn't do any housework. Why the fuck should he?

Full disclosure: Mr.JB works fulltime and takes care of our family so I can be at home fulltime, making all of this doubly true, but even if you do work, you shouldn't be making your husband do housework. Unless he wants to, of course.

Do you own throw pillows? Do you like the towels folded in a particular way? Are the things in your cupboards arranged the way they are because YOU arranged them? Does a dirty floor drive you nuts? Do you care about what the house looks like? Good.

It's because you are a woman and women have an attachment to their domestic space that men just don't have. Simply put, men don't give a shit about housework. Women bitch and moan about having to do a "second shift" of housework, but guess what? You CHOOSE to do that. Yeah, yeah, the laundry has to get done, food prepared and dishes washed. Maybe mop the floor every once in a while. The rest of the "housework" is 100% voluntary and you are the only one who gives a shit, so you should do it. Trust me, your husband and kids don't give a rat's ass if the beds are made, the placemats on the table match (or even if there are placemats) or the TV is dusted. Who gives a fuck? Oh, you do? Then get dusting bitch!

The number one reason you should not bully or harangue your husband about housework is that it is EMASCULATING. Are you a feminist? You might as well stop reading right now then, since emasculating men is the whole point of feminism. You gals WANT a kitchen bitch, and good luck with that. But for women who are interested in a happy, loving relationship with a man who acts like a man, there is nothing more emasculating that being ordered by your wife to scrub the bathtub.

Did you see what I just did there? It's not scrubbing the bathtub or the toilet or folding laundry or making lunch that is emasculating. It's BEING ORDERED TO by your wife. Mr. JB does a few things reliably around the house and they tend to be traditionally masculine chores. He takes out the garbage. All of it. He sorts the recycling. He cleans the bathrooms because that is gross and messy work and he agrees that I shouldn't have to do it. He brings the groceries in from the car. I have not once EVER ordered him to do these things. He does them because he wants to, because he wants to help me and because it makes him feel connected to his home. And if I get overwhelmed by something, or really, just don't fucking feel like unloading the dishwasher/cleaning the oven/picking up the damn toys, I can ask him to pitch in and help. And he will. Once in a while.

Here is a chore I do more or less every day that I know he doesn't give a shit about: I clear off the table, wipe it down until it shines, put on a table runner and a centerpiece. Ta-da! So lovely.

If I ask Mr. JB to clear off the table he takes the shit off the table and puts it all on the counter and there's that job done! Then he looks at me like I'm crazy because what fucking difference does it make if shit is piled up on the table or the counter?

Here's what I DON'T do: follow him around and order him to take all the shit off the table and put it where I have decided it goes. Yeah, watched a friend do this to her husband once and wondered why he didn't punch her in the face or at least tell her to fuck off. They're divorced now. Big surprise. Apparently, he was a lazy fucker. Or you know, she was a controlling, emasculating bitch. Take your pick.

Here's the thing: if you are going to define your domestic space as YOURS, and most women do, which is why there are MAN CAVES (hint: it's because the REST OF THE HOUSE has been claimed by the woman), then YOU are the one responsible for it. You don't get to decide that the blue throw cushions go on the chair and the crocheted rose throw goes on the couch and then DEMAND your husband follow your rules. Fuck that. And if you have blue throw cushions and a crocheted rose throw, then you better have a room your husband can sit in without feeling like he's invaded the ladies room at some posh joint.

Here's a solution to the dilemma of women doing more housework than men: LOWER YOUR FUCKING STANDARDS. Let go of the idea that you own your house and all the things in it, including your husband. He is not a robovac that can be turned on and put into service. If he doesn't give a shit about the housework, then maybe you should take his lead and give less of a shit yourself.

Or you know, DO IT YOURSELF. Which has some advantages. You wouldn't be so goddamn fat if you did more housework[96]. Cancel the gym membership and pick up the mop. You'll save money and be happier! And you won't have to cut off your husband's balls to achieve it.

Lots of love,

JB

---

[96] http://jezebel.com/5913577/study-claims-women-are-fatter-now-because-they-do-less-housework

It takes a village to raise a child? No, it takes a family, but that doesn't make the village unimportant.

It is often said that "it takes a village to raise a child", which is kind of a lovely sentiment, conjuring up images of houses clustered around a town square and a group of likeminded adults pulling together to take care of each other and each other's children.

That happy little scene is fractured by the modern interpretation of the aphorism to mean "let's hire some random in the village to raise our children for us because we no longer give a shit about our own children, never mind the children of others." Hillary Clinton herself wrote a book about it, and she would know, wouldn't she, with her cookie-baking mom sneer?

Yeah, fuck you Hillary. My cookies are awesome!

Mr. JB and I are extremely fortunate to have a life filled with men who are friends to us and to our children, and in an odd way, it's the idea of the village and of the ideology of feminism that makes it possible. Mr. JB works in an occupation that puts him in contact with lots of young adults, and over the years there has been a definite swing from mostly male colleagues to mostly female. Mr. JB has no objection to the women he manages and oversees, but he has a very healthy respect for the power they wield. The slightest hint of impropriety can destroy his reputation and career – he knows that, and so do the young women he works with.

And so he stays well away from them. He does not allow women in his office for more than a few moments. He will request they accompany him to some more public place in his workplace, and they hold their conversations in full view of other colleagues. He tries his best to match women to other women mentors, but few women are interested in mentoring their younger colleagues. Mr. JB takes a very active interest in promoting the careers and interests of the young people he works with, but because helping a woman could actually be taken as EVIDENCE FOR in the event of an accusation of sexual harassment or misconduct, he deliberately does NOTHING for the young women in his charge. So, hooray for insisting that ALL MEN everywhere are potential rapists and harassers, ladies. You've fucked yourselves nicely.

Mr. JB's very rational decision to protect his family, income and reputation FIRST by avoiding, as much as possible, interactions with women colleagues inevitably means that we are surrounded by men. Much of the promoting of young men's welfare comes in the form of socializing and informal conversations and just meeting with important people within their areas of interest. And since Mr.JB prefers to spend his time near his family, and I am an excellent hostess, a lot of this socializing occurs at our home. My children are growing up in a village filled with bright, hardworking, enthusiastic, educated, dedicated men.

A lot of those men have reached some very different conclusions about marriage and partnership and family, based on the time they spend in our home. Many of them have never seen a stay at home mother or a homemaker who makes her own bread (and cookies, too!) or a wife whose primary interest is in promoting her husband's career, because that's how she can "have it all".

Being surrounded by men is a wonderful antidote to counter the pernicious messages LittleDude gets at school about boys and how they should behave (answer: like girls). There is an attitude in the world at large that men should feel ashamed of being men; that proper men behave like women and that men should feel GUILTY about being faster, stronger, smarter and more adventurous than women.

And my girls are growing up with plenty of loving attention from men. It seems natural for men to be kind, generous, protective, guiding, reassuring and present, because that is all they see around them in the village. I do not allow my children to watch commercial television, so I have protected them from some of the grosser caricatures of men as unthinking, unfeeling, stupid brutes, but sooner or later, they will encounter these ideas. And hopefully dismiss them out of hand, because that is not the world they live in.

Today is International Men's Day, and I would like to take this moment to thank all the wonderful men in our own personal little village for their love, generosity, kindness and company. Our lives would be so much worse without you. We love you.

Lots of love,

JB

PS: Check out A Voice for Men at http://www.avoiceformen.com/ if you're interested in learning about some of the issues men face, and why an International Day to celebrate men is both necessary and kind.

The best gift for a stay at home wife and mother? Being at home, of course. But these things are nice, too.

According to the 2000 US Census, 70% of mothers with young children work outside the home, although a huge percentage of those women work only part time. The high-flying career woman who spends 15 minutes a day with her offspring is more a media creation than anything else. 30% of mothers with young children do NOT work outside the home at all, preferring instead to make the necessary sacrifices to give their children the best possible start in life, which is shockingly independent of designer clothes, frozen pizzas and a big screen TV. Children with mothers at home have what they need most: time, attention and love.

So, three out of every ten mothers are at home full time, and obviously that is the best possible gift a husband can give his wife: the opportunity to fulfil her most basic obligations as a mother. A word for a moment in support of men who would LOVE to have their wives at home, but have been raised in a school system rigged to advantage women and then forced into a work culture that outsources men's traditional work, but not women's. And another word in support of men who would LOVE to have their wives at home but have discovered themselves married to women who actually have no interest in providing anyone with the best possible anything, excepting themselves, of course. And finally a word in support of men who would LOVE to have their wives at home but who are all too cognizant of the fact that she can chuck him out of the home he paid for, turn him into a weekend Daddy while parading her latest fuckbuddy in front of her shell-shocked children and force Husband 1.0 to pay for the whole damn charade. Those men are scared, and rightly so.

Notwithstanding all of the above, three out of ten women with small children are at home, making the living their husbands earn worthwhile. And with the Christmas Season coming up, here are some suggestions for what to get your angel in the house.

Something inexpensive

It goes without saying that unless you are Mitt Romney rich, any decent wife will be completely horrified if you splurge on something terribly expensive. There are ALWAYS better things to spend the money on or just save (can the kid's trade school accounts have too much money?), so please, don't fall for the bullshit media message that she will value your gift in economic terms only. If she does, oh hell. You're in trouble buddy. Save that money. You're gonna need it.

The gift of time alone

One thing stay at home mommies don't get a lot of is time alone. That doesn't automatically mean time away from you or the children, although that can be nice, too. For me, personally, I like being alone in the house, but available to respond in case something terrible happens and one of the kids needs Mommy now! That's the whole point of being at home, isn't it? That you are available when the children NEED you, not from 7:15 to 7:25 AM and from 5:45 to 6:30 PM. Children can be very inconsiderate of corporate schedules, whacking their heads at any time of the day or discovering a monster under the dining room table at precisely the time you have a terribly important marketing meeting.

Time alone in the house is a treat, and here are some suggestions for how you can make that happen.

Bubble bath and a glass of wine

Oh, heaven. Even better, when you start the bath, pour the wine and have towels standing by. Then you herd the kids outside for a game of Find Daddy or upstairs to watch Power Rangers Dino Force for the 800th time. Either way, mom is relaxing alone but still available. Throw in a book and you will be the Best Husband Ever.

Dark roasted coffee (or a specialty tea, which ever she prefers), a box of chocolates and a magazine on a subject she loves

Let her curl up in bed for a few blissful hours and escape into her own private world of crafts/architecture/astronomy/fashion/whatever. A small caveat: please read the headlines and ask yourself if they are conveying what you want them to convey.

True story: one Mother's Day, Mr. JB forgot to pick anything up for the woman (me) who had just given birth to his chunky, happy little son (36 hours of labor – LittleDude has a giant head!). Oops! He rushed out the door and came back a few minutes later and sheepishly handed me a box of drugstore chocolates (all the good stores were closed on Sunday, and hey, it's the thought that counts, right?) and a magazine and the intention of letting me rest in bed all day. The magazine: Oprah.

WTF? We don't have commercial television in our home at all, and if we did, Oprah is pretty much the last fucking thing I would watch. It gets better though: the lead story was HOW NOT TO LOOK FAT IN A SWIMSUIT! I kid you not (wear heels is the answer. Fucking stupid Oprah.). Yes, six weeks after giving birth I got to contemplate whether I might look fat in a swimsuit. It was so outrageous, it was actually hilarious. At Christmas time, I had a beautifully wrapped box from Mr. JB that contained another Oprah magazine, this time with the headline screaming HOW NOT TO LOOK OLD.

Seriously, someone needs to fire the editor at Oprah. A lot of men got in shit over those magazines. So seriously, read the headlines before you buy! Save yourself some pain.

Yoga pants and a gift certificate for the local studio

Or whatever physical activity she prefers. I love walking myself, so warm socks and a map is a great gift for me. You probably know what she likes, so go ahead and give it to her. Time to focus on your strength and endurance and celebrate the wonders of a woman's body without having to stop to vacuum crushed goldfish crackers out of the rug or unclog the toilet is truly a gift.

Popcorn and a DVD of the movie she wanted to see in the theatre but never got a chance to

Tucking her up on the couch with her favorite movie while you take the kids swimming or to the park is an awesome gift for two reasons. First, she gets to watch a movie uninterrupted by any pee breaks except her own, and second, you won't have to sit through ANOTHER Ryan Reynolds movie. Win-win!

THE GIFT OF FEELING SEXY

One of the nice things about life before children is getting up, getting dressed, doing your hair and putting on makeup, leaving the house feeling and looking your best. Once children arrive, those things are no longer a priority (or they shouldn't be) and a bare minimum of effort is all you have time for. I think most moms miss that special preening time (I know I do) and there are a bunch of little things that you can do to bring that feeling of being sexy back.

An hour at the spa

A massage, hot rocks, deep conditioning treatment and the sounds of the rainforest. It's truly like heaven and an hour is plenty. I've noticed at the spa I like to go to the hour-long package is buried at the bottom of an exhaustive list of day long pampering options which, quite frankly, are too fucking expensive and all day? Really? I'd be bored out of my freaking mind. An hour is great, thanks.

A hair appointment

Women's hair is expensive. Two color highlights and a cut takes two hours and will cost more than $100 dollars, which is why I have mine done twice a year and touch up my roots by myself in between. I'm lucky though. My hair is still quite fair and I have no greys, yet. Women with darker hair and lots of grey will not be able to wait six months between appointments and still look good. If you can afford it and your wife happens to care, there is nothing like feeling that your hair looks great! Of course, this is a total and complete luxury, and if you can't afford that, then you can't. It's a box of Miss Clairol and that's life in the big city, kids. Ammonia smells terrible (the main ingredient in hair dye) but the kits come with gloves and instructions and if you really want to make her happy, help her. Feeling pampered is a key part of feeling sexy. Wait til the kids are in bed though. You do NOT want to chase a naked toddler through the house with that shit dripping everywhere. Trust me.

Lingerie

The key to buying lingerie for women is to buy what you think SHE likes, not what YOU like. She is the one who gets to wear it, so her comfort should come first. Victoria's Secret is my favourite because it's sexy, affordable and comfortable, the trifecta of perfect lingerie. Check the sizes, guys. Bras and panties both have little tags that tell you the size, in case you don't already know your wife's bra size. Sequins, lace that goes past the seams and ruffles are all itchy as hell. Give them a pass. Sparkly is awesome. Always. I'm very suspicious of people who don't like sparkly.

Beautiful nails

A manicure is a colossally stupid waste of money, which is why it makes the perfect Christmas gift. A gift you should give her a few days before so she can enjoy beautiful hands for Christmas day. Assuming she gives a shit about her nails.

THE GIFT OF YOURSELF

Mr.JB and I rarely spend a lot of time alone together. We are together almost all the time he is not at work, but not alone, and for the most part, that is how we like it. A while ago we found ourselves alone in the house, with all the children occupied elsewhere, and we went for coffee together and it was absolutely lovely. We don't like to pay for babysitters or be very far away from our children, but when Grandma and Grandpa are in town, we take advantage, and since Christmas is a time when there is very often family around, try and find some time to go somewhere together, just the two of you. Christmas is a great time to remind yourselves why you fell in love and married in the first place.

Merry Christmas, in advance.

And don't leave this shit til the last minute!

Lots of love,

JB

How many men want a marriage proposal from a woman? None!

The University of California at Santa Cruz is one of the most liberal, left-leaning college campuses in the US, so you would expect some pretty progressive attitudes about gender and social norms from the student body, and by progressive I mean gleefully emasculating and ideologically poisoned.

But guess what? Out of all the students surveyed[97] about their attitudes towards marriage proposals, not ONE SINGLE MAN OR WOMAN said they would prefer a woman to propose marriage. Raise your hand if you think this is MEN'S FAULT!

Yay! Good thinking! The desire for men to propose is SEXISM, and not just any sexism, but BENEVOLENT sexism. That means men think women should be cherished and protected and clearly, that is BAD because....well, I don't know why, but let's go with it, shall we? So men are benevolent sexists and this makes both men and women want MEN to propose marriage. Not just SOME women and men. ALL OF THEM. And they're hippies, too!

The researchers were SHOCKED. Shocked, I tell you. Why on earth weren't more women taking the lead and asking the man to marry her? Why in heaven's name weren't men delighted by the thought of the lady down on one knee with a ring for him?

Why indeed. Here's why: life is biology and biology always wins. Men are bigger and stronger than women. What women want most from a man is to feel protected. There is nothing whatsoever wrong with this.

"Consciously, most women would like their men to be kind, empathic, understanding, and respectful. But their inner cavewoman knows Doormat Man would become Sabertooth Tiger Lunch in short order", says Angela Knight, in A Billion Wicked Thoughts. Have you read that book? You should. It's a tour de force of evidence demonstrating that women are hard-wired to feel aroused by submission, that dominance in men is one of their most sexually appealing qualities. #sorryfeminists

It's interesting that even at Jezebel[98], not a very man (or woman) friendly site, many women are proud to declare their husbands proposed to them, and they have happily taken on their husband's name. In 2004,

---

[97] http://www.livescience.com/25198-who-should-propose-marriage.html

[98] http://jezebel.com/5965738/nobody-wants-heterosexual-women-to-propose-marriage-including-heterosexual-women

94% of married women in the US took their husband's name, and of course! It's a demonstrable testament to the fact that women want to be under the protection of a man.

Feminism as an ideology tries very hard to teach women that they should NOT want to shelter under the shield of a man's protection. "A woman needs a man like a fish needs a bicycle", said Gloria Steinem, famously. Who then went on to marry, of course. Baby boomer women did an excellent job of tearing apart the fabric of our society by teaching women to choose doormat husbands, and teaching men that their highest calling in life was to be that doormat. Lie down and let your wife wipe her boots on you.

And women have the law to back them up. They continue to divorce men at appalling rates, they are disproportionately awarded custody and child support and alimony and have never as a group been more unhappy[99].

A younger generation of women is now asking: where have all the good men gone? Look down. They're under your feet. And getting a little tired of your dirty boots.

And if you plan on marrying one of those men, don't even think about proposing to him and keeping your daddy's name. Not one person thinks that a good idea, and that right there is hope for the future.

Lots of love,

JB

Want to protect yourself from domestic abuse? Be a stay at home wife and mother.

Today the Daily Mail is reporting that women who have careers outside the home are much more likely to suffer domestic abuse at the hands of their partners than women who are full time stay at home wives and mothers[100]. 60% of career ladies reported their partners roughing them up, while only 30% of SAHMs said the same thing.

Hmm. Well, first of all, let's take a look at what constitutes abuse, shall we? According to the study's authors, abusive actions included having something thrown at them, being pushed, grabbed or shoved, slapped, hit, kicked or bitten or threatened with a gun or knife. Yikes! Those last few items are pretty scary indeed. Knives and guns and biting and kicking – good lord. That's some pretty serious fighting. What about having something thrown at you? I guess it depends on what it is, doesn't it? A basket of laundry that's been sitting on the table for two weeks is one thing. A bowling trophy is another. Being pushed or shoved or grabbed doesn't sound particularly pleasant, but it's a bit much to define it as abuse.

And of course, the great big blind spot in this study is HOW OFTEN ARE THE MEN SUBJECT TO DOMESTIC ABUSE? Ladies may not be quick to threaten with guns or knives (that's a fight they are likely to lose) but they don't throw things, shove their partners, grab them or push them out of the way? Bullshit. If we're defining abuse as those actions, then let's take a survey of men and see how often the ladies are dishing out what they damn well better be prepared to take.

---

[99] http://www.dailymail.co.uk/health/article-2033806/Depression-women-doubles-1970s-try-all.html

[100] http://www.dailymail.co.uk/news/article-2241324/Women-careers-twice-likely-victims-domestic-abuse-threaten-mens-authority-power.html

The researchers who conducted the study (women of course) have a theory about why career ladies are more likely to be on the receiving end of a shove. Raise your hand if you think it's MEN'S FAULT!

Of course it is, silly. Get ready for a ride in the WAHMBULANCE! Men are mean. Bastards! Ladies with jobs threaten authority and power in a marriage. Men don't like that, so they throw shit at their partners. Because men are stupid! Men suck! Big meanies!

The usual sneering contempt for women who stay at home and care for their families comes through loud and clear (we're domestic workers, ladies - not wives and mothers), and there is an interesting kernel of truth hidden inside the venom.

"When women are home-bound through their role as domestic workers, they lack connections to co-workers and the social capital that is produced through those connections, in addition to wages, job prestige, resources, and thus, power. In turn, they must rely solely on their male partner for financial sustenance and can benefit from the distinction that his employment brings the couple".

Ladies who work have prestige, money, power and social connections. All the things men are accused of having and abusing. Women, apparently, never abuse their power or connections. And they certainly never shove their big mean partners around. Nu-uh. Doesn't happen. La la la I can't hear you.

Is it possible that having two partners both working full time is a really shitty, stressful, unfulfilling awful way to live, and that when families are set up with two earners, both partners are equally likely to strike out in frustration and anger and disillusionment and just plain old exhaustion? Most families deal with the anguish of two earners by buying a whole lot of shit they don't need, that won't make them feel better and that is destroying our planet.

"Dual-income parents get to spend so very little time with their children on the average weekday, usually four or fewer waking hours. This becomes a source of guilt for many parents, and buying their children toys, clothes and other possessions is a way to achieve temporary happiness during this limited timespan.[101]"

Hey, I have an idea. Let's change the fundamental rules of the game. Stay at home with your children, buy less stuff, reduce competition in the domestic labor force (which will cause existing wages to go up to a family wage again) and when you get frustrated with how things are going, don't shove your partner!

Unless you're ready to get shoved right back.

Lots of love,

JB

My husband pays all the bills, so I OWE him blowjobs, right?

Many years ago, a young girl, the product of a broken family, decided to deal with her crippling depression and anxiety by swallowing copious amounts of fluoxetine, otherwise known as Prozac. She chronicled her journey down the rabbit hole of psychotropic medications in a book called *Prozac Nation*, which was an immediate bestseller, and launched a genre known as the "confessional memoir". Author Elizabeth

---

[101] http://business.time.com/2012/07/19/got-stuff-typical-american-home-cluttered-with-possessions-and-stressing-us-out/#ixzz2DuBlnprr

Wurtzel's use of selective serotonin reuptake inhibitors has led her, all these years later, into a life devoid of any accomplishment, affection or admiration.

"I have no husband, no children, no real estate, no stocks, no bonds, no investments, no 401(k), no CDs, no IRAs, no emergency fund—I don't even have a savings account".

Hey, sign me up for Prozac! Sounds like a world of good times. So here is Wurtzel, with no husband, fucked up beyond belief, weighing in on relationships:

"I am committed to feminism and don't understand why anyone would agree to be party to a relationship that is not absolutely equal. I believe women who are supported by men are prostitutes, that is that, and I am heartbroken to live through a time where Wall Street money means these women are not treated with due disdain".

Oh ho! Really? Really, Lizzie? We're prostitutes, are we? And due disdain? What the hell is that? Should all the housewives of New York be lined up, have their heads shaved and be marched down the streets while the proper women leave their cubicles to jeer and throw apple cores?

The idea that women who are financially dependent on men are prostitutes is not new, and in a way, doesn't bother me at all. What's wrong with being a prostitute? I think I have every right to determine the value of my sexuality and to trade it for cash, should I choose to do that. My body, my choice, right?

Then again, maybe not.

No, what I object to in Wurtzel's despairing accusation is that my relationship with my husband is a strict quid pro quo exchange of one service for another. It's Wurtzel's insistence that an equal relationship can only be measured by one metric: MONEY. A marriage is a vehicle for the EXCHANGE of wealth.

That leads to only one conclusion: If my husband earns all the money, I must OWE him something for that, and in Wurtzel's mind, that one thing is SEX. Wurtzel didn't say women who are supported by men are HOUSEKEEPERS, because that would mean I owe my husband a clean house. She didn't say women who are supported by men are CHEFS, because that would mean I owe my husband food. She didn't say women who are supported by men are NANNIES because that would mean I owe my husband childcare.

Nope. We're PROSTITUTES, so that means what I owe my husband in exchange for my keep is BLOWJOBS. Lots of them. What's the street rate for a blowjob? I'm not sure. Let's say $50? Does that sound fair? So we'll put Mr. JB's salary at $100 000/year (I'm not really sure, I pay very little attention to those details). That means I owe Mr. JB 2000 blowjobs every year.

Jesus. That's over 5 blowjobs a day, no weekends off!

As an aside, Mr. JB says I can have Sundays off, as long as I pick up the slack the rest of the week.

So in Wurtzel's mind, I have two choices: I can ante up and deliver my fair share of blowjobs, or I can get out there and earn some money, thereby reducing my blowjob workload. If I picked up a job for say, $50 000/year, I would be down to just over 2 blowjobs a day.

And that, ladies and gentlemen, is what a truly equal partnership looks like! Microsoft Excel is going to be useful in keeping track of all this. I'm also going to need some kneepads and probably a whole lot of Prozac to survive this kind of equality.

Is it any surprise that Wurtzel finds herself without a husband or children? When you view the most private and intimate relationships as merely a vehicle to exchange things of value, you end up alone with nothing of any value at all.

Here is what DOES get exchanged in a marriage: love, first and foremost. That feeling of knowing someone else, and being known. Of accepting someone else, for all their flaws and foibles, and being accepted in return. Knowing yourself to be valued and respected and adored, and waking up every morning next to someone you yourself value and respect and adore.

Dignity comes in a close second. Putting together a life that includes a home and friends and children and pets and enough time to enjoy all those things in a meaningful way is a lot of work. One person needs to earn the money to make all that possible, and the other person needs to do the work to make it all fall together, and there is tremendous dignity in succeeding, or at least trying. My husband doesn't look at me and think "you lazy bitch, where's the cash"? He looks at me and thinks "thank you for this life". And the feeling is mutual.

Modern marriage can be a real trap, especially for men, who tend to earn more money than women, and in a culture that sees marriage as primarily a vehicle to exchange things for cash value, the highest earner has the most to lose. Women like Elizabeth Wurtzel, who promote the idea that a marriage between equal partners can only be measured in terms of dollar values are the principle reason marriage is such a mess. Why enter a contract in which love and respect and dignity and value are seen as superfluous to the real measure of value: a bank account statement?

She's a good cautionary tale, too. Wurtzel has nothing. So that theory worked out well, didn't it?

Let's be clear: sex in marriage is an absolutely fantastic thing. It's the glue that keeps couples together. Sex promotes the production of hormones and feelings that drive human pair bonding, and it's just a whole lot of fun.

Love is an art, but it's a science, too. Here's some advice from a woman who has been married for 13 years and counting: when your husband pisses you off – like, really pisses you off – take off all your clothes and make love to him. Then discuss your issue. You will find your rage has dissipated, the problem (whatever it is) becomes surmountable and he will probably give you whatever you ask for. It works. Trust me.

Check out these cute boots!

Wait! Did I just say that? I had sex with my husband so he would buy me cute boots?

Er, yep! God, I'm such a whore!

Lots of love,

JB

Shit, I'm doing this housewife thing wrong!

Katie Baker, writing at Jezebel[102] has noted something interesting about interns who work for no pay: they're the new housewives of the corporate world! Neat! And by housewife, of course she means "highly

---

[102] http://jezebel.com/5973293/are-interns-the-new-housewives

motivated, dedicated, autonomous, self-directed, multi-tasking and with a skill set of astonishing range and flexibility".

Oh wait. No she doesn't.

By housewife, she means "compliant, silent, submissive and obedient". I had to run that one by Mr. JB. His response? "Shit honey, you're doing it wrong".

I'll say.

Leaving aside, for the moment, the issue of unpaid internships, what is up with all this housewife hate at Jezebel? Could it be that the Shrews of Gawker media have sensed a change in the air? Check out this comment from Hannali:

Just wanna point out that all of the housewives I know are strong, intelligent, competent women. I'm not sure where this myth came from that all housewives are doormats. Quite frankly, it's a lie. Are there men that abuse their stay-at-home wives? Yes, but that doesn't mean that all stay-at-home wives are abused. This stereotype has been around for far too long. I am eighteen years old, in college, with my own job, and yet my dream job is still to be a stay-at-home mom. Nothing would make me happier than to love, to nurture, and to make a home for my family. It makes me sad that society trashes the concept.

Young women like Hannali must scare the bejeebus out of an older generation of feminists. Her ambition in life is to love and make a home for her family.

The pendulum swings back, as it always does.

According to Forbes Magazine[103], opting out is the new dream for American mothers. According to the annual Forbes survey of working mothers, "**84% of working women say that staying home to raise children is a financial luxury they aspire to**".

84%

I wonder if that 84% knows that once they become housewives, they will also have to be silent, submissive and obedient?

It's interesting, isn't it, that Jezebel likes to portray housewives as some horrifying caricature of femininity stuck halfway between a character out of *Les Miserables* and an antebellum slave. When 84% of women surveyed by Forbes ASPIRE to be housewives, where can this caricature come from?

I think Simone de Beauvoir said it best: "No woman should be authorized to stay at home to raise her children. Society should be totally different. Women should not have that choice, precisely because if there is such a choice, too many women will make that one."

Now, who is it again that wants women to be silent, submissive and obedient? Was it the patriarchy, which understood that women do not like to be parted from their children and created a society that kept families together as a functioning unit, or feminism, which also understands women do not like to be parted from their children BUT DOESN'T GIVE A FUCK WHAT WOMEN WANT?

Shut up, sit down and take it. Yeah?

---
[103] http://www.forbes.com/sites/meghancasserly/2012/09/12/is-opting-out-the-new-american-dream-for-working-women/

Well fuck you Simone de Beauvoir and fuck you feminism. Also, fuck you unpaid interns. Get a degree in something that actually gives you some skills and hey guess what? People will PAY YOU MONEY.

And Hannali, if you're gonna keep reading trash like Jezebel, I hope you even it out with some JudgyBitch.

nolite te bitchardes carborundorum

Don't let the bitches grind you down.

Lots of love,

JB

Hey married dudes! Want to have more sex? With your wife, I mean. STOP DOING HOUSEWORK!

File this one under "no shit Sherlock", but it turns out that married couples who adhere to a gendered division of household labor have more sex than those who don't.

Yep, it turns out that playing out traditional masculine and feminine roles has an impact on sexual desire, and therefore on sexual frequency. Guys who take out the garbage, mow the lawn, pay the bills and take care of the vehicles are getting laid 20 more times a year than the kitchen-bitches slaving over a hot stove. And obviously, the inverse is true, too. Ladies who cook, vacuum, fold the laundry and make the kid's dentist appointments are getting love 20 more times, too.

Why should this be? I have a theory: I think it has to do with respect. Feminism has spent a long time trying to convince both men and women that gender is socially constructed. That in and of itself is not a bad thing, necessarily. Stupid, but not bad. Where feminism went really wrong was to define femininity as POSITIVE, all the while ignoring the not so pleasant qualities associated with the feminine, while simultaneously defining masculinity as NEGATIVE, all the while ignoring the wonderful things about masculinity.

Feminism is straight up a theory of female supremacy.

Ladies rock! Men suck!

Of course by ladies, we mean white ladies, so don't get excited, all you ladies of color. You are here to do all the shit-work the white ladies don't want to do anymore. So get your mops and get at it.

Once you accept the premise that the feminine is a priori superior to the masculine, the plan of attack becomes quite obvious: men must become feminine or be forever defined as inferior and unworthy. It's a tongue in cheek aphorism that feminists hate men, but of course, that's not true. They love men. As long as men act like women.

Of course, Jezebel[104] responded to the research, conducted at the University of Washington using a sample size of 4500 (that's a good sample) with reason and rationality. They took a careful look at the data and then tried to come up with some hypothesis that might explain why couples following traditional gender roles might have increased sexual desire for one another.

Yeah, right. Nope. What they did was mock and ridicule the data, and then set up some kind of bullshit sexytime dollars, which is pretty rich, considering the data indicates that SEX is exactly what they won't be

[104] http://jezebel.com/5980298/cleanliness-is-next-to-manliness-the-chores-that-will-get-a-guy-laid

getting. Well, not as often as the couples in the study who rejected the idea that women's work is man's work and the two are interchangeable.

Look at how they titled the piece: Cleanliness is next to manliness, which chores will get a man laid?

There you have feminism in a nutshell. Sex is something WOMEN give to MEN as a reward for doing whatever SHE defines as necessary.

Good dog!

Sex as an act of bonding, an expression of the deepest love and care, a mutually satisfying and pleasurable experience does not even occur to these women. Nope. Sex is a tool, a weapon, something you can use to coerce men into doing whatever shit these women want.

And oh my! We have a word for coerced sex. We do! I know it! It's on the tip of my tongue. Give me a second...

Oh yeah!

RAPE

Now isn't that fascinating? A long time ago, a gorgeous, svelte, luscious lady, the pure embodiment of femininity, said that "all heterosexual sex is rape".

By which she means MEN are raping WOMEN.

Here's a new one for you: all sex with a feminist is rape. Women raping men.

Dudes, if you are getting laid tonight in exchange for cooking dinner or sweeping the floor or folding the laundry, AND YOU WOULD NOT OTHERWISE HAVE DONE THOSE THINGS, you are getting raped. Hey, lots of men love to cook, and good for them. The best cooks in the world are men # sorryfeminists.

But when you have been ordered into the kitchen by a sulky bitch who figures "it's your turn and if you don't do it, I won't have sex with you", then you sir, are being coerced, and that is rape. Down with rape culture!

NO MEANS NO!

No, I won't cook dinner

No, I won't vacuum

No, I won't pick up all those fucking Barbie shoes

No, I won't fluff the throw cushions

No, no, no!

Give the rape a pass, dudes. Traditional gendered division of labor is how you put more sex into your relationship. Sex based on love and affection and respect and admiration and desire.

Take a page from Marilyn's book:

Sex is a part of nature. I go along with nature.

Marilyn Monroe

Me, too!

Lots of love,

JB

It's been fifty years since Betty Friedan tore apart her home. Thanks for nothing, you whiny bitch.

Both Slate and Jezebel are running pieces today on the 50th anniversary of the publication of Betty Friedan's *The Feminine Mystique*. The book was a grenade tossed in the cultural landscape and when it detonated, it left American families shattered, women of color sidelined and the millions of children without fathers.

Good work, Betty.

In all fairness to Noreen Malone, writing at Slate, she does acknowledge that "...work doesn't automatically put you on the road to self-actualization (as Friedan implies it does), and the degree to which it contributes to it probably waxes and wanes at different points in a person's life. What about women (or men!) who genuinely do find the bulk, or even part, of their creative fulfillment in more traditional homemaking tasks, or at least less corporate ones, and who derive their sense of mission from helping people—even if mostly the ones related to them?"

Work doesn't automatically put you on the road to self-actualization. When you consider the "work" women actually do, that's a giant NO SHIT SHERLOCK. What exactly is so fulfilling about being a secretary? Still the number one occupational category for women. Jezebel, in an uncharacteristic recognition of reality, has noted that women still haven't achieved very much, despite 50 years of college degrees and boisterous cheerleading telling them they can do everything men can do, backwards, in heels!

The idea that we may be on the wrong track, culturally, naturally never occurs to old Jezzie. Nope. If what we have isn't working, well then, we must need MORE OF IT! Genius. In service to this idea, they have created a "reality check" for young women. I'll give you the summary:

- Teach girls to angrily blame others for their choices, emphasis on anger
- Force them into STEM fields, against their curiously stubborn lack of interest in those fields
- Teach them to be sluts and just call it "sexuality"
- Teach them to be activists in supporting important causes like "slutwalks"
- Teach them to put their own inflated sense of ability and worth at the center of their life narrative
- Force them into creative fields (I thought we wanted STEM?)
- Teach them a sense of entitlement to leadership
- Teach them to choose only the choices preapproved by Feminist White Ladies™

Wow. Gee, I sure hope my daughters grow up to be feminists. Sounds like a world of happiness, right there.

To celebrate the 50th anniversary of the worst book every written for women, I'd like to offer my own "reality check" for girls and women.

Let's start by teaching young women to calm the fuck down. There is no conspiracy/patriarchy designed to enslave you in the kitchen wearing nothing but an apron and Chanel No.5 (although that sounds like fun).

Feminism, by and large, has confused two separate ideas: patrilineage and aristocracy. Patrilineage is simply the custom of having children bear their father's surname. When a family unit is formed, the family shares a single surname and in our culture, that surname belongs to the father. It says nothing about the personalities or the quality of the relationship between the two individuals who have formed the partnership.

It always makes me laugh to hear women say "I kept my own name". Uhm. No you didn't. You kept your FATHER'S name, or if you are the product of a single mother, you kept your GRANDFATHER'S name. That's just how we roll. Our names come from our fathers. Get over it.

The word "patriarchy" is thrown around by feminists to describe this mythical place wherein all women were oppressed and exploited by all men, who had all the rights and privileges of both citizenship and sex.

Wrong.

Most MEN had no rights or privileges of any kind. They were just as oppressed and exploited as women. By whom?

By an aristocracy of both MEN AND WOMEN. Queens Victoria and Elizabeth are the longest reigning sovereigns in the written history of the world, and neither of them took any particular interest in the plight of the working class, unless forced to by the circumstances of history.

The last men in England, for example, did not win the franchise until 1885. One generation later, women secured to right to vote, too. Until then, almost all men and women were peasants slaving on lands owned by a ruling elite.

You want to hate something? Hate the crown. The rich (both men and women) are the ones who oppress and exploit, and confusing "rich" with "men" misdirects our anger and our strategies for redress.

Let's teach young women that their interests and proclivities tend to be dramatically different than men's and that's okay. It's okay to let men dominate in STEM fields, where they continue to discover and invent technologies and tools that astonish us and transform our world. Forcing women into these fields against their natural instincts or abilities is only going to slow that rate of discovery. Women who WANT to be there should be, just as men who WANT to be first grade teachers should be.

Let's tell young women the truth about their sexuality, and their fertility. Most women will want to have children. That's the instinct that keeps us alive as a species, and all the iPhones and Pinterest boards in the world isn't going to change that. And most women will not only want to have children, they will want to BE WITH THEM. Women's fertility peaks at 25 #sorry feminists. After 35, you are on a long, painful road to Clomid and IVF and after 40, the deal is pretty much done. You will not be having any children.

We need to teach young women to respect their fertility and to plan their lives around that. Biology. Always. Wins. Heading off to college and trying to launch a "career" (most likely as a secretary) during peak fertile years is a recipe for total disaster, as global birth rates in the feminized world demonstrate.

The best possible scenario to raise children is a nuclear family (two parents, gay or straight) splitting responsibilities and sharing labor. Since women FEED babies, that means that the domestic labor is hers, and productive, economic labor falls to her partner.

All of that strongly implies monogamy and fidelity. Teaching women that acting like sluts and having sex with a lot of different men outside the bonds of a loving relationship (whether that results in marriage or not) is somehow empowering and evidence for their strength and independence has had devastatingly predictable outcomes for young women: cutting, drug addictions, depression, eating disorders, suicide.

Feminism tells young women pernicious lies about their own desires: most women want loving, stable relationships with men they care about and feel deeply connected to, and they will want to have children and raise those children in the context of that sort of relationship. Young women need to be encouraged to make the kind of choices that will allow them to fulfil those desires.

Let's teach young women that there is a difference between what you WANT to do, and what you are ABLE to do. This is toddler-ville, people! No, you can't be anything you want. How does this even seem like a sensible thing to tell anyone?

True story: When LittleDude was three years old, he got a pair of Superman pajamas with a little cape and he was soooooo excited. He stripped down and could barely hold still while I helped him don his new suit, then he climbed up on the back of the couch and flung himself down on the hardwood floor! It was a nasty landing. Poor little guy. I picked him up, sobbing, and he said to me, "Mommy, these don't work!"

He really, really, really wanted to fly. He could not have wanted it more.

Guess what? He can't.

Teaching young women that they can be firefighters or astronauts or combat soldiers or the President or a unicorn trainer when they grow up is encouraging them to ignore what they are ABLE to do and just focus on what they WANT. Hey, for any women who are in fact, ABLE, every opportunity should be open, but the fact is that most of them are not capable of taking on physically demanding jobs that require enormous strength of either body, will or mind.

When we teach young women to focus on their ability rather than their desire, we encourage them to take rational stock of themselves, and we counter the cultural pressures towards self-absorption and narcissism. Be who you are, to be certain, but know who you are and what you can do, first and foremost.

Let's teach young women that there is nothing wrong with being First Officer. The USS Enterprise D has a crew complement of 1014 and only one of those people is the Captain. Most people, men and women, are not cut out for the Captain's chair and that is just fine.

#startreknerd

We can't all be Captains, obviously. Teaching young women that they are not ambitious enough, that they will never be fulfilled, that their accomplishments amount to zero unless they are in the Captain's chair does a huge disservice to all the many men and women who are happy to be crew members and gives permission for women to sneer at other women who are happy with their lower ranks.

It goes by the name "The Mommy Wars" in popular culture, and it is essentially a movement to devalue, discredit and shame women who would rather care for their own families than earn money caring for someone else's. When the only measure of a woman's value comes in the form of dollars earned, women who stay at home to care for their families have no value at all.

That's nice, isn't it? Feminism: making women feel like shit for 50 years.

And finally, let's teach young women that they are not special. Young women need to know they are not better than men, they are not morally or ethically or legally superior to men, and we need to encourage them to start agitating for changes in the law and culture that will make those truths the reality. Let's make young women activists? Oh hell yeah.

Insist on equal treatment before the draft board. Insist on equal custody agreements when marriages dissolve. Insist on the right to bodily integrity for both boy and girl babies. Insist on fair schooling that respects both boys and girls. Insist on equal health care and social spending. Insist on the right to raise your own children without shame.

How's that for a reality check?

Lots of love,

JB

Women change their names when they get married precisely because identities DO matter. And for most women, husband > daddy.

Jill Filpovic, writing at the Guardian, wants to know why the sweeping majority of women still take their husband's name upon marriage. "Identities matter, and the words we put on things are part of how we make them real."

Exactly, Jill. That is exactly correct. Identities DO matter and the words we put on things ARE part of how we make them real. Do you know what marriage does? It creates a new family. And in our culture, we choose our family names according to patrilineage.

pat·ri·lin·e·age (ptr-ln-j)

n.

Line of descent as traced through men on the paternal side of a family.

Let's stop for a moment and consider WHY we have established the custom of patrilineage. I think Satoshi Kanazawa has it right:

Patrilineal inheritance of family names, where children inherit their last names from the father, not from the mother, evolved as a social institution as one of the mechanisms to alleviate paternity uncertainty. Like all mammalian males, human fathers can never be completely certain of their paternity, but, unlike most mammalian males, they are asked to invest very heavily in their offspring.

Satoshi Kanazawa! You mean that EVOLUTIONARY PSYCHOLOGIST?!

Yep. I mean him.

What is it about evolutionary psychology that gets feminist knickers in a knot? Feminists HATE evopsych with a passion that is almost unparalleled. Evolutionary psychology is an offshoot of evolutionary biology, which is uncontested by any rational person, because sexual dimorphism is just so fucking obvious. You can scream EQUALITY to the high heavens and it will not change the fact that men, on average, are bigger than women.

One set of evolutionary biologists got around to thinking, hmmm, if our physical characteristics evolved so differently, is it possible that we also have psychologies that evolved differently to reflect what it is we DO with our bodies?

And evolutionary psychology was born.

The earliest feminists and suffragettes of the First Wave had absolutely no problem acknowledging that women had a special role to play in society: as the mothers of all citizens, they had a vested interest in what happened to those citizens.

> "A woman's place is in the home; and out of it whenever she is called to guard those she loves and to improve conditions for them."
>
> Nellie McClung

The Second Wave feminists, however, rejected maternal values, since they strongly implied that women were not constitutionally or psychologically equipped to center their lives on competition, ingenuity and survival. Women's psychology evolved to prepare them to live inside a perimeter, guarded by men, with the primary goal of ensuring the survival of their offspring.

Well that sucks. "Fuck that noise" was the rallying cry of feminists everywhere! And off they went, out into the wild blue yonder, to compete head to head with men in a battle of wits, guts and glory!

Aaaaaaaaand 70 years later, most women are working as support staff and paid caregivers, safe inside their little perimeters while men skulk out the edges of human knowledge and possibility. And what happened to the offspring? Where the babies at? Oh, yeah. We don't have any. Not enough to replace ourselves, at any rate.

What an ingenious plan! Let's not have any children! And the ones we do have, we'll pay some other woman to raise! Hello, ladies with brown skin. Get over here and raise my one kid, would you? Don't ask for too much money, though. I have gel manicures and throw cushions to buy with this money I earned as a secretary for some man doing the real work.

A, B, C, D .... Now where does G go again?

Know why 90% of women change their name when they get married, Jill? Because there is something deeply, profoundly psychologically satisfying TO WOMEN about feeling that you are under a man's protection. You leave your father's name behind and place yourself under your husband's shield, and you share a name and identity with the children you have together.

When Jill writes about identity, she wants women to cast off their identity as a WIFE and MOTHER. For women, HER identity should only include HERSELF. No one else could possibly matter.

That feels pretty shitty for most women, and most of them reject that definition of self. Then they sally forth into a wider culture that tells them at every possible turn that, honestly, husbands and children DO NOT MATTER. Women abandon the few children they have to the care of women poorer than themselves, divorce is easy, cash flows like water from their ex-husbands and taxpayers and the search for something more, something better, something else continues, in defiance of what actually makes women happy.

Today is International Women's Day. How about we celebrate it by cheering for all the ladies who are married to the fathers of their children? Those are the women who are helping to create a world filled with happy, productive, stable and caring people.

Oh, gosh, but that would make men an essential part of International Women's Day wouldn't it? Well we can't have that. We need to celebrate the day by EXCLUDING MEN, because Patriarchy! Privilege! Power! Oppression!

All across the globe, women will march and cheer and gather to celebrate women. 90% of the married ones will have their husband's name. Too bad 90% of them won't KEEP their husband's names. They'll take the name of Husband 2.0. And 3.0. And 4.0. As for me, I'll be celebrating by going about my day, safe in my perimeter, with the father of my children. And I'll sign all the school permission slips with my husband's name, which is also my name. After all, it's part of my identity.

It's part of what makes me real.

Lots of love,

JB

Yes, I take my husband for granted. What do you want anyways? A standing ovation every day?

I have a friend, whom I love very much, that I haven't seen much of lately, mostly because she doesn't really like my husband, and that makes being friends a little difficult. NurseRatchet is fun and witty and super intelligent and just generally a great person to hang out with, but she misunderstands my relationship with Mr. JB and that often leads to tension.

You see, Ratchet was a woman of stunning beauty when she was younger. She still is a very fine looking woman, but in her youth, oh wow. She looked eerily like Kim Basinger. And she had a great deal of attention from men as a result. She turned down two marriage proposals, one from a cardiologist and one from an airline pilot, thinking that the glory days would never end.

But they did.

She ended up married to a man who has a bit of a spotty employment history, had two children in quick succession and now finds that she must work fulltime to have any sort of decent standard of living. Ratchet bitterly regrets casting away the doctor and the pilot, and she hates working. She envies my life and I suppose that is the basis of our friendship. Ratchet understands completely what a wonderful luxury it is to be at home, dependent on a man, and wishes she could have the life I have.

She absolutely sees what I do as work, but that is where our perspectives diverge. Ratchet thinks that Mr. JB does not show enough appreciation for the things I do – that my work goes unnoted. Her own marriage is a little more, egalitarian, shall we say, in terms of how domestic labor gets done, although she generally ends up doing more than Mr.Ratchet, and that makes her unhappy and angry and she feels "taken for granted".

That feeling is one that women seem to complain about much more frequently than men, and it can have a very devastating impact on marriage.

What does it mean to be "taken for granted"? Essentially, it means that the work and effort you put into your relationship and life together is not acknowledged with either verbal or romantic gestures, and that communication about your daily lives has broken down, and by that definition, yes, Ratchet is correct: I am absolutely taken for granted.

I am also smart enough to see that the traffic on that street goes both ways. No, Mr. JB doesn't thank me after every meal, and he doesn't stand around applauding when I fold the laundry or unload the dishwasher. Guess what? I don't thank him for going to work every day or for paying the bills, and quite frankly, I really don't know what he does at work all day, nor do I particularly give a fuck. I have a general sense of what his job his, but the details, to me, are mind-numbing and I don't want to hear about them.

Sometimes Mr. JB will try to explain some technical aspect of his job to me and I will slowly slump down to the middle of the kitchen floor, pretending that I am in a coma. That kind of irritates him, but I think it's hilarious. Like he wants to hear about all the issues I had clarifying with the spice store that Cimarron is actually a type of oregano and I NEED it to make barbacoa properly?

Nope. He doesn't give a shit what spices I use, just as long as it tastes good.

Honestly, it's kind of hard for me to imagine what our relationship would look like if we were constantly communicating with each other about what we do all day and if we had to stop and acknowledge each other for every little contribution. Jesus, that would be a full time job, not to mention the fact that I DON'T CARE what he does all day, nor does he care what I do all day. At the end of the day, he wants to come home to a warm, friendly, reasonably clean house and something fabulous to eat, and I want to hand him the bills and never give them another thought.

We absolutely take each other for granted.

I think that when Ratchet looks at our relationship, she completely forgets what Mr. JB contributes: all the money to pay for our life. Because she imagines herself in my role, she only sees the work that I do, and she notices that it doesn't get acknowledged very often, ignoring the fact that I don't acknowledge what Mr. JB does very often either. I mean, not explicitly. My whole life is an appreciation for him, as is his for me. That just seems....self-evident.

The Sparkly Princess Cupcake narrative is looking more and more to me like the single most destructive cultural story out there. I find it interesting that while we have all the Disney movies in our house, they have never been the favorites for any of my children. My kids have always preferred the teamwork stories. The go-to videos feature a group of people working together to solve problems: *Bob the Builder, Power Rangers, The Wiggles, Thomas the Tank Engine, Go Diego Go* – they're all about a team pulling together. And that's not because I've imposed it, or even given it much thought. Those are just the stories my children are drawn to, likely because they are a reflection of how their own lives work.

I think a great deal of women's unhappiness stems from the notion that they should be the star of their own show. No matter what it is they actually do, the spotlight should always be on them. And the applause must be deafening! Adulation! Glory! Me! Me! Me!

Not only is that a completely ridiculous way to live, it wouldn't even be fun! Let's say I took Ratchet's advice to heart and gave Mr.JB the "we need to talk" look. I know my husband well enough to know exactly how he would respond. He would listen to me complain that he doesn't say thank you enough and he doesn't acknowledge me enough, and he needs to notice all the work I do in an explicit way (flowers!) and he needs to spend more time thinking about me and he would be having the following conversation with himself:

Oh fuck, here we go. Is this worth it? Do I really want to listen to this shit for the next twenty years? Is this worth fighting over? Should I tell her to go fuck herself and point out that she doesn't exactly do cartwheels every time she turns on the tap and there's hot water?

And he would reach the following conclusion:

Nope. Not worth it.

Then he would create a list of all the things I do every day, set up calendar alerts on his phone, write some sort of algorithm so that the alerts appear to be random, and text me little notes of acknowledgement when his phone reminds him to do so.

None of that would be because he truly, genuinely, deeply appreciates all those things. It would be because he doesn't want to put up with any bitchy sulkiness and the whole thing would just be one giant pain in the ass. Maybe it's just me, but my goal in life is not to be a whiny toddler my husband has to placate over and over again.

You see, Mr. JB DOES show his appreciation when he is truly moved to do so. I recently pulled off a magnificent dinner party for 38 of Mr. JB's colleagues and the senior administration including the President of the organization Mr. JB works for. It was a stunning, resounding success. We got home from that party, and Mr.JB was absolutely overcome with gratitude and love and pride and he decided to show it. You should know that I am 5'6 and 130 lbs and Mr. JB is 6'2 and 200 lbs – so he's quite a bit bigger than me.

He picked me up off my feet and gave me one of his Big Bear Hugs and ….

Oops!

A little too much gratitude.

He broke my rib.

No seriously. He really did. He was, and is, completely wretched about it. It was a one in a million thing. And I recently had a bone density scan! Bones like concrete!

Snap!

It really hurt, too. Took almost 6 weeks to heal! And of course, it took about two seconds for all the gallows humor to come out in our friends. I got lots of fridge magnets and flyers for domestic abuse hotlines, and lots of comments about how I should probably listen next time, blah blah blah.

And, as always, there is a silver lining in that cloud. Who thinks I played the "oh my poor broken rib!" card to win every little spat we had for months on end?

Of course I did! I used it yesterday, as a matter of fact. Mr.JB takes out the garbage in our house, and yesterday, he took care of that yucky little task on his way out the door to a meeting, but he FORGOT TO PUT A NEW BAG IN! So I texted him at work about it, knowing that when he is in a meeting, his phone will only go off if he gets a message or phone call from me.

You forgot to put the bag in the garbage can. Can you please come home and do it?

That irritates the hell out of him, and yes, this really is the kind of petty shit we argue about. When he got home he started to lecture me about abusing the fact that he never sets his phone to silent and always takes messages and calls from me no matter what, so naturally I responded by saying

What are you going to do? Break my other ribs?

Boom! Score one for JB! I win!

I never told Ratchet about the whole broken rib thing, because I really don't think she would understand at all. It was an accident, and one that Mr. JB feels terrible about. In all fairness to Ratchet, she would feel that she was protecting me by taking sides against Mr. JB, but that is because she so deeply believes in the Princess story. She truly believes that women should be pampered and catered to and acknowledged and applauded and obviously, never, ever have their ribs snapped.

But that isn't how life works. Accidents happen. Dealing with them with humor and fun and lightheatedness and genuine forgiveness and understanding leads to a much happier life. I go through life taking for granted that all the irritation and annoyance and frustration that comes along is secondary to the bigger picture.

I take a lot of my life for granted. I don't think that's a bad thing. It certainly helps me to understand that I am taken for granted in return, and that isn't a problem that needs to be solved! It's the basis for security and happiness and contentment. I take for granted that the members of Team JB are all working together, and I trust them to take for granted that I am, and always will be, pulling right beside them.

I don't need daily acknowledgement of all the work I do. And I wouldn't like having to live with somehow who wanted a constant stream of approval and back-patting. Gratitude, when genuine, is always appreciated and always nice, but it doesn't have to be frequent.

I only have so many ribs!

Lots of love,

JB

Work for THE Man = Freedom. Work for YOUR Man = Slavery

I found the following tweet by Private Man very interesting: "feminism has the muddled idea that women are free when they serve their employers, but slaves when they help their husbands.

I have a feeling he was responding to this article by our favorite screechy wingnut, Amanda Marcotte[105], but not necessarily:

What's an ambitious woman to do? Obviously, the price tag put on your employment is just another version of the pay gap, and for some reason, the elegant solution of professional women refusing to have children until someone fixes this situation has been taken off the table. It's a major conundrum. So why not look to men for answers? Men have managed the sticky situation of both having a job and having a home life for decades now. Their solution is possibly even more elegant in its simplicity than the "don't have children" one: Marry a woman.

---

[105] http://www.slate.com/blogs/xx_factor/2013/03/22/leaning_in_man_style_women_just_need_their_own_housewives_to_get_ahead.html

Wow! A treifecta of cluelessness, as we have come to expect from dear old Mandy. Let's unpack this picnic basket, shall we? Who thinks we're gonna come up a few sandwiches short?

..the elegant solution of professional women refusing to have children until someone fixes this situation has been taken off the table

By whom? Oh, wait! You mean ladies with careers eventually figure out that having children is actually really, really important to them? Why, even lifetime harridans end up chucking all their hard earned bucks at fertility clinics long after their eggs have expired and their ovaries have shrivelled into prunes to match their bitter faces?

Whodda thunk it? This is the number one reason I think feminism as a political movement needs to die: it outright, unashamedly, remorselessly LIES to women about how they will feel about babies and then tries to make them feel guilty about loving their children more than they could ever love their jobs. The reality is that most women die inside dropping their children off at the day orphanage for some other woman to raise. Most of those women would much rather be at home, especially when their children are very young.

It's true in most of the modern Western world, and absolutely true in the United States as well. Want to find out HOW true? Offer paid maternity leave. In countries where paid maternity leave is available, the sweeping majority of women TAKE it. Why? Because they WANT to be at home with their children. I don't actually support maternity leave as an institutional policy because all it really does is fuck with the labor market, and it has no impact on the birth rate. The countries with the most generous maternity leave policies tend to have the lowest birth rates.

So what's the point of maternity leave? Oh, we'll get to that. Just keep in mind that childless Amanda thinks a potential solution is just not have babies. How clever.

So why not look to men for answers? Men have managed the sticky situation of both having a job and having a home life for decades now.

Uhm, no they haven't. Show me the man with any kind of career, any kind of job, who was there to witness his baby's first steps (unless PooterPie starting walking at night).

Show me the man who never missed a dance recital. Show me the man who went to every ballgame. Show me the man who never had a late night meeting or a client to deal with after hours or picked up a swing shift to pay for the ballet shoes. Show me the man who was fully and completely involved in his children's lives AND had a career at the same time. Men have always had to make trade-offs and there has been shockingly little whining and weeping from that group of grown-ups.

Life is about choices.

You have them.

You make them.

You own them.

Why is it that men seem to get this while women gnash their teeth and wail at the unfairness of it all? Could it be that women are tormented by separation from their small infants in a way that men are not? Oh no! Evolutionary psychology again! And let's be clear: I am in no way saying that men do not feel every bit as emotionally attached to their infants as women do. Nonsense. Men are just as invested and care just as deeply about their children as women do, but they express that very differently.

By providing. They work longer hours at more difficult jobs for higher pay, and that ain't for shits and giggles, folks. Those men are working for their families. The pay gap has more to do with men's deep instincts to provide for their families than anything else. Men WANT to work. Women don't.

Well, not outside the home anyways. Not when they have small children.

The whole idea that men have it all and women don't is just straight up bullshit. Here's where Amanda's article gets interesting: her deep love and respect for both men and women just shines right through.

Their [men's] solution is possibly even more elegant in its simplicity than the "don't have children" one: Marry a woman.

So when men marry women who stay at home and take care of the house and the children, they are exploiting them and enslaving them, and the solution is for women is to enslave other women?

Nice.

Not far off the truth though, is it? Who picks up all the slack work when women are out working (in jobs that barely differ from the work they would be doing at home)? Oh yeah. That would be other women.

Obviously, Amanda is writing this piece as satire, but as far as biting commentary goes, it falls a little short. What it does reveal is the second big lie feminism tells both young men and women: that being dependent on a man for even a short period of time is the most frightening, terrifying thing a woman could ever do.

Why?

Well because men are evil, obviously. They might abandon you and the children to starve in the streets! Their own children! Starving like dogs in the barrio! They'll probably abuse you and you'll be helpless to stop them! They will trade you in for a younger wife! A man's life is just one giant effort to make the woman he loves and the children they have together as miserable and terrible and awful as possible.

Look at the divorce rate! Oh wait. Most of those are initiated by women for spurious reasons like "I don't feel connected anymore". Okay, well think about all those deadbeat dads who don't pay child support. Oh, oops. That's a crock of shit, too. It's actually women who are less likely to pay the child support they owe.

The U.S. Census Bureau's most recent data shows that non-custodial mothers are far less likely to pay the support they owe than are non-custodial fathers. So fathers pay 61.7% of what they owe while mothers pay only 54.6%. Forty-two percent of fathers pay everything they owe but only 34.1% of mothers do. But more interesting than that is the fact that so few non-custodial mothers are ordered to pay support. Some 54.9% of non-custodial fathers are the subjects of child support orders while only 30.4% of mothers are. In other words, fathers are about twice as likely as mothers to be ordered to pay support.

It's no wonder young women are so confused and unhappy and guilt-ridden about very normal, natural, instinctual desires for children and a meaningful relationship with a man. The two big lies of feminism are in direct conflict with what nature and biology has intended them for:

You won't care about your babies or want to be with them

Depending on a man is a colossal mistake

That's really what maternity leave policies are designed to address: the enshrined belief that the worst thing a woman could ever do is depend upon a man. Paid maternity leaves allows women to be with their children without having to depend on that child's father for financial support, and the most direct impact of those policies can be felt in the institution of marriage itself.

Marriage has turned into a means for WOMEN to have their personal, mostly irrational desires fulfilled. Her husband plays the role of the groom on the Big Princess Day, and then he exists to flatter her vanity and ego and romantic illusions, and the moment he stops doing that, out the door he goes, to be replaced by the next sucker who stands as a mirror to reflect only the reality she perceives. She has been told from birth that she is special and unique and utterly deserving of having her every whim indulged, and that she is better than any man and she must never, ever count on a man, except for all those times when she should.

Ask me out

Pay for dinner

Buy me flowers

Propose to me

By me a giant ring

Come to my rescue

But don't expect anything in return for that.

These are all, obviously, the desires of young, immature women who have yet to face the reality of their lives. Eventually, young women grow up and then they find out what they really want:

Marriage

Family

Children

Some women don't grow up until it's far too late, but you know what? Boo fucking hoo. You buy the lie, you pay the price.

Everything in life comes with a price. That doesn't mean the price isn't worth paying. My new iPhone5 is worth every penny (my husband spent). So is my dishwasher. And my new Lululemon yoga pants. Price is a reflection of value, so what is the value of being able to raise your own children?

Incalculable.

What is the price? You depend on a man, for the short time that you are at home, and if you are smart, you make sure he knows YOUR value by showing gratitude and appreciation and by actually doing the work being at home entails - cooking, organizing, cleaning, budgeting and lots of sex won't hurt either.

Working in the labor market for cash (generally doing some sort of housewifely job) for some other man isn't freedom. Being chained to a cubicle while your children are cared for by other people while your heart bleeds isn't independence. Having a client dictate how you spend your hours isn't autonomy.

That's enslavement.

Working for your man, your husband, taking care of your family on the schedule you decide and you control – that's freedom.

But it's not free. And until women understand that marriage is about two people pooling their resources for an entire lifetime, and using those resources to raise the children they have together, they will continue to yearn for a wife of their own.

Know why?

Bollywood said it best: *because there's no life, without wife.*

Lots of love,

JB

Feminist Housewife? I don't think so.

Aww, it's so cute to watch the lovely feminist ladies at Jezebel[106] try to make sense of the housewives profiled in New York Magazine[107] who value men and babies more than money and cubicles. How can this be? First up, we get class snarkiness. Why, one of those ladies is rich and she lives in Manhattan, of all places! I wonder which part of **New York Magazine** led them to believe that women in Wyoming would be profiled? Gosh, now that is a mystery.

"I'm really grateful that my husband and I have fallen into traditional gender roles without conflict", says Patricia Ireland, one of the housewives interviewed. You know, those traditional gender roles that lead to a more satisfying sex life, greater wealth and just general overall happiness. My goodness! Why would any woman choose that? Jezebel twists herself into a big knot trying to deny that there is some biological imperative for women to WANT to be at home with their small children. No, no, no. Gender and gender roles are 100% socially constructed. The only reason women prefer to be in the company of children is socialization. It's a nefarious plot of the patriarchy to ensure that women are actually happy and fulfilled denied the opportunity to pay someone else (another woman, usually) to raise her children while she files papers or works as support staff or takes care of other people for less money than her husband earns.

I find it interesting that the MORE intelligent a woman is, the MORE educated she is, the MORE likely she is to be at home with her small children.

Know why that is?

Because those women dodged the bullet previous generations of women aimed straight at them in an effort to shatter a social structure that has delivered incalculable luxuries and technologies and privileges and protections and comforts. Everything from antibiotics to iPhones, from flushing toilets to push-up bras has been invented by men, and those older ladies were pissed to the hell, neglecting to recall that all of those men had MOTHERS who made it possible for their genius to shine.

See, feminism is all about choice. Women should have all the same choices as men, at the same time. Except two:

---

[106] http://jezebel.com/5991343/the-feminist-housewife-is-such-bullshit

[107] http://nymag.com/news/features/retro-wife-2013-3/

No housewives.

No hookers.

Hmm. The two things women are really good at. The two oldest professions. The two women interviewed by New York Magazines identify as feminists themselves. Now how's that for some cognitive dissonance? No, you can't be a housewife AND a feminist. That's like being a creationist AND believing in evolution. The whole point of the one is to deny the other.

What is the rationale behind the vitriol against housewives at Jezebel and across other feminist websites? I think they are responding to a change in the cultural tides, and one that does not bode well for the theory of female supremacy. More and more young women can see the truth, that a woman's highest calling is caring for her own children under the protection of the children's father.

Marriage

Family

Children

The problem isn't, and never has been, women's ambitions to work outside the home. The problem has been the uncritical acceptance of a male timeline to accomplish those goals. Most women won't work at anything particularly productive or useful and our society will hardly crumble without their epic levels of artistic or scientific or technological genius.

And that's okay.

There is nothing wrong with women having a different sort of genius. The problem comes in denying that difference in service to an ideology when the facts and the biological realities are so very different. Young women feel torn that their most heartfelt desires are for a relationship with a man, and they live in a culture that tells them they should feel guilty to long for husbands and children more than accolades (which will be few and far between) and accomplishments (also pretty scant).

Contrary to what a lot of readers seem to think, I think women are smart and capable and assertive and perfectly adept of sorting through the conflicting messages the dominant culture sends them, and they seem to be doing just that, in ever increasing numbers. There are two giant problems that need to be addressed before we will see the re-emergence of the nuclear family as the primary social unit.

Women first need to throw off the shackles of an ideology that insists they are exactly equal to men and whenever they aren't (hello faculty of engineering) it must be the fault of men. That kind of thinking denies reality and encourages women to see themselves as perpetual victims, and there is nothing quite like the self-fulfilling prophesy of the victimhood mentality.

Remember all those second wave feminists who didn't need any bicycles and who hated babies? Gloria Steinem? Germaine Greer? Ring a bell? Yeah. Married and throwing cash at IVF clinics in a futile bid to have those hated babies now. Victims of their own misguided and utterly false beliefs about the importance of men and children and relationships and families and love.

Don't make that mistake, ladies. You'll regret it. We need a new celebration of the fact that women are not better than men, nor worse: we are different. That's not just okay, it's wonderful!

The second major problem we need to address is that there are now almost ZERO incentives or rewards for men to support a wife at home with children. Why should they work long and hard to provide all the material comforts of life to women, only to have those women walk away with all the spoils AND the children too, in divorce? Marriage has turned into a rotten deal for men.

Now that women are starting to see that, oh, oops, marriage and being a stay at home mother is actually a super-sweet deal, it's time to start sweetening the deal for men, too. That will take some concerted political effort, since so much of the bitterness for men is actually enshrined in law. Divorce, custody and spousal support laws all have to change. The importance of fatherhood needs to be openly celebrated and acknowledged.

That won't be easy. But it's very necessary.

The first thing we need to do is ignore the mewlings of liberal feminists with their kitchen-bitch husbands and their kids being raised by some poor woman while they moan about how unfair and difficult their lives are. Most of those women would be at home, too, but they "have to" work. Because they made crappy choices. They believed the lies. And now it's just sour fucking grapes. Being angry at women who made sure they DID have choices is not the answer. If you want to be angry, be angry at the women who don't think you should have the choice at all.

You don't actually need feminism's authorization to do anything. But if you want to be at home raising your own children, you will need a man who is willing to support you. Just what feminists hate. That's okay. I hate them right back.

You should, too.

Lots of love,

JB

"Lean In", says Sheryl Sandberg. That way you won't miss when you chuck your husband and kids under the bus.

Sheryl Sandberg's admonition to women to "lean in" to their careers has ignited quite the debate in the media, especially amongst all the rich white ladies to whom she is speaking. As expected, she gets lots of sneering contempt for being a rich white lady, mostly from other rich white ladies, who are just not quite as rich as Sandberg. The not-quite-as-rich white ladies resent Sandberg's implication that they need to work a bit harder.

Kudos to Sandberg for at least admitting that the real problem with lack of women at the top of the corporate world is that they simply don't make the kind of effort and sacrifice required to be there. She's absolutely correct with that analysis.

Where she goes off the rails is by suggesting that women deliberately, purposefully and strategically COMPLETELY AND UTTERLY IGNORE the needs of anyone they care about, and focus solely on themselves. Don't feel bad about abandoning your infants to the care of poor women, she says. Focus on your career and put those little buggers in daycare for MORE time. Consider it an investment in yourself.

Well, isn't that precious? How delightful for the children.

Most women see instantly that Sandberg is full of shit and more and more of them are choosing their children and husbands over a corner office, which is a heartening trend. Susan Faludi, who wrote a very famous book called Backlash: The Undeclared War Against American Women, takes Sandberg to task on her views about the importance of mothering, but she spins it in a very interesting, and quite frankly, alarming direction.

In a piece at CNN called Sandberg Left Single Mothers Behind, Faludi lays out a vision of the future that is both depressing and infuriating at the same time.

Our economic framework is founded on women's subjugation.

The power structure that Sandberg wants to feminize was built to cement the power of (some) men, and on the backs of (most) women, who would not only stay out of the power suites but would make all the power plays possible by assuming every backstage duty, from minding the kids to handling the least glamorous and lowest-paid work. It's in capitalism's DNA, and no cosmetic paste-ons at the top are going to change the dynamic without significant change on the bottom.

Faludi goes on to quote Charlotte Bunch, who claims that "class distinctions are an outgrowth of male domination". Faludi doesn't appear to have any problem with that statement. It's such a clever little semantic trick isn't it? On the one hand, Faludi and her furious friends acknowledge that power is concentrated in the hands of some men (mostly rich, mostly white) and then they use that as evidence that most women are shut out of the power structure while completely ignoring the fact that SO ARE MOST MEN, and then in a nice big giant spin of the hamster wheel, they declare our entire society to be male-dominated.

IN AN ARTICLE ABOUT A RICH POWERFUL WHITE LADY.

In order to advance the theory of patriarchy, you need to do two things: ignore the fact that most men are just as powerless as most women, and ignore the fact that some women are just as powerful as some men. It's unusual to see that played out so blatantly, though. How in the hell can you look at an argument like that and not see the flaws? It boggles the mind.

Ah well. So it is.

Let's look at the rest of Faludi's article. After declaring that male-dominated society perpetuates class as a means of maintaining their domination, Faludi turns her attention to a large class of subjugated women: single mothers. She has a little moan about the fact that single mothers are held responsible for their own choices, and has a little weep over the fact that in the US, taxpayers are ever reluctant to hand over their cash to pay these women for making terrible decisions.

The U.S. provides the worst support structure for single parents of any economically comparable nation, a recent major study by Legal Momentum found.

And it's only getting worse, as politicians aim to slash welfare programs, enforcement of child support, child tax credits and anything else they can think to deny single mothers, as they blame them for all that's wrong with society.

Oh, boo hoo. That's so mean. Why can't I have a baby with no means to pay for it? Why can't you pay for it? What, you're paying for your own children? Well too bad. Pay for mine, too!

Now Faludi gets to the heart of her vision for the future: why, she asks, can't women like Sandberg CHAMPION single mothers? Promote them as the ideal vision of what our society should be? Single mothers, you see, are the key to women's independence.

She is an adult woman with responsibilities who is not supported by a man. Symbolically, she stands for the possibility of women to truly remake the patriarchal structure. That would require a movement built not around corporate bromides, but a collective grassroots effort to demand the fundamental social change necessary to grant independent mothers a genuine independence

Let's look at this very carefully, shall we?

She is an adult woman with responsibilities who is not supported by a man.

Except for the 47% who receive child support payments. From a man (potentially the biological father of the child, but not necessarily). And except for the 35% who receive government benefits, which, astonishingly, do not grow on money trees in the fairy garden. Most of that money comes from MEN, who carry more of the tax burden than women, because they tend to make more money than women. In the UK, for example, men pay over 70% of the taxes collected. So anyone receiving state benefits is most certainly dependent on a man. On all working men, in fact.

Symbolically, she stands for the possibility of women to truly remake the patriarchal structure.

Leaving aside for the moment that the power structure is an aristocracy in which both rich men and women exploit the poor who, are also both men and women, what is this power structure going to be transformed INTO?

Faludi answers her own question:

Consider instead the benefits of a campaign that bore down on the causes behind the negative endings that mar so many single mothers' lives. It would not only be confronting a problem that affects huge numbers of women, it would be mounting a significant challenge to a system that will otherwise continue to stand between women and full emancipation.

Emancipated from what, pray tell? And now we have the entire point of the theory of patriarchy, don't we? Women are to be emancipated from the domination of men. Men will contribute two things: sperm and cash. Give me babies and give me money. And then kindly go fuck yourself.

I can't quite figure out why men object to this. It's not like we're going to DOMINATE you, lads. We're just going to make the most of what you have to offer. Money and babies, money and babies, la la la la la.

That would require a movement built not around corporate bromides, but a collective grassroots effort to demand the fundamental social change necessary to grant independent mothers a genuine independence

Know how to grant single mothers genuine independence? Let them pay for themselves. Let them lie in the beds they have made. You want to have a child without a man's support? Then accept that you will NOT HAVE A MAN'S SUPPORT. Why the hell should MEN pay for a social system that is designed to reduce them to strict utilities, unless some woman graciously consents to allow them to be fathers and husbands and yet retains the right to reduce them to functionality at any given moment?

The whole point of the early women's movement was to ensure that WOMEN were not treated as mere cattle to bear offspring, although that was never the case to begin with. While women were considered the "property" of men, men had the corollary obligation to pay for the upkeep of their "property". Obviously, that is distasteful and the declaration that women are not property was both necessary and just.

How is it possible that Faludi cannot see that she is arguing for a cultural change that would define MEN as property? The collective property of all women. And how on earth can she imagine, for one second, that men won't fight back?

You wanna talk Backlash, Susan?

Just watch.

Lots of love,

JB

Husband ≠ Friend

Yesterday morning, Mr.JB was feeling very affectionate and lovey, and on his way out the door, he kissed me and told me I was his "best friend".

Aww. How sweet.

First of all, you should know that he's leaving on Sunday to attend a conference in a really big, glorious, proper city, and he's giddy with joy at the prospect of getting out of our little town. Mr. JB is a city boy at heart, and there is pretty much nothing he loves more than the sound of traffic and sirens and the sun bouncing off skyscrapers and the hustle and bustle of millions of people shoving their way down crowded sidewalks.

Me? Not so much.

What he really wants to say is "See ya later, hillybilly! I'm outta here!", but it comes out as a smooch and "You're my best friend". It's straight-up bullshit, but funny bullshit, so I don't mind. But it did get me thinking....

Mr. JB is a great guy, obviously, and I love him to pieces, but he is NOT my best friend. My best friend is Pixie, by far, followed by GloryGirl, SuzyQ, SnowWhite (who is in France for the year with her husband and kids, but she'll be back in September), JudgyAsshole, Prince Charming, CleverGuy and NurseRachet. Those eight people form the core of my circle of friends. They are the ones I complain to, ask for advice, laugh with, discuss endless amounts of minutiae and just generally share the details of my life with.

On the one hand, it would be awesome to be married to Pixie. She does laundry! And she cooks! And she sends the most hilarious ecards about how much cooking and laundry sucks! We spend many days counting down the hours until wine o'clock and no one appreciates my contempt for internet assholes quite like Pixie.

On the other hand, I wouldn't like to fuck her. Oh, she's super cute and hot and has awesome hair, but the whole girl thing doesn't do it for me.

So there's that.

After the "best friend" comment yesterday, I thought I would try a little experiment on Mr.JB to see just how good a friend he is. I copied and pasted him, the whole morning, on all the texts I sent to Pixie. Here are the main issues in my life at the moment:

> The hamster is loose in the ductwork. (Don't ask, it's a long story).
>
> The stitch marker fell out of the slouchy hat I'm making for LittleDude, and now I've lost my place and the whole thing is fucked up.
>
> Who the fuck gives a four year old Sharpie markers? How do I get Sharpie markers off the coffee table?
>
> Do these yoga pants make my ass look fat?
>
> I don't have any lime juice to make the barbacoa. Can I use lemon juice instead?
>
> What the fuck is wrong with Amanda Marcotte?
>
> The *Catching Fire* trailer will be out on April 14th! Squee!
>
> Do I have to wait until the kids get home from school before I have a drink?
>
> On a scale of one to ten, how hot is Chris Hemsworth?

Just as I predicted, shortly after 11AM, my phone rang. I have a special ringtone for when Mr. JB calls: It's the Imperial Death March from Star Wars, and when I hear it, I know this shit is serious. He never calls unless it's really important.

"Dear, what is all this bullshit you are sending me? Am I supposed to do something about this?"

Then of course, I drop the F Bomb.

"But I thought you were my friend! My best friend! Don't you want to know how my day has been?"

crickets

"Let's not be friends."

You see, I think there is something totally and utterly destructive in the notion that your spouse should be your friend. Your best friend, even. Friends are people who share your interests and who are going through some of the same stages and having the same issues and confronting the same obstacles that you are. And sometimes, when friends pass into different stages of their lives, the friendship loses some of its intensity and value and there is a disconnection and often those friendships drift into fond acquaintances and that's it.

Graduating, getting married, having children (especially having children), buying a house, moving cities, moving countries, changing jobs, managing health problems – all those things can change a friendship into something less.

Sometimes, it's just time to move on.

I'm incredibly fortunate that my best friend has been my best friend for almost 20 years now. Pixie and I have been inseparable since our first year at college. I've known SuzyQ for 13 years. CleverGuy's older brother was the best man at my wedding, so while I have only known him really well for 5 years, I have known his family for a long time. CleverGuy is a really good friend. I can talk to him about tons of stuff that doesn't interest my other friends, but he is about to graduate from an engineering program, and who knows where he will end up? If he moves very far away, we'll still be friends, but not as close as we are now.

And that's okay. That's life.

Friends fill in little voids in your life that your spouse either isn't interested in, doesn't care about, or just can't fill in! There is no way Mr.JB can ever appreciate how valuable cimmaron is when making Mexican-fusion dishes. JudgyAsshole, who is a wonderful cook, can. JudgyAsshole's dad has brilliant advice about flower arranging. No way in hell Mr.JB will EVER have an opinion on that subject.

At the moment, I happen to give a shit about those topics, and I am lucky to have friends who can share those interests with me. It's conceivable that my interests will change in the future, and I'll need a different set of friends to reflect what's new in my life. And that is absolutely a two way street. I don't care what Mr.Jb's Xbox score is. I don't give a shit which part of the budget will be used to fund a new hire. I do NOT want to watch Naked Gun. I don't give a fuck how much trouble linen pants are. Text your friends, dude. Don't bother me with this shit.

But what happens when your spouse is your friend, and your interests change? Then what? You start feeling disconnected, alienated, lonely. When you ask your spouse to meet your needs as a friend, you run the very real risk that your needs will change, and your spouse won't be able to meet those needs.

That's a tragedy. The solution is NOT to trade in your spouse for a new one. It's to STOP asking your spouse to be your friend.

So if Mr.JB is not my friend, what is he?

It's very simple: he's my husband. I'm his wife. We are partners in an enterprise that matters deeply to both of us: our family. Of course, we have shared interests and I find him hilarious and fun to be with and when he's gone, I miss him deeply. He's also really great to have sex with. But ultimately, we are partners, not friends.

If all my friends were to suddenly disappear, I would indeed be very lonely and sad and unhappy. But that wouldn't be my husband's fault, nor would it be something he could solve. Getting rid of my husband wouldn't change the fact that I am friendless. It would just mean that I am without the protection of a partner.

And it would mean, that in a very real way, I would lose most of my most cherished memories. In a long term partnership, like the one we have, we are the repositories of one another's memories. Our shared life together exists in one another's minds. Our life is a tapestry of tiny threads, woven together, into a work of beautiful art.

Chains do not hold a marriage together. It is threads, hundreds of tiny threads which sew people together through the years.

Simone Signoret

I don't need my friends to create art. I just need my fellow weaver. When I find the work frustrating or irritating, I don't turn on my partner or throw away the whole project. I text my friends.

That's what friends are for.

Now, does anyone have any ideas about how to get the hamster out of the air ducts?

Lots of love,

JB

Rocket scientist figures out that a woman's life isn't rocket science.

Yvonne Madelaine Claeys was born on Dec. 30, 1924, in St. Vital, a suburb of Winnipeg, Manitoba. Her parents had separately immigrated from Flanders, in Belgium. Her father was a carpenter. After the University of Manitoba barred her from the engineering program, she studied mathematics and chemistry instead and graduated at the top of her class. Her lack of an engineering degree did not prevent her from getting a job with Douglas Aircraft in Santa Monica, California. "Nobody had the right degrees back then, so it didn't matter," she told The Star-Ledger of Newark in 2010. "I didn't have engineering, but the engineers didn't have the chemistry and math."

Yvonne Brill is rare example of female genius defined in traditionally male terms, and as I've argued before, when women of tremendous talent and ability and intelligence are born, the culture almost always makes room for them to rise. The University of Manitoba barred Yvonne from the engineering program because there were no accommodations for women at an outdoor engineering camp. Really? What kind of accommodations would she need? A menstruation hut? Her own tent? That kind of challenge was insurmountable for engineers? How stupid.

I'm guessing there was just very deep suspicion that women could actually perform in a discipline as demanding as engineering. These are some of the smartest people on the planet, and the higher up the intelligence distribution curve you go, the greater the gender disparity. Men outnumber women eight to one on the curve after IQ measurement reaches 145.

Eight to one!

That's not sexism. It's biology. But it still didn't stop Yvonne. She was the one, up against the rightfully suspicious eight.

Engineering is out?

Well then, math and chemistry are in. Easy peasy. "You just have to be cheerful about it and not get upset when you get insulted," she once said.

Exactly, Yvonne.

Jezebel threw a spaz[108] because Yvonne, who went on to marry and have children, planned her life around her husband and her children, and seems to have been very happy to do so. She preferred to be called Mrs.

---

[108] http://jezebel.com/5993068/new-york-times-obit-for-rocket-scientist-yvonne-brill-rhapsodizes-about-her-beef-stroganoff

Brill, and when her children came along, she stepped out of the workforce for eight years to care for them. Apparently, she also made a beautiful beef stroganoff.

Well shock and horror!

The lovely Mrs. Brill, at home in an apron with her children, knowing that her genius wasn't going anywhere, and that supporting her husband's career was just as important as her own ambitions. Mrs. Brill followed her husband around as he changed jobs, and according to her son, Matthew, she was perfectly content to do so. "Good husbands are harder to find than good jobs."

Amen, Yvonne.

Here's what pisses me off about the Jezebel article, among other things: It should go without saying, but the problem with the original obituary is that a male scientist would never — NEVER — be hailed as a "the world's best dad" before being hailed as an important scientific innovator.

First of all, although she sounds like she really was a wonderful mother, nowhere in the obituary does it say that Yvonne was the world's greatest mother. It says she made beef stroganoff, took time off to raise her children, preferred her husband's name and felt that a good husband was a far better investment than a good job.

Leaving that little sneering bit of contempt for mothering aside, it took me approximately two seconds to find an obituary for a male scientist that spoke of his family upbringing, what he liked to eat and the importance of his wife. Okay, he didn't make a mean stroganoff, but apparently the rice and evaporated milk diet was important enough to mention[109]. Ah yeah, and he liked lizards and frogs, too. And it took a further two seconds to find an eminent scientist who works cooking into his lectures[110]. In an article titled *Ten Things You Need to Know About Stephen Hawking*, the Mirror[111] felt that four of those things should be about his upbringing, his family, his children and his hobbies.

These things are not buried in some deep, dirty, secret part of the internet that is almost impossible to access. It would have taken Jezebel ten minutes to find out that articles and obituaries that refer to male scientists are just as likely to talk about their family, their spouses, their children, their hobbies.

So what is the source of feminist bitterness about women, incredibly intelligent, accomplished, brilliant women who are capable not only of building propulsions systems that keep satellites in orbit, but ALSO of making beef stroganoff, being great moms and loving wives?

Personally, I think it's the order of priorities that pisses feminists off. The feminist ideal is this:

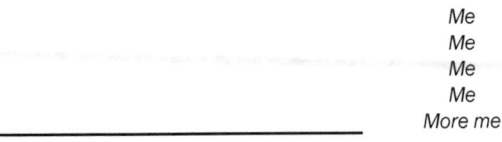

Me
Me
Me
Me
More me

---

[109] http://www.telegraph.co.uk/news/obituaries/science-obituaries/9920933/Hobart-Muir-Smith.html
[110] http://www.seas.harvard.edu/brenner/Home.html

[111] http://www.mirror.co.uk/news/uk-news/stephen-hawking-10-things-you-171089

My cat
More me
Yoga
Book club
Shopping
Pissing and moaning
How much will I get if I divorce him now?
Should I fuck the new intern? He's kind of hot.
I hope that asshole doesn't think I'm making dinner tonight
Shit, I chipped my manicure
Should I get a venti or a grande?
My house
My kid
My husband

Women like Yvonne have an entirely different set of priorities:

Husband
Children
Work

In that order. You would be hard-pressed to find a lady smarter than Yvonne, and she put that intelligence to work in BOTH caring for her family and designing rocket propulsion systems. Because you see, you CAN do both. But not at the same time. The simple reality of women's lives is that we are on a time line that has built-in constraints, and if we want children, we need to have a completely different set of priorities than men.

Oh, and we need men, too. And that's the real burn. Fish DO need bicycles, and those bicycles aren't free. Why should they be? It comes down to realizing that women and men are not identical, and in feminist theory, that means we are not equal. According to feminism, the only way women can be equal to men is to meet them head on, achievement for achievement, and to deny, in the face of all evidence, that there are real, measurable differences in terms of what we can accomplish.

Rather than embrace a woman's special genius, feminism denies femininity altogether. A rocket scientist who was also a mother, wife and excellent home cook? Only one of those things is worth mentioning. By denying that even the smartest women on the planet are still women, feminism inadvertently (or perhaps consciously and deliberately) hates women.

Why would I embrace a theory that hates who I am? Why would any woman? Loving your husband, taking care of your children and making a terrific stroganoff are not things to be embarrassed about or ashamed of. Nonsense. They are the very things that make us happy.

All of us.

It's not rocket science.

Lots of love,

JB

Should greedy wives walk away with all the spoils?

Today I'd like to introduce you to a blogger/columnist I think you will find quite interesting. Her name is Claire-Louise Meadows. Claire offered her take on a Daily Mail article titled *We fought for equality. So why do greedy wives still sponge off their ex-husbands?* and today, I want to offer mine.

Let's start by playing a game of what if...

What if I woke up tomorrow and decided, you know what, this not buying me flowers bullshit is a deal breaker. I want a divorce. I have not contributed money to my marriage for the past 11 years, but goddamn it, I have contributed value.

I want the house, the car, the kids and all the furniture. I want child support, half of Mr. JB's pension and alimony to cover the time it will take me to find a job. Oh, five years ought to do it.

And I'm going to get it. All of it. I have the courts on my side and the law to back me up. And I will have all the sympathy of our friends and family. Remember that time he picked me up in a bear hug and broke my rib?

I think I remembered that wrong. He actually got really mad at me and he beat me up. Punched me in the ribs. No, wait! He pushed me down the stairs. He did whatever it is you have to do to break someone's rib. I don't know. I'll figure out the details later. I can make this shit up as I go along.

Jesus, it can take DECADES for a woman to recover from that kind of abuse. I may never have to get a job! I can live off his salary until the pension kicks in.

Super win for me!!!!

It sounds like a joke, but IT'S NOT. I could do all of those things. I could walk away with everything. And if I did, it would be his fault. He should have bought me those fucking flowers.

These are the kinds of divorces the Daily Mail is talking about, and I agree with both Claire-Louise and Liz Hodgkinson that this shameless fleecing of men needs to stop. The laws governing divorce were created when the world was a very different place, and they are now being used to abuse men and reduce them to what amounts to indentured servitude.

Yes, that's for you, Liz.

In my circle of friends alone, I know of countless men who have fallen foul of greedy ex-wives who seem determined to see the men they married reduced to penury.

It's easy for an attractive woman to use her charm and wiles to entrap a rich man, all the time calculating the cash they receive when they can call time on the marriage.

One friend had been married for about 20 years when his wife decided she wanted a divorce. There were no particular grounds, and no one else was involved. Each sought out a lawyer, and the wife was awarded 85 per cent of the joint assets.

There were no children and she had never worked. After the divorce, she moved into a small cottage with enough money to see her out. He had just enough money to buy a small flat, and had to start all over again. He got virtually none of the marital assets accumulated over the years, including a house worth £800,000.

But, I can also see another side to this argument.

Let's play another round of what if....

The sad truth is that I'm getting older. I haven't really let myself go, but I'm not the taut, firm twenty-four year old I used to be. Three pregnancies have left their marks on me, and I spend an awful lot of my days in yoga pants and UGG boots. They're fucking awesome UGG boots, but still. Mr. JB looks at me, and it just isn't there anymore. And I make him feel old.

You know who doesn't make him feel old? That twenty-four year old PhD student he met at work with her perky tits and firm ass. The way she giggles and flirts with him makes him feel amazing. Like he's still got it. She thinks everything he does is hilarious and she's in awe of his experience and knowledge and expertise and once he starts banging her on his desk, it's all over.

He's trading me in for a younger, hotter wife who is also not quite such a mouthy, judgy bitch. Of course, he has no idea that ten years from now, she's gonna be in yoga pants, complaining that he doesn't buy her flowers, but no matter. Right now, he feels like a god!

So he sits me down and gives me the talk: I want a divorce.

Oh yeah? Fuck you. I have spent the last decade of my life making it possible for you to excel at work, keeping you healthy and happy, caring for your children and your home, and those things are now mine. You wouldn't have the income and position you have without me, and you WILL pay me for those things.

That's the kind of scenario that divorce and alimony laws were designed to address.

I'm not certain where the statistic comes from, but I have come across it repeatedly: 17% of divorces are caused by infidelity.

I sincerely doubt that ALL of infidelity was committed by men, and furthermore, that the cheating partner went on to marry their paramour. But let's assume it's true. Every divorce in which infidelity is cited as the main reason for the divorce involves men cheating on their wives, and every single one of those men went on to marry their mistress.

It would still only be 17%!

That's a very small number. The other 83% fall under the "irreconcilable differences" label. All of this suggests that the first scenario I described is the most likely one. Most divorces are initiated by women. And most of them are for completely bullshit reasons. The top two reasons cited[112] are verbal abuse and emotional neglect. He called me a bitch and didn't buy me flowers. Most men are blindsided when their wife requests a divorce. Because she has never given any indication that anything is wrong[113].

I call it "The False Okay." I think a lot of women tell the very same lie for years on end. They say "okay" when they don't mean it. They tell their husbands, "everything's fine," even when it's not. "Keeping the peace" is what they call it. They are, they tell me, getting through the day. It is all about the argument they simply do not want to have.

Part of the reason women don't have the argument they need to have is that there is no consequence for letting shit build up for years and years and years without saying a word. If women knew they would walk away with NOTHING, they might be a little more inclined to open their mouths and speak. That is why,

[112] http://divorcesupport.about.com/b/2012/06/24/why-most-divorces-are-initiated-by-women.htm

[113] http://www.huffingtonpost.com/lynn-toler/why-so-many-men-never-see_b_815502.html

despite the headache of administering such a program, we need to bring back the concept of fault to divorce. Spouses who want to walk away from a marriage should be free to do so for any reason they like, but when it comes to dividing assets and determining custody, we need to return to the concept of guilty and innocent.

You're not happy and don't feel fulfilled anymore? Okay, sweetie. That's too bad. Off you go, but you will NOT be taking the house and car and kids with you. Get your clothes and your shoes and your self-help books and GTFO. Personally, I think infidelity is a stupid reason to end a marriage, but if that's going to be the reason you cite, then you'll need some proof. Screen-cap those sexts, honey. You husband has been abusing you? Prove it. You can't just SAY IT. You need to prove it. And that proof will guide judges when it comes to the division of assets.

As it stands, the law does an excellent job of protecting those few women like myself from being left destitute should my husband decide to trade me in. It's doing a piss poor job with the others, though. Even divorcees admit that divorce is far too easy to obtain, removing all incentives for couples to grow the fuck up and deal with their issues. And by "couples", I mostly mean "women", since they are the initiators in the majority cases.

And that's what it comes down to. Women refusing to engage their husbands when they have a problem, allowing resentment and bitterness and unhappiness to build until it becomes unbearable, and then blaming all of that on their husbands. And we give them no reason NOT to do that. If we brought the concept of fault back to divorce, women would have some pretty damn good reasons to work on their marriages rather than heading for divorce courts where they can rest assured they will walk away with most of the assets and the children.

You want a divorce? Okay. You'll need a reason. And if your precious feelings are the only reason you can come up with, well, don't let the door hit you in the ass on your way out, sweetheart. The door will be staying attached to the house your husband and kids will continue to live it, with or without you.

Oh, and as an aside, I should tell you that Mr. JB now buys me flowers quite regularly. He fucking hates it, but he does it. Because he knows I like them. Know HOW he knows that?

I told him!

Lots of love,

JB

Sulky little bitch can't manage her money, threatens her husband with divorce if he doesn't give her more. Sulky bitch is clearly also a stupid bitch.

I love reading advice columns, and Dear Prudence is one of my favorites. Jesus, that bitch is clueless. Her advice usually consists of "go to therapy", and she appears not to realize that most "therapists" are retards who took psych degrees and can't find any other job.

She's always good for a laugh, though, and her response to this writer[114] is one of the best I've had in a long time:

114

http://www.slate.com/articles/life/dear_prudence/2013/04/dear_prudence_my_daughter_lied_about_bei

Q. Married but Financially Separate: My husband and I have been married for five years and have totally separate finances—bank accounts, credit cards, nothing is shared. He makes significantly more money than I do and pays all of the bills with the exception of the mortgage, which I pay. He "gives" me money weekly for groceries and incidentals. Regardless, I am pretty much broke all of the time. We don't have a joint credit card or bank account and I get really resentful when he spends lots of money on something and I am relegated to the local discount store, a place he wouldn't consider gracing. He refuses to join our finances or have a joint credit card. This isn't a partnership. As he would say, what's mine is mine and what's yours is yours. Is he on a power trip or paranoid? I know I blew it by not discussing how we would handle our money before getting married but I didn't and now this is a serious issue for me.

Let's take this apart, shall we?

My husband and I have been married for five years and have totally separate finances—bank accounts, credit cards, nothing is shared.

Hmm. I wonder why? Anyone get the feeling that something is being left out here? Totally separate finances for five years feels like some sort of reaction, no? I wonder what cupcake would like to DO with that joint bank account and what she intends to purchase with the shared credit card?

Oh, let's just start with the assumption that MEN SUCK and this guy is no different. He's a big mean asshole who won't foot wifey's bills.

In which case, why did you marry him?

I'm seeing some excellent judgement from cupcake right off the bat.

He makes significantly more money than I do and pays all of the bills with the exception of the mortgage, which I pay.

Oh boo hoo. Does he have some actual, real, marketable skills that translate into an income and you don't? Let me guess. Women's studies major? Psychology? Art history? And he pays all the bills! What a jerk! YOU have to pay the mortgage? Well, that's bullshit. Why should you have to pay any bills at all?

I wonder how much the "bills" amount to after the mortgage is paid?

According to the Department of Labor statistics[115], the average couple spends about $10 000/year on housing. Out of an annual expenditures budget of just under $50 000. So cupcake, who has to pay the mortgage, is likely spending about $10 000 per year, leaving her husband, who pays all the other bills, on the hook for $40 000 a year.

That's so mean! He pays, on average, FOUR TIMES MORE for all the bills, and this bitch is whining?

He "gives" me money weekly for groceries and incidentals. Regardless, I am pretty much broke all of the time.

So basically, she doesn't earn very much money, has to pay a quarter of their expenses, he gives her money ON TOP of that, and she's still broke most of the time. Sounds like a really responsible sort of person, no?

ng_a_stripper_for_years.html

[115] http://www.thesimpledollar.com/2010/01/04/how-the-average-american-family-spends-their-income-and-how-to-trim-it/

Gosh, this is a perplexing situation indeed. Why on earth doesn't he want to give her access to his bank account?

We don't have a joint credit card or bank account and I get really resentful when he spends lots of money on something and I am relegated to the local discount store, a place he wouldn't consider gracing.

Awww. You get wesentful? You don't wike him spending money on himself? You have to go to the discount store? Hey, I have an idea! Get a better job! Or a second job. Or, you know, shut the fuck up.

He refuses to join our finances or have a joint credit card. This isn't a partnership. As he would say, what's mine is mine and what's yours is yours. Is he on a power trip or paranoid?

Let's see. By your own admission, you are resentful of your husband, you don't earn much money, you can't manage the little money you DO earn PLUS what he gives you on top of that and you are broke most of the time. Hmm. Is he on a power trip or paranoid? I'm not sure how you are defining those terms, but if you mean "is he responding rationally and prudently to an immature sulky little bitch of a wife who can't even manage her allowance", then yes to both!

I know I blew it by not discussing how we would handle our money before getting married but I didn't and now this is a serious issue for me.

You know what, sweetpea? I'm thinking he's having the exact same thoughts. He blew it by marrying you, and he doesn't intend to blow it any further by giving you carte blanche access to the family resources.

So what is Prudie's advice?

MAKE HIM PAY FOR MARRIAGE COUNSELING!

And if that doesn't work, get a divorce.

A: Since you don't mention other more pleasant aspects of life that you do share, I'm wondering if there is any part of your union that does feel like a partnership. (I hope your weekly stipend isn't for services rendered.) If not, what are you doing in it? There is something you two need to do together and for which your husband should pay: marriage counseling. Tell him that you thought you married the handsome prince, but you feel like Cinderella before the ball. Explain that you have become so resentful of your disparate financial conditions that your marriage is at stake. Do keep in mind that since you are chronically broke, if you two do split, you're going to have to learn to live within your own means.

At least Prudie has the good sense to remind Cupcake that she will be paying all her own bills should she decide to go that route. Well, depending on whether or she can secure alimony. Odds are pretty good she'll get a few years worth of access to that bank account, which just might be enough time to line up the proper Prince Charming who will grasp that she is not Cinderella BEFORE the ball, she is Cinderella AFTER the ball.

Having read this column, I am now even more grateful that I have a husband who shares not just his life with me, but his money, too. True story: Once NurseRatchet was over for a visit and Mr. JB came home and took my wallet out of my purse, looked over all the receipts, took them, counted the cash I had and then put my wallet back in my purse.

After he left, Ratchet threw a fit! How dare he? He checks your purchases? Just goes in your purse whenever he wants? Counts your money? Do you have to grovel for that money? Do you have no privacy at all?

Ratchet is kind of a bitch. I don't really see her anymore, but that's another story. The point here is how she assumed that our finances were something deeply personal and separate. They're not. Mr. JB checks my wallet pretty much every day because he files all the receipts in the event that I need to exchange or return something. If it was up to me, I would never find a receipt ever. I can barely find my keys, never mind a receipt for the hairdryer I bought six weeks ago. He also likes me to have a certain amount of cash in my wallet, in case I want coffee or need to buy some small thing. I never check to see if I have money before I go somewhere, because I KNOW that I do.

I have access to our bank account, but I never touch it. If I'm not going to bother learning how our budget works (and I'm not), then I figure I have no business messing with it. I use my Visa or the cash in my wallet for whatever I want or need to buy. Anything bigger than $40, I run by Mr. JB first. I'm not asking for permission, I'm asking if that purchase will mess with his budget. It works very well for us, because I'm not a big shopper and I don't spend a lot of money (except for the bookstore – I can be pretty deadly in the bookstore).

And once I go back to work, none of this will change. I will have whatever money I earn deposited into our joint account, which I will then proceed to ignore completely and I'll keep using my Visa and trusting that my wallet is filled with cash. It works because I'm actually a grown-up with some concept of how money and budgets work. We never carry credit card debt and I would consider it a huge personal failure to ever blow our family budget to the point that was necessary. It's just not going to happen.

What happens when you marry someone like cupcake who can't manage her allowance and is perpetually broke?

You keep your accounts separate. Seems pretty reasonable to me. If cupcake wants to be Cinderella AFTER the ball, she can get her ass out of that pumpkin and go earn some money. Prince Charming is hardly likely to foot the bill for some resentful little bitch who thinks the solution to her problems is the Prince's cash and a joint credit card.

You know, I just realized something. I never put my wallet in the same place twice. Right now I have no idea where it is. That means Mr.JB has to go hunting for it every day to make sure I have money. That must be really fucking annoying.

I'll have to work on that.

Baby steps!

Lots of love,

JB

What do women want from marriage? Oh, everything. Is that so much to ask?

In the past five years on our street, we have seen two marriages disintegrate.

I'll preface all of this by saying no one really knows what's going on in any marriage except the two people in it, but it's fun to speculate! Up close and personal, these two marriages seem rather instructive.

The first couple were highschool sweethearts who had been together for 18 years, married for 10 of those. They went away to college together, both became geologists, graduated, got married and had a daughter.

The original plan was that GeoGal would stay home with the baby and GeoGuy would continue to work and support them. Sadly, maternal instinct seemed to have passed GeoGal by, and she hated being at home with the baby. Absolutely hated it. GeoGuy, on the other hand, was utterly smitten with his little Peanut and couldn't bear to part with her, so they switched places, and GeoGuy became a full time stay at home daddy with a baby.

We moved in next door when Peanut was 8 months old. GeoGuy is a huge nerd and we bonded instantly over our love of Star Trek costumes and crocheted baby Yoda hats and our mutual dislike of housework. I was pregnant with LittleDude when we came to this town, and soon we both had babies and each other for company, which was really, really nice.

We also live on a street with a superhuge blabby-mouthed busy-body who had me and GeoGuy involved in a sordid love affair in no time flat. That irritated the shit out of me mostly because by the time she really started yapping, we had four children under six between us! I seriously doubt there was one single day of those first few years that one or the other of us did not have babypuke, urine, snot or dried food stuck on us somewhere. One baby produces an enormous amount of disgusting fluids. Four takes "gross" to a whole new level.

So sexy.

And just when, exactly, did Blabby think me and GeoGuy were getting it on? And who was taking care of the children while this was happening? Actually, GeoGuy had the best response to that little rumour! He said, "yeah, we're homeschooling. The kids are majoring in sex ed".

Well, I thought it was funny.

GeoGuy was and IS a really great father, but the more domestic he became, the more invested in his child and his home, the more his wife started to despise him. She was jealous of the bond he had with their daughter and eventually, she asked him to put the baby in daycare and go back to work so she could respect him again.

He refused.

And that pretty much spelled the end of the marriage. Five months before Peanut was ready to go off to the first grade, and GeoGuy was ready to go back to work, GeoGal filed for divorce. It was completely devastating for Peanut, who had never experienced daycare before and she was suddenly thrust into it because Mommy threw Daddy out and he had to go to work.

He had no trouble finding a job, but it killed him that GeoGal wouldn't wait five months for their daughter to start school and let him help her make that transition.

It's not uncommon, though. Women scream that they want men more involved in their children's lives and then show nothing but contempt when men do exactly that. The stay-at-home dad is great in feminist THEORY, but in practice, those men get nothing but scorn and disrespect.

Man up, you lazy fuckers. Get a job!

The truth is that once a woman loses respect for a man, she loses attraction for him, too, and that pretty much spells the end of the fairytale. Young women are being sold a version of marriage and relationships that is pretty much guaranteed to end with women despising their male partners. They get advice like make men sign contracts to do housework. Or trick your man into doing what you want, the way you want it done. Reward him with sex if he follows your orders.

Aaaaaaand, in the shock of the century, men hate that shit and pretty much won't put up with it. Leading to the second shock of the century: women aren't happy. Single women aren't happy because they aren't married and married women aren't happy because oops, they married an actual person, and not a Ken Doll they can use as a perfect accessory to complement both their outfit and the curtains in the living room of their DreamHouse!

According to sociologists Karyn Loscocco and Susan Walzer in *Gender and the Culture of Heterosexual Marriage in the United States*, women are pissy about marriage because MEN, obviously.

Forget about "two becoming one" when a man and woman marry; in fact, what we really experience is a "his" and a "hers" marriage – a husband's and a wife's. In general... ...marriage generally benefits the hubby more than the wife.

I'll let all the guys who have been through the divorce ringer have a good chuckle over than one. Marriage benefits men more than women?

No.

It makes men happier than women because men approach marriage as realists. They understand that marriage isn't going to be a Disney story. Parts of it are great and parts of it suck, and that's life. Women see marriage as a home improvement project, with hubby being the project that needs improving. I think a lot of this stems from the fact that so much of marriage occurs in the domestic sphere, which women tend to define as their own.

True story: about five years into my marriage, I realized that all the things I found irritating and annoying about Mr. JB were NOT going to change. I honestly thought they would. Part of me was sold on the idea that I would be able to mold my husband into the perfect little wedding cake-topper groom that I wanted him to be. And, like most women, I couldn't do that, because it turns out that my husband is a person with his own characteristics and traits and his own reasons for doing the things I find annoying.

And I was frustrated and unhappy.

Almost ready to swallow the idea that I deserved more. I deserved better. I deserved a husband who would just do whatever the fuck I told him to do, and do it with a goddamn smile, too! Looking back, it seems so ridiculously petty, but at the time, it felt like a serious issue. Mr. JB, you see, is super uptight about his stuff. His clothes, his books, his papers, his shoes, his glasses ... you name it. He is careful with his stuff and if I happened to treat his things a little roughly, he will get really angry with me.

One day I threw his shoes down the stairs.

I was going to put them in the closet, so I chucked them down and planned on getting to them later. And then he was mean and yelled at me. I took that to mean waaaaah – he doesn't love me! He loves his stuff more than me! He cares more about his fucking shoes than me! Waaaaah!

And I was getting more and more sulky.

You don't take care of me the way you take care of your dress shirts! And why are all your shirts blue? Can't you buy another color for fuck's sake? Ignoring, of course, the fact that he spends his entire life taking care of me. By paying all the bills. All of them. No matter what color they are.

Hamster logic!

Then one day, we were going out somewhere, and at the last moment, I couldn't find the coat I wanted to wear. Or my wallet. Or my keys. Which is normal. I never put stuff in the same place twice. I don't know why. I just don't. I never have any idea where my sunglasses are or where the cordless phones are or what I did with the book I was reading. I have to go looking for them, and when we are in a rush to get somewhere, that's annoying.

On this particular day, Mr. JB flipped out on me. He was furious and just lit into me. "Why don't you ever put any of your shit in the proper place? You would think after five years you might have picked up at least ONE good habit from me!".

Bingo!

I remember laughing hysterically when he said that. He had been hoping that I would change, that his habits might rub off on me, just as I had been hoping he might learn to be a little less uptight.

And we were both wrong.

We spent the next few days talking about the fact that we needed to accept that the other person was not going to change, and in realizing that I was just as annoying to him as he was to me, all my bad feelings disappeared. It helped so much to talk about the things we can't stand about each other. First, it makes it really obvious that most of this shit is just so petty. Second, it makes both of us understand that we aren't being ourselves for the express purpose of annoying one another. It's just who we are. He needs to know where his things are. It unsettles his mind if he doesn't know where his keys are. I could care less where my keys are. I just assume I'll find them when I need them.

And in those flaws are the things we love about one another. He is calm and centered and stable and he orders our world with precision and makes sure that everything is taken care of properly and reliably. I never have to worry about any of the practical details of how our life works, because he takes care of all of that. I am flexible and cheerful and optimistic and I assume that everything will work out and I just go with the flow of everything around me for the most part, and that makes it very easy for me to accommodate changes in plans or the conversation we had just ten minutes ago: "Six people are coming for dinner in four hours. Is that okay?"

Yep. It's fine. No worries. I got it covered.

What it takes for women to be happy in marriage is to look in the mirror and understand that WE ARE NOT PERFECT. That's hard to do, and women get no encouragement from the wider culture to understand themselves as personally flawed. It's quite the opposite. Women are encouraged to believe that what they want, how they see the world, what they expect from relationships – all those things are automatically correct and a woman should sacrifice everything to ensure that she has what she wants.

Thereby guaranteeing she gets nothing she wants.

It starts and ends with the very simple concept of respect. Respect for your partner, as a person. That means you understand that he or she is a completely different person than you are, and it is NOT up to you to change or alter who that person is, even if you find some aspects really irritating. No one is perfect, including yourself. Women who don't respect men, in particular, are not going to be able to love them. If you force your partner into behaving in a way you can't respect, you are quite literally destroying your love for him.

That's the mistake that is making so many women unhappy.

That second marriage on our street that collapsed? Let's call them Brad and Susan. Susan enrolled in college, got a degree, got a promotion, started earning way more money than Brad, cultivated interests like theatre and shopping trips to the Big Apple and found she just couldn't respect Brad anymore. So she traded Brad in....

For GeoGuy.

Yep. GeoGuy and Susan are now living together. So Blabby was right about GeoGuy getting busy with one of the wives on the street. She just had the wrong wife. We'll see how that relationship works out. Any guesses?

Holy shit, I have six people coming for dinner tonight! I should probably run out and get a bit more wine.

Now where the hell are my keys? Anyone seen my wallet? Dammit!

Lots of love,

JB

Being a mother isn't a job? Bullshit. Is it the toughest job? Hahahahahahah! Nope. But it's definitely a job.

Lots of interesting commentary around the recent Parents survey that reveals 92% of all mothers agree with the statement "There's no tougher job than being a mom". There are a number of different factors at play when we talk about "mothering" and what constitutes a "job" and what makes a job "tough" – let's tackle them one by one.

Predictably, Jezebel begins with the old Simone de Beauvoir "being a stay at home mother and wife should be banned" bullshit.

No woman should be authorized to stay at home and raise her children. Society should be totally different. Women should not have that choice, precisely because if there is such a choice, too many women will make that one."

- "Sex, Society, and the Female Dilemma," Saturday Review, June 14, 1975.

Feminism: giving women choices. Except the one they would most prefer. Jezebel has a long history of slagging on women who do their work outside the formal economic structure of the marketplace, and it's not the JOB they hate, so much as the women who do the job for their OWN families rather than for strangers.

Is working in daycare center a job?

Is running a housekeeping service a job?

Is owning a catering business a job?

Of course it is, but only if you are selling your services in the formal marketplace. Provide those services for the family you love, and you are a pitiable dupe of the patriarchy. Because someone has to earn the living, right? And if Mommy is at home, it must be Daddy doing the productive economic labor.

Oh, dear. Too much power for Daddy. Out there every day slogging in some job he may or may not enjoy so he can have the pleasure of lording it over the woman who gets to do whatever she wants, whenever she wants, all day long.

I find it interesting that when a family has TWO Daddies, they are more likely to embrace the traditional division of family labor, and have one Daddy at home full time. In his seminal book *A Treatise on the Family*, published in 1981, the Nobel Prize–winning economist Gary Becker argued that "specialization," whereby one parent stays home and the other does the earning, is the most efficient way of running a household, because the at-home spouse enables the at-work spouse to earn more.

Guess who is most likely to specialize? Gay dads[116].

When you take the ideology of gender and feminism out of the equation and ask a couple raising children to make the most sensible economic choice, the traditional family wins out. If the debate were really about what makes the most financial sense, then having a parent at home would be a no-brainer. But that is not what the debate is about. It's about giving women the power to game a system that ensures that no matter how hard a man works, his wife will always be able to control the family assets and access to the children.

And that conversation starts with denying[117] that the at-home parent is even doing an economically productive job at all.

But the thing is, being a mom is not a job—if it were, you'd get time off, maybe some health insurance, and most importantly, paid for all your hard work.

Naturally, what Jezebel refuses to consider is Becker's evidence that having one parent at home allows the other parent to be more productive, earning a premium, and that premium is the income the at-home parent contributes. Even if you are going to hold fast to the idea that cooking dinner every night only counts if you sell the dinner to your neighbor, not feed your own family, you can STILL measure a wage increase attributable to the at home parent.

Hey, the Nobel Prize committee thought it was pretty compelling evidence for specialization, but what do they know, right? If millions of women decided "fuck this cubicle shit, I'm going home", and millions more young women decided "screw $50 000 worth of student debt so I can work minimum wage, I'm getting married", it would have a dramatic impact on both the marketplace and marriage.

Not very men want the pleasure of supporting a fat, nagging hag with a permanent bitch face. Creating a union in which one person is dependent upon another requires some slightly different attributes than a union in which two people compete for resources rather than cooperate. Remember the Princeton mom who encouraged women to look for husbands at university? She was roundly spanked in the media, but she has a book deal! I can't wait for that book. Publishers know there is a market for a book like that. Personally, I think the market is growing, too. Young women especially are seeing that the whole housewife gig is a far cry from oppressive and dreary. It's actually the best damn job any woman could have!

[116] http://www.theatlantic.com/magazine/archive/2013/06/the-gay-guide-to-wedded-bliss/309317/2/

[117] http://jezebel.com/being-a-mom-is-not-a-job-747142586

That brings us to our second point: being a mother is the toughest job in the world.

Excuse while I laugh hysterically for a moment.

10 most dangerous jobs:

Timber cutters
Fishers
Pilots and Navigators
Structural metal workers
Driver-sales workers
Roofers
Electrical power installers
Farmers
Construction workers
Truck drivers

What do all these jobs have in common? They are physically and/or intellectually demanding, some are highly dangerous and the vast majority of the workforce in these occupations are men. Maybe I'm doing it wrong, but so far, mothering has not included any dynamite, out of control flames, chemical spills or crude oil. Hell, I don't even deal with clogged toilets or drains.

I text my husband for that shit.

I will add the caveat that having a newborn in the house is physically EXHAUSTING labor, but it's not physically demanding in the way that construction or roofing is. Not even close.

So why is it that so many mothers agree that being a mom is not just a tough job, it's THE toughest job?

Because most of them are shit mothers. That's my theory. I'd like to see how many stay at home moms agree with that statement. Those of us who spend our days making cake pops for the kids dance troupe fundraiser (I have to make TWO THOUSAND by September 1st!), ignoring the housework and blogging in our spare time might have a thing or two to relate about how "tough" our lives are.

Women who leave the house every day, dragging sleepy, sobbing children off to the day orphanage, trying to get one modicum of "work" done in their cubicles then racing to the grocery store to pick up some shitty processed food to microwave for dinner might find mothering a "tough" job because it's hard to cram in around all the other "priorities".

Some of those women have so many other "priorities" that they completely forget they are supposed to drop off the baby for some other woman to raise, and they leave the baby to cook to death in the back seat of a hot car.

20 children have already died in hot cars in 2013. You know what kills me? What just kills me? The advice to avoid doing this to your own baby is to put your mobile phone in the baby's seat or your purse on the floor near the baby. You know, something important. Something you would never forget. Something that has top priority in your life.

YOUR FUCKING PHONE IS MORE IMPORTANT THAN YOUR BABY?

And it makes me rage when I hear sanctimonious commenters say "it could happen to anyone". Like fuck it can. I do not mentally check out of my baby's life for eight hours a day, expecting someone else to be responsible. The odds that I would "forget" my baby in the car are ZERO!

IT WILL NOT HAPPEN.

Failing to make mothering your primary job means that babies die. And the ones that don't die are still miserable and unpleasant and angry and unsettled and really, really hard to take care of. They're not being cared for in the way every neuron in their brain tells them is necessary. They need an attachment to a primary caregiver, and when they don't get it, bad things happen[118].

'No one can deny that daycare increases aggressiveness of toddlers. A toddler raised at home with a single carer is six times less likely to be aggressive than one enduring more than 45 hours a week daycare and the more daycare a child has, the greater the aggression. This aggression is sustained and predicts greater problems in primary schools.'

That Parenting survey was missing a word: Being a SHITTY mother is the toughest job in the world.

Yep.

Now I have to go and get started on those cake pops. I need to make around 80 a day (weekends off) to hit 2000 by September 1st. This is the first year I am in charge of fundraising. I figure we'll clear $4000 our first event. That's quadruple the amount the squad made last year for the WHOLE year.

Oh, but don't worry. I won't consider it work. And I sure won't delude myself into thinking making cake pops is "tough". It's actually a lot of fun! Look at the things you can do with a cake pop! Beats being a garbage collector any day. I wonder if the garbage crew would enjoy a cake pop the next time they swing down our street?

I think I'll find out.

Lots of love,

JB

Appease the shrieking feminists and they will STILL piss and moan. Jane Austen is the WRONG sort of woman to grace a bank note. She liked men. And she understood economics. Obviously, Jane sucks.

Regular readers will know that I am a huge fan of period costume drama and Jane Austen is hands down my favorite author, across all time and space forever. She is the greatest writer to have ever picked up a quill and anyone who doesn't agree with me is wrong. Anne Elliot and Frederick Wentworth are the sine qua non of beautiful couples, unmatched by any other.

So there.

I was, naturally, quite thrilled to hear that Jane Austen will be replacing Charles Darwin on the British ten pound bank note. Anything with Jane on it wins in my book, but despite my enthusiasm for the Lady of the Letters, I was still able to pause for a moment to consider that the accusation that there is a dearth of

---

[118] http://www.dailymail.co.uk/news/article-2275962/A-generation-little-savages-raised-nurseries-daycare-linked-aggression-toddlers.html

women on British currency is utterly laughable. Indeed, given the reach of the Commonwealth of Nations, surely the majority of the world's currencies feature a woman?

54 nations, under the aegis of Her Majesty, Queen Elizabeth II. Yeah, no women on currency around the globe at all.

Oh, but the Queen is not a role model for modern young women, so she doesn't count. She's just loyal and dutiful and practical and booooooooring. The petitioners argued that while Queen Elizabeth's face graces the front of every banknote, the monarch hardly represents the women of England—she's on the currency because of her bloodline, not her merits. Apart from the Queen and Fry, Florence Nightingale is the only other woman whose face has appeared on a British banknote. (Nightingale was featured on the 10-pound note from 1975 until 1992).

Florence Nightingale and Elizabeth Fry were more to the ladies liking. Florence, of course, established modern nursing. Never married, with some "close" relationships with other women. She did, of course, prefer the company of men, saying: "I have never found one woman who has altered her life by one iota for me or my opinions."

Oops.

Oh well. She still looks better on the surface than that silly Jane who adored the company of other women, her sister Cassandra and her many nieces in particular, and of course her beloved characters. And Elizabeth Fry, well, she was a married mother of eleven children, deeply moved by the plight of prisoners and the homeless. She worked tirelessly to improve their conditions, all the while managing her own substantial brood and some fairly disastrous family finances.

Pretty much zero British people have any clue who or what Elizabeth Fry was or what she did. She has no grand mystique surrounding her, like Nightingale or Austen, and therefore is also a safe choice for bank notes.

Jane, of course, has an entire cult of admirers who have kept her stories alive and loved across the centuries. Jane's books were prescribed to shell-shocked veterans of World War I, for "providing "great comfort" in a "crazy" world. So what is the opposition to Jane taking over from Charles Darwin on the ten pound note[119]?

"And what really irks is that the best woman the banking bods can think of is one who writes about finding a husband and waits quietly for her turn."

Quietly waiting for her turn? Clearly Susie Boniface has never read Austen. Lizzie Bennet quietly waiting for her turn? When Mr. Darcy proposes marriage, Lizzie has this to say to him: *"And those are the words of a gentleman. From the first moment I met you, your arrogance and conceit, your selfish disdain for the feelings of others made me realize that you were the last man in the world I could ever be prevailed upon to marry."*

Yep, pretty meek there, Lizzie!

Fanny Price fends off the advances of Edward Crawford, Anne Elliot stalwartly refuses her cousin Mr. Elliot and outright refuses Charles Musgrove, Emma literally shoves the obnoxious Mr. Elton out of the carriage and asks him if he is drunk when he proposes, and Elinor Dashwood scoffs at her brother's insistence that

---

[119] http://www.mirror.co.uk/news/uk-news/jane-austen-10-banknote-wrong-1998982

she grab up Colonel Brandon before her ovaries shrivel into dust at the ripe old age of nineteen. Yeah, yeah, Emma Thompson is a bit older, but in the book, Elinor is nineteen! None of Austen's ladies are meek or sit around "waiting for their turn".

But they are intent on finding a husband they can love, respect, admire and prosper under.

And that, if you ask me, is the real opposition against Jane Austen on the British currency. Jane lives on in popular imagination as the woman who wrote detailed, exquisite stories about women's search for a husband. She has been updated as Bridget Jones, another woman desperately seeking Mr. Right, to hilarious ends. Emma becomes the delightful Cher in Clueless, incapable of seeing what is right in front of her face. The man in the "friendzone" is the one she wants.

Marriage.

That's what Jane Austen stands for, and it is something modern feminists hate with a passion. Oh, they like marriage, all right. The legal entitlement to a man's assets, but that all rests on the assumption that the natural conclusion of any marriage is DIVORCE.

Interestingly enough, it seems like men are starting to really clue into just how vulnerable marriage makes them. Normally, the discussion of why men don't want to get married engages some variation of the immature, stupid, lazy man-child playing video games in a Cheetos-dusted Superman t-shirt in his mom's basement.

Helen Smith, writing at the Huffington Post offers some slightly more accurate perspectives on men's growing reluctance to tie the knot. Here are her 8 reasons[120] men no longer see marriage as a particularly great deal:

1. You will lose, rather than gain respect when you marry

2. Your wife will get fat and sex will be a pleasant dream

3. Your friendships will suffer

4. Your wife will take over the entire living space and declare it hers

5. You'll lose your kids and your money (even if the kids are not biologically yours)

6. You'll get fucked in court, no matter what

7. Pay up, or you will go to jail

8. Why buy the cow when you get the milk for free?

On the one hand, it's refreshing to see a writer actually discuss what is happening with the state of marriage rather than just whinge about how men are lazy assholes who won't grow the fuck up. On the other hand, it means that both men and women who are truly, deeply interested in a permanent union with one another are up against a social tide that looks increasingly dangerous to men.

Why should men get married? What are the benefits? According to Men's Health[121], there are still some pretty damn good reasons to get married.

---

[120] http://www.huffingtonpost.com/helen-smith/8-reasons-men-dont-want-t_b_3467778.html

1. Increase Your Pay

A Virginia Commonwealth University study found that married men earn 22 percent more than their similarly experienced but single colleagues.

2. Speed Up Your Next Promotion

Married men receive higher performance ratings and faster promotions than bachelors, a 2005 study of U.S. Navy officers reported.

3. Keep You Out of Trouble

According to a recent U.S. Department of Justice report, male victims of violent crime are nearly four times more likely to be single than married.

4. Satisfy You in Bed

In 2006, British researchers reviewed the sexual habits of men in 38 countries and found that in every country, married men have more sex.

5. Help You Beat Cancer

In a Norwegian study, divorced and never-married male cancer patients had 11 and 16 percent higher mortality rates, respectively, than married men.

6. Help You Live Longer

A UCLA study found that people in generally excellent health were 88 percent more likely to die over the 8-year study period if they were single.

I'm interested in those contradictory statements about sex. Which is it? Do married men have more or less sex than their single counterparts? I suspect the duration and quality of the marriage has a lot to do with it. A topic for another day.

If men are the most vulnerable in marriage, then it stands to reason that picking a partner is of vital importance. How do you know which woman will give you the benefits, and which ones will detonate the divorce grenade?

Tough call. I've taken a stab at that subject before, but now I want to add another flag to look for. Does she like Jane Austen? If your lady friend has a copy of *Pride and Prejudice*, or *Emma* or the swoon inducing *Persuasion* on her bedside table, or a well-worn copy of *Mansfield Park* tucked in her bookshelf, she just might be a woman who is looking for permanent love.

A woman who doesn't like Jane Austen?

That is a woman to avoid. She will never pierce your soul. She may leave you in agony, but never in hope. She is best left behind with her cat and her Scum Manifesto. But it's early yet to despair. The continuing popularity of Jane Austen and her beautiful stories suggests there are LOTS of women who value love and companionship and the enduring loyalty and comfort of a happy marriage.

---

[121] http://www.menshealth.com/mhlists/benefits_of_marriage_and_commitment/

You just have to keep looking.

> There is nothing lost, but may be found, if sought.
>
> Jane Austen

Lots of love,

JB

Advice for Women Who Don't Want to get Divorced

After 16 years of marriage, Gerald Rogers finalized his divorce and wrote down some advice he wished he had received a long time ago. His Facebook posting went viral, with over 10 000 likes and 100 000 shares at last count.

I'm not divorced, nor do I have any plans to be, but I thought I would give my perspective on Gerald's advice, and then offer my own advice for married women who would like to stay that way.

MARRIAGE ADVICE I WISH I WOULD HAVE HAD:

Obviously, I'm not a relationship expert. But there's something about my divorce being finalized this week that gives me perspective of things I wish I would have done different... After losing a woman that I loved, and a marriage of almost 16 years, here's the advice I wish I would have had...

1) Never stop courting. Never stop dating. NEVER EVER take that woman for granted. When you asked her to marry you, you promised to be that man that would OWN HER HEART and to fiercely protect it. This is the most important and sacred treasure you will ever be entrusted with. SHE CHOSE YOU. Never forget that, and NEVER GET LAZY in your love.

Oh dear. Courting, dating and taking for granted are all different things. Life doesn't always leave room for courting and dating, neither of which has anything to do with taking someone for granted. You should not be asking your husband to PROVE his love to you, over and over again. He has already proven it. It happened the day you got married. What you SHOULD do is be grateful. Say thank you. Acknowledge all the little and big things he does for you. And make sure you reciprocate. Don't keep score. Life is long and it will all balance out in the long run, which is what you are in for.

And most importantly, understand that men and women show their love in different ways. Women tend to like to talk about it. Men tend to show it. Neither is better than the other. Don't try to bend him to your way of communicating. Listen to the love,

2) PROTECT YOUR OWN HEART. Just as you committed to being the protector of her heart, you must guard your own with the same vigilance. Love yourself fully, love the world openly, but there is a special place in your heart where no one must enter except for your wife. Keep that space always ready to receive her and invite her in, and refuse to let anyone or anything else enter there.

Okay, sure. Protect your own heart. But at the same time, don't make the mistake of thinking your husband will be the one person to fulfil all your needs, and all your desires. The only person who can do that, ultimately is YOU. There will be many passions in your life that come and go, and some of those you will share with your husband, and some you won't. That's okay.

I think one of the biggest myths we cherish about love and marriage is that there is one, and only one person meant just for us. That really doesn't make any sense. There are 7 billion people on the planet! The idea that only one of those humans is the perfect match for you is nonsensical. You are both going to meet people with whom you feel a spark, a connection, a sense of compatibility and mutual attraction.

So what? Accept that there are many, many people with whom you could create a happy, harmonious life, and then let it go.

You've made your choice. Whatever problems you are experiencing at any given time, whatever part of you is going unfulfilled or unsatisfied, understand that trading in for a new partner won't change that. You'll just have new problems.

3) FALL IN LOVE OVER and OVER and OVER again. You will constantly change. You're not the same people you were when you got married, and in five years you will not be the same person you are today. Change will come, and in that you have to re-choose each other everyday. SHE DOESN'T HAVE TO STAY WITH YOU, and if you don't take care of her heart, she may give that heart to someone else or seal you out completely, and you may never be able to get it back. Always fight to win her love just as you did when you were courting her.

No. I hate this. Marriage is not and should not be conditional on how you happen to feel at any given moment. Yes, you will both change. People change. Marriage vows are about navigating those changes together. As one. Even the not so great changes.

...to have and to hold from this day forward, forsaking all others, for better or for worse, for richer, for poorer, in sickness and in health, to love and to cherish; from this day forward until death do us part

4) ALWAYS SEE THE BEST in her. Focus only on what you love. What you focus on will expand. If you focus on what bugs you, all you will see is reasons to be bugged. If you focus on what you love, you can't help but be consumed by love. Focus to the point where you can no longer see anything but love, and you know without a doubt that you are the luckiest man on earth to be have this woman as your wife.

Again, I disagree completely. Make a list of all the shit that drives you absolutely nuts about him! The things you want to kill him for! The stuff that makes you scream and want to tear out your hair! The things he does that makes you take stock of just where the knives are.

And now, for every item on your list, write down the shit that YOU do that makes him go insane. For every irritating, annoying, infuriating, frustrating thing that he does, I guarantee you, you do something equally exasperating.

And then laugh about it. Humans are annoying. Everyone has their own quirks and foibles and idiosyncrasies and all those things tend to annoy the shit out of the people they have to live with. That's just life. You don't need to ignore the fact that your husband irritates the shit out of you on occasion. Just keep in mind that you yourself return the favor.

No one is perfect. There is no need to pretend they are.

5) IT'S NOT YOUR JOB TO CHANGE OR FIX HER... your job is to love her as she is with no expectation of her ever changing. And if she changes, love what she becomes, whether it's what you wanted or not.

Yeah, I agree with this one. Don't expect your partner to change, but at the same time, know that he will. It's not up to you to decide how or when or in what direction he changes. And if you don't like the change, talk about it with him, but understand that the tables will turn soon enough, and it will be him not terribly happy with how you have changed.

6) **TAKE FULL ACCOUNTABILITY** *for your own emotions: It's not your wife's job to make you happy, and she CAN'T make you sad. You are responsible for finding your own happiness, and through that your joy will spill over into your relationship and your love.*

These things are not mutually exclusive. Yes, it is your husband's job to make you happy and he most certainly CAN make you sad. And yes, it is YOUR job to make him happy, and you most certainly can also make him sad.

But that's not the same thing as saying ALL your happiness will come from your partner. It won't. A marriage in which both partners are devoted to making the other person happy is a joy indeed. That's really the key to how you make a marriage work. You make your husband's happiness YOUR priority and he makes YOUR happiness his. That's how the whole deal works. That doesn't mean you turn yourself into a self-sacrificing martyr dragging the burden of other people's well-being like a cross through life. Nonsense.

Making the people you love happy is what will make YOU happy. It's not just true for the people you love, either. Making other people happy is what makes us happy. It makes us human.

7) **NEVER BLAME** *your wife If YOU get frustrated or angry at her, it is only because it is triggering something inside of YOU. They are YOUR emotions, and your responsibility. When you feel those feelings take time to get present and to look within and understand what it is inside of YOU that is asking to be healed. You were attracted to this woman because she was the person best suited to trigger all of your childhood wounds in the most painful way so that you could heal them... when you heal yourself, you will no longer be triggered by her, and you will wonder why you ever were.*

You were attracted to this woman because she was the person best suited to trigger all of your childhood wounds in the most painful way so that you could heal them

Yikes! Well, that certainly wasn't the reason I chose my husband, and I'm almost sad to read that Gerald chose a woman that brought back all the pain of his childhood. I understand how the wounds of childhood can be painful, and that relationships can indeed help to heal them, but I personally found that I let go of all the pain of my own blighted childhood by being the kind of mother I never had.

I can understand marrying someone like your opposite sex parent if that relationship was principally loving and affectionate, but on the whole, I don't think I would advise anyone to marry someone who triggers pain and a sense of being wounded.

8) *Allow your woman to JUST BE. When she's sad or upset, it's not your job to fix it, it's your job to HOLD HER and let her know it's ok. Let her know that you hear her, and that she's important and that you are that pillar on which she can always lean. The feminine spirit is about change and emotion and like a storm her emotions will roll in and out, and as you remain strong and unjudging she will trust you and open her soul to you... DON'T RUN-AWAY WHEN SHE'S UPSET. Stand present and strong and let her know you aren't going anywhere. Listen to what she is really saying behind the words and emotion.*

This is really beautiful, and absolutely true for women, too. When your husband is upset, it's your job to hold him and let him know that everything is okay. Sometimes you will need to be the pillar on which your husband can lean. All too often, I think women don't truly appreciate that men can be floored by an emotional reaction. Men can receive staggering blows. Men have all the same emotions and reactions and feelings as women, as sometimes those will be overwhelming.

Don't run away or act disgusted when confronted by your husband's emotions. Don't be afraid of anger or physical expressions of inner states of being. When women get really angry or upset, they tend to cry. When men get really angry or upset, they like to kill things in virtual reality. One isn't better than another. And both are felt with equal depth. Don't sneer at how your husband expresses his emotions.

9) BE SILLY... don't take yourself so damn seriously. Laugh. And make her laugh. Laughter makes everything else easier.

Absolutely. But if your idea of a laughter filled weekend involves a Benny Hill/Three Stooges marathon, maybe give your wife a pass to go to a period costume drama at the theatres with her friends?

Just a thought.

10) FILL HER SOUL EVERYDAY... learn her love languages and the specific ways that she feels important and validated and CHERISHED. Ask her to create a list of 10 THINGS that make her feel loved and memorize those things and make it a priority everyday to make her feel like a queen.

Aww. This is sweet. Make sure you do the exact same for your husband. He will have a love language all his own, and a list of specific things that makes him feel loved and cherished. Be the Queen. Absolutely. Don't be a Princess. A Princess is a spoiled brat who thinks Daddy should give her everything she wants by simple virtue of existence. A Queen knows that she has a job: she rules a realm with a King at her side. She has privileges and rights, and she knows they come with responsibilities and obligations. You can't have one without the other.

That's a marriage.

11) BE PRESENT. Give her not only your time, but your focus, your attention and your soul. Do whatever it takes to clear your head so that when you are with her you are fully WITH HER. Treat her as you would your most valuable client. She is.

Oh god no. This comes across as way too much attention. Life has so much drudgery and routine and things that just need to get done and sometimes the loveliest feeling in the world is just getting through the work knowing the other person is there. He doesn't have to be the sole focus of your whole life, nor do you have to clear your mind so you can focus only on him, him, him.

And please don't think of your husband as your most valuable client. Your marriage is not a transactional relationship. Viewing your partner as a client to whom you are obliged to deliver services reduces the whole relationship to one of functionality. And when the relationship doesn't function any more?

You replace it.

Marriage isn't a commercial relationship. Don't turn it into one.

12) BE WILLING TO TAKE HER SEXUALLY, to carry her away in the power of your masculine presence, to consume her and devour her with your strength, and to penetrate her to the deepest levels of her soul. Let her melt into her feminine softness as she knows she can trust you fully.

Ladies, be willing to be taken sexually, to be carried away in his masculine presence, to be consumed and devoured with strength, to be penetrated to the deepest levels of your soul. And be willing to return the favor.

Again, make his pleasure your primary goal, and let him make your pleasure his. It reinforces how the whole relationship works.

13) DON'T BE AN IDIOT.... *And don't be afraid of being one either. You will make mistakes and so will she. Try not to make too big of mistakes, and learn from the ones you do make. You're not supposed to be perfect, just try to not be too stupid.*

Yep. Good advice. Just try not to be too stupid.

14) GIVE HER SPACE... *The woman is so good at giving and giving, and sometimes she will need to be reminded to take time to nurture herself. Sometimes she will need to fly from your branches to go and find what feeds her soul, and if you give her that space she will come back with new songs to sing.... (okay, getting a little too poetic here, but you get the point. Tell her to take time for herself, ESPECIALLY after you have kids. She needs that space to renew and get re-centered, and to find herself after she gets lost in serving you, the kids and the world.)*

Yes. Very true. And remember that sometimes your husband will have those moments when he feels like nothing more than a walking wallet. Like an ATM machine whose purpose in life is to grind out cash and hand it over. Of course, you are all living in the same life, and all benefitting from everyone's work, but that doesn't mean he won't occasionally feel like his usefulness boils down to a number on an IRS form.

Be sensitive to those moments. Make sure your husband knows he is more than just a tool the family uses to survive. Set aside money just for him to spend on what he likes, and make no comments. Give him time and space to go and be the man he is, and not just an instrument you find particularly useful.

15) BE VULNERABLE... *you don't have to have it all together. Be willing to share your fears and feelings, and quick to acknowledge your mistakes.*

Yep. Every one screws up. Say you're sorry. And when it's his turn to fuck up and ask for forgiveness, be gracious, accept the apology and then let it go. Don't bear grudges. You screw up, too. If he screws up big time, consider it money in the bank for some future transgression on your part.

(I'm kidding!)

16) BE FULLY TRANSPARENT. *If you want to have trust you must be willing to share EVERYTHING... Especially those things you don't want to share. It takes courage to fully love, to fully open your heart and let her in when you don't know i she will like what she finds... Part of that courage is allowing her to love you completely, your darkness as well as your light. DROP THE MASK... If you feel like you need to wear a mask around her, and show up perfect all the time, you will never experience the full dimension of what love can be.*

Again, the alternative to wearing a mask and pretending to be perfect is not complete transparency. I don't need to know everything going on in my husband's mind. Jesus. I don't want to! And I'm pretty sure he would go insane in about five minutes if I shared everything going on in my mind with him.

Somethings are better left unsaid. Somethings are just things you THINK. No need to share. Again, think about his happiness. Will telling him X or Y add to that happiness or detract? Make his happiness your priority and text your girlfriends about your frustrations.

17) NEVER STOP GROWING TOGETHER... The stagnant pond breeds malaria, the flowing stream is always fresh and cool. Atrophy is the natural process when you stop working a muscle, just as it is if you stop working on your relationship. Find common goals, dreams and visions to work towards.

Yes. This. No matter what life brings, what changes come your way, you find a way to work together. Til death do you part.

18) DON'T WORRY ABOUT MONEY. Money is a game, find ways to work together as a team to win it. It never helps when teammates fight. Figure out ways to leverage both persons strength to win.

Well, you can worry about money, but don't fight about it. Fights over money are apparently a huge source of conflict in a lot of marriages. I would seriously consider NOT marrying someone if you can't agree on the ground rules for how to manage money.

19) FORGIVE IMMEDIATELY and focus on the future rather than carrying weight from the past. Don't let your history hold you hostage. Holding onto past mistakes that either you or she makes, is like a heavy anchor to your marriage and will hold you back. FORGIVENESS IS FREEDOM. Cut the anchor loose and always choose love.

This is probably the key thing Gerald gets right. And of course the biggest thing to forgive in any marriage is infidelity. Some people consider infidelity a deal breaker. Have sex outside the marriage and the marriage is over. I don't take that stance at all. My principal interest would be in what motivated the infidelity.

Sex on the side, as a little entertainment, is annoying and I wouldn't be especially pleased about that, but I wouldn't end my marriage over it either. I have made it clear to my husband that if he IS going to have sex with someone other than me, he chooses a professional. For one thing, the risk of disease is considerably lower. And the risk of pregnancy and other emotional complications is also much, much lower.

My strategy for keeping my husband faithful is to have a lot of sex with him. Leave him with no energy or desire to consider professional alternatives. Seems to be working.

Sex with another woman he loves would be a much bigger problem. I personally would still not end our marriage over that kind of infidelity, because we have children and I am not going to punish them because I have neglected my husband to the point that he has a full emotional relationship with someone else.

That kind of infidelity would indeed be very troubling, but I would accept partial responsibility for that scenario, and turn my attention towards working on our own relationship, and that wouldn't be possible without forgiveness.

Gerald is right. Forgive. And forget. And then work on what led to the problem in the first place.

20) ALWAYS CHOOSE LOVE. ALWAYS CHOOSE LOVE. ALWAYS CHOOSE LOVE. In the end, this is the only advice you need. If this is the guiding principle through which all your choices is governed, there is nothing that will threaten the happiness of your marriage. Love will always endure.

As long as "always choose love" means "put the other person first" then I agree. But that MUST be reciprocal. If he is not going to put you first, not going to forsake all others, not going to make you his priority, then you are wasting your time and your life.

And so is any man. None of us exist to be a tool for others to use. It's absolutely true that marriage works best when the other person is the top priority, but if the feelings and actions are not returned, the relationship is just an elaborate exploitation of one person by another.

And the sad reality is that marriage really has become a vehicle for one person to exploit another, until they get tired and decide to trade in. What I take away from Gerald's post is that he deeply regrets not supplicating his entire personality and needs to the woman he loved. That may be cruel, but it's the feeling I am left with. There is so little sense in his writing that any of their marital problems were caused by her. It feels like he accepts complete and total blame.

There's something heroic in that.

And something bitter, too.

Everyone knows that ultimately, marriage is a gamble. There are no guarantees. But when the odds are stacked so horribly against you, why would you take the risk at all? In my opinion, Gerald's advice doesn't help, over all. Encouraging men to yield everything they can to women, without insisting that women yield the same to men, is only handing women a sword.

That tends not to work out very well.

> *I gave 'em a sword. And they stuck it in, and they twisted it with relish. And I guess if I had been in their position, I'd have done the same thing.*
>
> Richard M. Nixon

Why would a man fight a battle he knows he can't win?

Lots of love,

JB

Food = Love

Captain Capitalism[122] has a theory that people whose political inclinations tend to lean left are less physically attractive than those who lean more to the right. According to the Captain, looking physically attractive takes work and effort and leftists have a strong tendency to look for someone else to blame for their problems, including having a huge ass and a muffin top that makes the People of Walmart look positively lithe.

I do NOT believe liberals and leftists are born uglier than their average conservative counterpart. It's not like they're genetically inferior or anything. What I am talking about is that they put A LOT LESS EFFORT into their physical appearance. Ergo, this is not a criticism of their basic, physical beauty, let alone their genetics, but it IS a criticism of their psychology. You could take that Prius-driving, 45 year old, gray haired, super skinny yoga woman who never wore make-up, never did her hair up, give her a make over and she'd come out looking just fine. Just as you could take the cowering, tubby orbiting beta with the Seth Rogen beard, through him in the gym for 3 months and have him come out looking just fine.

But that's the not the point.

The point is to your average leftists such working out and maintenance requires effort. That AND the added risk they may still "fail" in attracting a mate. It is their pure hatred and fear of effort and competition that not only drives their political and economic ideologies, but also drives their "romantic" or "mating" ideology.

[122] http://captaincapitalism.blogspot.ca/2012/09/why-leftists-tend-to-be-uglier.html

I don't want to discuss Cappy's theory per se, other than to point out he cites some research that suggests he may be on to something, and that more feminine looking women tend to be Republicans. It's colloquially known as the "Michele Bachmann" effect[123]. What I want to discuss is how an entire worldview can play out in various aspects of one's personal life without necessarily any awareness on the part of the actor. Liberals may not realize that in blaming the "Man" for why they have a shitty job, they are also providing the justification for not hitting the gym, but the relationship exists nonetheless.

And I want to discuss that in the context of the woman who made 300 sandwiches for her boyfriend after she made him a sandwich and he told her she was on her way to earning an engagement ring, because to him, the act of making a sandwich was an act of love. And why else do you get engaged if not for love? To him, sandwiches are like kisses or hugs. Or sex. "Sandwiches are love," he says. "Especially when you make them. You can't get a sandwich with love from the deli."

It's actually pretty funny to see the feminist ladies at Slate's Double XX blog and Jezebel try to understand how a woman, ANY woman, could possibly want to indicate her love for a man, and make that the basis of a potential marriage.

Who does that? Who shows a MAN they are loved and then thinks love is something that can sustain a marriage?

Amanda Hess[124] is particularly hilarious trying to parse out the relationship between love and actions that demonstrate love.

How do we make sense of love in the time of "I'm 124 Sandwiches Away From an Engagement Ring"? The traditional romantic structures that previously organized our physical and emotional connections to other people are crumbling fast. Nobody buys one another root beer floats anymore. Everybody's touching everybody else before they marry anyone. There are no boyfriends here. In the face of all this romantic disruption, some lovers are frantically constructing new frameworks—diamond-fishing sandwich blogs, for example—in a desperate attempt to reduce our strange and wonderful human experiences into another rote mechanical exercise. Stop. Love each other. Eat sandwiches. Don't trade either of them for anything.

Don't trade either of them for anything.

How can she not see that sandwiches and love are ONE AND THE SAME THING? Love is not just something you say. It's something you do. Every day. For the rest of your life. For someone else. If you're a heterosexual woman, that someone else is going to be a man.

And there's the problem.

It doesn't have to be a sandwich. It can be anything. Pizza. Cookies. Bread. A different handmade pasta every day for 300 days. Those things take skill, though. The beauty of a sandwich is that anyone can make one, regardless of their familiarity with the kitchen and the tools therein.

What it takes is a particular mindset.

---

[123] http://www.sciencedirect.com/science/article/pii/S0022103112001758

[124] http://www.slate.com/blogs/xx_factor/2013/09/25/just_300_sandwiches_for_an_engagement_ring_step hanie_smith_s_300_sandwiches.html

Your whole worldview needs to change to do something like make 300 sandwiches. You have to put the other person first, and take time out of your day, every day, to make a special effort to please another person. You think about their comfort and feelings and well-being and you put those things ahead of your own, not forever, not always, not in every single situation you will ever confront in your life together, BUT FOR THE TIME IT TAKES TO MAKE A SANDWICH.

What is that? Maybe 15 minutes? 15 minutes of your day, every day, is dedicated to the care of the person (man) you love.

And that's just too much to trade, is it?

How sad. It's not hard to imagine Amanda's response, is it?

Well, what does he do for ME fifteen minutes a day? Get out the spreadsheets and start tabulating. 15 seconds to open the door for me. 45 seconds to go to the bedroom and fetch my purse because I have my boots on already and I forgot. 3 minutes to select an excellent Shiraz for our evening meal (South Africa! Try South Africa!). 8 minutes to run a hot bath and fill it with vanilla scented bubbles.

Keep careful tabs, and if he doesn't hit the 15 minute absolute perfect trade-off mark, then fuck him and his sandwich. Chuck it in the trash. We're after perfect equality, right? And the best way to achieve that is to be a temporal bean-counting bitch.

Yeah, okay. Good luck with that.

Jezebel[125] wonders just how piss-poor a sandwich can be offered. If you're gonna make someone a sandwich that he interprets as a gesture of love, then you want to put the LEAST amount of effort into that as possible, right? And maybe even try to trade off for blow-jobs instead?

Even though we now know, collectively as a Lady Monolith, how to please men, collectively as a Man Monolith, a few loose ends were left untied in Smith's piece. Namely: how complicated a sandwich are we talking here? Would Eric still light up Stephanie's ring finger if she just half assed the last 124 sandwiches by making him a pile of peanut butter on folded bread monstrosities? What is the minimum number of ingredients required for Eric to count it as 1/300th an engagement ring? Are there any substitutions for sandwichmaking? What's the sandwich-to-blowjob conversion rate (my boss suggested that 1 BJ is worth 2 4-or-more-ingredient sandwiches; I'm inclined to agree)?

Where on earth does the stereotype of feminists as sulky, sour, bitter, loveless bitches come from? It's such a mystery. There is just so much love and affection in that quote, isn't there?

Let's look at some of the comments. They're so cute!

cassiebearRAWRU

Deli sandwiches don't have love?

Why the fuck would I want love in my sandwich? That just takes up room that could be used for sliced jalapeños and bacon. Yesterday 12:46pm

Straight up denial. Food is not love.

---

[125] http://jezebel.com/lady-earns-engagement-ring-by-making-300-sad-sandwiches-1383822830

quashitlikeitshot

Exactly. I am a great cook, and my husband loves my cooking. He has never, ever, once made me feel bad for not cooking. There is a difference.

This guy is an ass, and he can certainly kiss mine. Yesterday 1:02pm

Point right over the head. He never made her feel bad. On the contrary. He told her that the love she put into making to sandwiches was NOT going unnoticed, and that he was prepared to love her forever.

Wenchette

This morning I made a piping hot cup of disappointment for my husband. Rich black disappointment, tinged with regret and a sense of impending loss, served piping hot with two sugars and some cream. Yesterday 12:47pm

This is funny in the way that watching socially impaired people try to interact is funny. You feel awful at the same time. Schadenfreude. That's what the word really means. You laugh at someone's misfortune, but at the same time you feel absolutely terrible for them. The second part has to be there in order for the word schadenfreude to be the correct choice. Laughing at someone's misfortune is just sadism.

Trust me.

My father speaks German as a first language and it always drives him nuts when people confuse sadism with schadenfreude. This comment made me laugh, but at the same time, holy fuck, what a bitch! I feel sorry for her and her husband.

One commenter acknowledges that buddy in question is no slouch in the kitchen, but it has no effect on the Jezzie ladies.

see you in rach-hell

I guess I'm the only person who has read her blog and realizes that their relationship seems fine, he cooks an equal amount for the both of them, and it's not really as serious crazy-woman-desperate-to-get-married-to-a-misogynist as this article makes it sound.

Some might say the idea is sexist. "A woman in the kitchen—how Stepford Wife of you!" a friend argued. I say come over for dinner, and watch E whip up roasted duck breast with a balsamic and currant sauce with a roasted parsnip puree and shaved pickled beets in no time, and you'll see who spends more time in the kitchen.

Some say I'm just desperate to get engaged. Hardly. I don't have to be. E didn't say "cook me 300 sandwiches or I'm leaving you!" He gave me a challenge—a dare, to some degree—and the type-A, Tracy Flick side of me can't stand being challenged. I will prove to him and the rest of the world I can make the 300 sandwiches.

Seems hyperbolic to me. Yesterday 1:22pm

Nope. That kind of reasonableness won't play here.

InterrobangUsee you in rach-hell391L

Her premise is revolting. That her husband cooks changes nothing about the fact that her blog is about making enough sandwiches to "earn" an engagement ring.

Or, you know, maybe that demonstrating the willingness to care and make an effort to provide for the other person is mutual? Seems like Stephanie has the better deal here, with Eric pureeing parsnips to go with roast duck.

Seriously, these women just can't STAND the idea that any woman would demonstrate love by providing food for a MAN even though he obviously takes the time to provide food for her.

That is what brings me back to Captain Capitalism's theory. Women who embrace feminism don't seem to be able to perceive that they are encouraged to blame men for all their problems and actively hate men, and simply REFUSE to make a fucking sandwich because severe cognitive dissonance kicks in and it is impossible to reconcile all the contradictions of feminism as a philosophy.

"We don't hate men" claim the feminists.

But make them a sandwich? Oh hell no. That will be interpreted as love and we love men so we can't do anything that shows we love men.

Remember my advice on how to pick a wife? I mentioned providing food as being a critical condition, and I am now inclined to believe it may be the ONLY flag you need to look for.

Food = love.

A woman who doesn't provide food for you doesn't love you. She doesn't have to be Julia Child. Anyone can make a sandwich. Anyone can order pizza. Anyone can fry bacon.

"Make me a sandwich?"

It really means "do you love me"?

I'd listen to the answer very carefully. A woman who refuses is likely very much a feminist, even if she won't use the word to describe herself.

And that's not a woman you want.

Lots of love,

JB

Made in the USA
Charleston, SC
09 June 2016